The New York Times

DINNER FOR EIGHT

The New York Times

DINNER FOR EIGHT

40 GREAT DINNER PARTY MENUS
FOR FRIENDS AND FAMILY

....

DENISE LANDIS

Foreword by AMANDA HESSER

ST. MARTIN'S PRESS ❧ NEW YORK

www.stmartins.com

Design by Kate Nichols

The author is grateful for permission granted to use or adapt
some recipes previously published in *The New York Times*.
A list of those recipes appears on pages 269–270.

Library of Congress Cataloging-in-Publication Data

Landis, Denise.
    Dinner for eight : 40 great dinner party menus for friends and family / Denise Landis ;
foreword by Amanda Hesser.
        p. cm.
    Includes index (p. 275).
    ISBN 0-312-32581-9
    EAN 978-0-312-32581-7
    1. Dinners and dining.   2. Menus.   I. Title.

TX737.L39 2005
642'.4—dc22   2005046594

10   9   8   7   6   5   4   3

For **JD** *and*

SARA, JACOB, *and* **BENJAMIN,**

my first and best audience

Contents

· · · · · · · · · · · · ·

Foreword

by Amanda Hesser

. . . .

PART FORMULA and part poetry, the best recipes set down the mysterious language of cooking while captivating the senses. But a good recipe is not just a well-written one. It's well tested and leaves no room for questions to trouble the worried cook's mind. When a recipe says the sautéed onions should be soft after ten minutes, they are. When you don't have the right pan, it offers an alternative. And when you must use cream and nothing else, it insists.

Great recipes are rarely the work of one person. Food writers and chefs may compose recipes, but they rely on recipe testers to add the critical details that will make them work without a hitch—the addition of parchment paper to line a baking pan, the use of a wooden spoon to cook jam. Testers, working in anonymity, are the culinary gurus behind recipes in magazines, newspapers, and cookbooks. They guide cooks down the right path, always with an eye to providing a safety net for inexperienced cooks while speeding the experienced on their way. The best recipe testers are fine technicians and wordsmiths. They can help you bone a leg of lamb without a diagram. They know that a recipe's sensual detail—a caramel's straw hue in the early stages of cooking; the elasticity of properly whipped meringue—adds immeasurably to the joy of cooking.

Denise Landis is such a guru. She has worked for more than a decade as a *New York Times* recipe tester. By the time I began collaborating with her eight years ago, she was a seasoned tester with a newspaperman's sensibility. Denise is economical in her use of words, sensitive to a cook's concerns, and precise in her descriptions of technique.

And because Denise works out of her home in New Hampshire, she is in many ways the *Times* writers' link to reality. In New York, butchers always carry foie gras and grocers always stock Maldon sea salt. And when you aren't cooking for a family, it is easy to convince yourself, as a writer, that readers really do want to cook soufflés on weeknights. As Denise has pointed out to all of us at one time or another, they don't. Nor do they want to shell eight pounds of fava beans or strain a sauce four times, even if it's for a recipe by Ferran Adrià.

A mother of three, Denise serves the reader as the voice of the modern home cook—adventurous and ambitious but keenly aware of the number of hours in a day. She shops in a regular grocery store, Shaw's in Stratham, New Hampshire, not in Whole Foods or Citarella. If I send her a recipe containing grains of paradise, she will seek them out online, but if I start asking her to order crates of mandarin oranges from California, she puts her foot down. And with Denise the proof is always in the pudding. A recipe is not a success if it simply works, if the proportions are accurate, but only if she and her family like it.

Testing for the *Times* means that Denise has prepared recipes from every region of the world and every kind of cook. Over the years she has tested lima bean ice cream (which she said tasted like frozen sweetened lima beans), Vanna White's favorite dessert (a concoction of Cool Whip, cottage cheese, and powdered lime Jell-O), a chicken dish that involved juicing sweet potatoes, and Italian wedding soup (a three-day affair). The breadth of Denise's experience makes her more knowledgeable than most chefs. Denise can tell you the difference in cooking times between a braised lamb shoulder and a braised lamb shank, the best temperature for frying oysters, and the percentage of butter in a proper scone.

I remember one particular week when I sent Denise recipes for migas (an egg and tortilla omelet), calas (southern fried rice balls), Derby pie, milk punch, "Corpse Reviver #2" (a drink involving Lillet, pastis, gin, and a maraschino cherry), and poke (a Hawaiian raw fish salad). Poke calls for a "reddish brown seaweed such as limu kohu or ogo" and a tablespoon of "ground kukui nuts." Each time I pressed "send" on my computer, I flinched, waiting for an angry phone call from Denise. But nothing came. A few days passed and six perfectly written recipes arrived in my in-box with one asterisk. Denise had indeed tracked down the limu kohu and kukui nuts—at the Takahashi Market in San Mateo, California—and she noted, to save me from any embarrassment, that "poke is pronounced 'poh-kee' or 'poh-kay.'"

It is a boon to cooks that Denise has finally sat down and recorded her own recipes. They capture the spirit of a confident and unpretentious cook. Denise knows she doesn't need to chase the latest trends, so she offers dishes that have held up for decades, such as penne alla vodka, deviled eggs, and strawberry shortcake. And yet she has an eye for the combinations that stimulate an intrepid cook, like short ribs with porcini-prune sauce and Poire William ice cream.

Denise has arranged the recipes in menus for parties of eight, an approach that's both practical and optimistic. Menus are what we need for parties, and, of course, we should all be having more parties!

When my husband and I throw dinner parties, all my entertaining anxiety gets played out up front as I sketch out the menu. Sometimes this will take me days (my husband might say weeks). A great menu gives shape to a party. Once it is set, the rest of the work—the shopping, the cooking, the table setting—can be done with a sense of purpose. Without a good menu, the party planning just clunks along. I once decided to bake very fragile butter cookies to serve as dessert for a large party. These cookies could collapse in a strong breeze, but convinced that they were too delicious to resist, I put them on the menu. The first batch fell to dust. The second batch crumbled, too. At midnight before the party, I decided to make ice cream in case the third batch also crashed and burned. They didn't. But the ice cream kept me up until three in morning.

Denise protects us from such debacles because she has done the work for us. Her well-designed menus mean no fretting. And in each recipe you will find a voice of experience, a razor-sharp palate, and, perhaps most important, someone who cuts out unnecessary steps whenever she can, because Denise does her own dishes!

Introduction

·······

MY INTRODUCTION to the food world began with dinner parties. I had always enjoyed eating good food, but fresh out of college I was a young archaeologist traveling from job to job with little chance to practice cooking. I made do with whatever battered pots and pans were in the accommodations I shared with my fellow archaeologists. Seasoning consisted of salt, pepper, and oregano for communally made spaghetti sauce. I marvel to recall the vast quantities of fast food I consumed.

Early in my marriage I was unemployed by choice, staying at home with first one small child and then two. My husband, a wine collector, urged me to have small dinner parties at which he could serve his finds to guests. I cringe when I remember some of those dinners: a disastrous paella, underdone chicken, a dinner for a professional chef who said not a word about the food except to comment condescendingly that the soup (which had taken three days to prepare) was "yummy."

Gradually, I found my stride. I learned how to recognize a good recipe. I learned to be organized. I learned to plan ahead. I was still so distracted by food preparation that I often found myself rising from the table at the end of the meal with my apron still tied over my "dressy" clothes. Since I favored (and still have a soft spot for) hand-sewn aprons from the 40s and 50s that I picked up at flea markets and church sales, I must have looked ridiculous. Sometimes I would be so obsessed with the food that the guests (often business acquaintances of my husband) seemed incidental to the party. A shy young woman who looked completely unfamiliar once greeted me in the street and had to explain—to her obvious chagrin and my mortification—that she had been a guest in my home a few days before.

I acquired cookbooks and then kitchen equipment, and finally I learned to relax. One day my husband casually mentioned that a coworker, a renowned cookbook editor, had mentioned she needed someone to try out some recipes from a cookbook she was considering for publication. My reaction—*I want to do it!*—was reflexive. I was ready for a job, even part-time, even temporary, especially if I could do it at home. All I had to do was make the recipes and say if I liked them. It didn't seem like enough, so I wrote a few paragraphs critiquing each one: the method of preparation, how it tasted. The work was exciting and the rewards were immediate: I got to eat the results of my labor. The job lasted for two years. Sometimes while I cooked, baby Ben would bounce in a swing suspended in the kitchen doorway and toddler Jacob would stand near me on a stepladder by the spice rack, carefully opening each spice, sniffing it, asking its name, and then carefully replacing it. Sometimes I cooked late at night while my husband worked at his desk and the children slept. When I made food that would not keep until the next day—éclairs, soufflés, and other fragile foods—I brought a filled plate to the basement of my apartment building for the Polish-speaking night staff, who must have been baffled but clearly were pleased.

After two years of testing recipes for cookbooks, I heard that *The New York Times* was looking for a recipe tester. I applied and was hired. That was fourteen years ago. In those years I have become a knowledgeable cook, recipe tester, editor, and giver of dinner parties. I do all the cooking alone, am never nervous, and know without a doubt that everything, from soup to nuts, will be better than *yummy.*

ABOUT THIS BOOK

Recipe testing allowed me to learn to cook the best possible way: by trying out recipes and asking questions of the people who wrote them. All the recipes I have tested for cookbooks, newspapers, and magazines have been written for a moderately experienced cook working in a home kitchen. I discovered early in my career that if a recipe didn't work for me, it wasn't a result of my lack of knowledge or experience but because the *instructions* were at fault.

When I am testing another cook's recipes, I never combine the work with entertaining. Testing a recipe takes longer than following a finished, edited recipe. I work alone in the kitchen, reading and rereading the original recipe, going a step at a time, making notes and corrections. I catch errors and omissions, change weight measurements to volume (cups), clarify language, adjust seasonings, and try substitutions for obscure ingredients. Sometimes a recipe fails, and I have to figure out why. Most of the time the final product is delicious, and my family is the beneficiary.

In my household designating a recipe a "keeper" is significant. My husband's expertise is in matching foods and wines, and he provided the wine pairings for this book. It's fair to say that my children, now young adults, have been raised from birth to be food critics. We all discuss food and wine with the same maniacal interest with which some other families discuss sports. When a recipe is unanimously and enthusiastically applauded, it becomes a part of our family culture. My children and I keep handwritten collections of our favorite recipes. Many of those recipes are in this book.

I am more interested in actual finished dishes than in who has created them. Most recipes published in *The New York Times* are written by professional chefs and food writers. But some excellent recipes come from small-town cafés, others from somebody's grandma, and others from inexperienced but talented young chefs. I have no favorite kind of food or favorite cookbook. There is simply too much to choose from, and so much of it is extraordinary.

This book contains some of the best recipes I have collected over the years as well as recipes I have written based on what I have learned from many talented cooks in the past sixteen years. The menus have been assembled so that most of them can be prepared conveniently ahead of time and served easily and elegantly.

THE DINNER PARTY

Hosting a dinner party usually inspires a mixture of pleasurable anticipation and anxiety. A dinner party offers the chance to bring together old friends and introduce new ones, and to show off your cooking skills and your home in a relaxed atmosphere. But the host who wants to do the cooking faces a dilemma: how to cook and mingle with guests at the same time, particularly when preparing a formal sit-down dinner.

It *is* possible to host a dinner party and have time to spend with your guests. How? By choosing a menu carefully and planning ahead.

The menus in this book combine recipes that can be made ahead of time with recipes that can be made (or finished) easily at the last minute. Each menu includes an hors d'oeuvre that is intended to be eaten as a finger food while standing (or sitting) with a drink or wine. When guests are called to the table, they are served a first course, a main course and accompaniment, and finally dessert.

While the menus combine recipes that complement one another, recipes from different menus and even different seasons can be put together. Menus, like food preferences, are largely a matter of taste.

NOT EVERYONE APPEARS at a dinner party at exactly the same moment. I like to serve three hors d'oeuvres while guests are arriving and greeting one another: two simple foods such as marinated olives or seasoned roasted nuts to nibble on, and one dish that requires some cooking or assembly. Guests should be given a drink of some kind as soon as they have removed their coats and have been introduced: wine or a mixed drink or a festive nonalcoholic drink. I like to begin with sparkling wine or, for nondrinkers, strong homemade lemonade mixed with sparkling water. If I am serving a hot hors d'oeuvre, I bring it out when most of the guests have arrived and the party can begin.

I usually plan to serve my first course about an hour after I have asked guests to arrive. I expect guests to arrive within fifteen or twenty minutes of the time dinner was called for, and allow half an hour to forty-five minutes for hors d'oeuvres. This gives me time to mingle with guests, make introductions, and return to the kitchen for any last-minute preparations.

A RECIPE-TESTER'S KITCHEN

In sixteen years of testing recipes I have developed a kitchen that is a cross between a normal home kitchen and a commercial one. I have ordinary, though high-quality, appliances, and I am accustomed to doing all the prep work, cooking, and most of the cleaning myself. The features I most love about my kitchen are those that provide space and convenience. A brick chimney in the center of the kitchen has two floor-to-ceiling poles attached that have iron crossbars which support an array of heavy pots and skillets. An island nearby has two deep, lidded drawers, each holding two steel-lined bins for whole wheat flour and white flour, granulated sugar and confectioners' sugar. A cabinet with swing-out shelves holds hundreds of spices, and behind another door is a swing-out holder for bottles of oils and vinegars. An extra-large wood-burning stove keeps the kitchen warm through our long New Hampshire winters, and in the cold months it often has a large pot of stock simmering on it. These are all luxuries, but the overall effect and utility are not very different from what is found in kitchens in many homes.

Where my kitchen departs from the average is in the number of cookbooks I have for pleasure and reference—about fifteen hundred, housed in a large bookcase in the kitchen, in an upstairs room near my tiny office (which itself is large enough only for a desk, chair, and filing cabinet), and overflowing shelves in my basement. In the basement I have a large deep-freezer, many shelves of cooking wines and spirits, and a pantry housing spices, condiments, dried mushrooms of all kinds, and boxes of candles for dinner parties. Large industrial shelving units hold cans of tomatoes, broth, and beans, and plastic bins hold pasta in all shapes and sizes. More shelves and boxes hold kitchen equipment of every description: Crock-Pots, thermometers, George Foreman grills, cake pans, mandolines, ice cream makers, and jelly jars. All these supplies allow me to test practically any recipe at a moment's notice.

I haven't forgotten what it was like to cook in our New York City apartment, in a kitchen so cramped I would squeeze in chairs and stools so I could use the seats for extra counter space. It's not necessary to have a lot of space in a kitchen, a trove of cookbooks, or even a flotilla of pots and pans. Good recipes, fine ingredients, a little equipment, and a sense of humor will take you a long way.

EQUIPMENT

I use all kinds of cookware, including ovenproof glass, stainless steel, ceramic, cast iron, and anodized aluminum. The only cookware I avoid is nonanodized aluminum because it is flimsy and reacts to acidic foods (such as lemon juice and wine). Nonanodized aluminum tends to be very inexpensive and often is poorly made. (Anodized aluminum, which has a hardened surface that renders it nonreactive, is used in many high-quality products.)

If you have the means and the space, it's possible to amass a large collection of cookware from around the world: clay pots from Spain, kadhais (also called karahis) from India, woks from China, and copper pans from France. However, if you have a small space or favor simplicity, a few essential pans will serve you very well.

A 12-inch cast-iron skillet: Preferably get one with an ovenproof glass lid (which may be purchased separately). Cast iron, unattractive when new, becomes beautiful as it ages. It will be gray at first and probably coated with a substance to protect it from rust. Scrub it well to remove the coating, dry it, and rub it all over with vegetable oil. I do not believe in trying to season cast iron; good seasoning only really happens with time and use. Do not try to cook delicate foods in an unseasoned cast-iron pan; they will stick. Instead, cook meats or chicken breasts or vegetables, using a bit more oil than you normally would and occasionally sliding a sturdy metal turner under the foods to help prevent sticking. Clean the pan in water without soap, using a plastic scrubber and kosher salt as an abrasive. Wipe the pan dry and rub again with vegetable oil. You'll find that the pan ages quickly with use, turning black and eventually almost completely nonstick. Do not cook acidic foods in cast iron because they will react with the metal and be affected in color and flavor. Once the cast iron has developed a black patina it can be washed lightly with soap, but always dry it thoroughly and coat it with oil on all sides before storing to prevent rust.

One or two nonstick skillets: Even if you have a seasoned cast-iron skillet, you will need at least one nonstick skillet. I recommend buying a small one (6 to 8 inches) and a large one (10 to 12 inches). Save your iron skillet for cooking over high heat and use a nonstick pan for cooking eggs and crepes, sautéing, making sauces, and cooking acidic foods. This is an item in which you should invest as much money as you can. Higher-quality nonstick surfaces are more durable, and good quality pans are less likely to warp and dent. Try to buy a pan that is ovenproof to 400 degrees or more and has a handle that will stay cool when used on the stove top. (Bear in mind that all stay-cool handles will become extremely hot when the pan is placed in an oven.)

A covered casserole or Dutch oven: If you have only one casserole, it should be a large, wide one that can be used on top of the stove or in the oven. A few years ago I discovered a pan that has become my favorite: Calphalon's 8½-quart Dutch oven, 12 inches in diameter and 4½ inches high. It is shallow enough to sauté in, has two short handles, and is deep enough to use as a casserole dish. It has a flat, snugly fitting lid. It's ideal for recipes that require sautéing, stove top simmering, and finishing in the oven. It can be used for stews, soups, and stock. It is also the perfect size for boiling spaghetti: The strands fit sideways in the pan.

A large roasting pan: A roasting pan is about 4 inches deep, has handles, and can be made of stainless steel, enameled steel, lined copper, or anodized aluminum. Roasting pans are also available with nonstick surfaces. The prices can range from very cheap (for enameled steel) to quite expensive (for lined copper). If you don't already own a sturdy roasting pan, you may be surprised at how useful it can be. In addition to holding everything from a leg of lamb to a half-dozen game hens, it can roast vegetables and serve as a bain-marie (water bath) for a cake pan or individual soufflé dishes. Toss wedges of potatoes with olive oil, garlic, and rosemary, and roast them in a large, heavy pan to make them crisp and brown outside, fluffy and white inside. It's not necessary to have a covered pan. A heavy-bottomed pan has the best browning capability, and large sturdy handles enable you to pick it up easily.

A chef's knife: Last, you should have a good chef's knife. This is a large, heavy knife with a wide triangular blade. Buy the best-quality knife you can afford and ask someone to teach you how to use it. If you take proper care of your knife, you will find it well worth your investment. Never soak a good knife in water or put it in the dishwasher. Protect the sharp edge by keeping it in a knife block or on a magnetic wall strip; do not allow it to clatter loosely in a drawer with other utensils. Also, do not allow the edge to grow dull; sharpen it often with a small handheld sharpener. Inexpensive knife sharpeners may be found in kitchenware stores and hardware stores. Most handheld sharpeners are simple to use and come with easy-to-follow instructions.

INGREDIENTS

If you are lucky enough to live near a good supermarket and/or in a city, you should be able to find most of the ingredients for this book very easily. A resources list at the back of the book will guide you to sources for less common or especially high-quality ingredients. The same list also includes a few sources for equipment and uncommon cookware, such as earthenware pie plates.

Some seasonal produce, such as heirloom tomatoes, is best found at farm stands or small local markets. Don't overlook health food stores as a source for some hard-to-find items such as shelled hazelnuts, short-grain rice, orange flower water, and rice flour. Many mail-order catalogs, such as King Arthur Flour (baking ingredients and cookware) and Adriana's Bazaar (spices), are happy to give advice over the phone about ingredients and cooking.

In the recipes, certain ingredients are defined as follows:

- **BUTTER** refers to salted butter unless otherwise specified (that is, unsalted butter).

- **SHELLED NUTS** refers to nuts that have been removed from their shells. Shelled pistachios, hazelnuts, and pumpkin seeds can often be found in health food stores or ethnic food markets such as Middle Eastern or Indian markets.

- **ONIONS** are medium yellow onions unless otherwise specified.

WINES

by J. D. Landis

There are generally three wine recommendations in this book for most appetizers and main courses. The three wines are listed in order of likely expense, from low to high. Their order does not indicate one's greater compatibility with the food. And it's always a mistake to assume that better wine comes at greater cost (just as it is often a mistake to assume that it doesn't).

White wine or red (not to mention rosé) can be drunk with many dishes: salmon, pork—all kinds of food really. The best wine for a particular recipe is frequently determined not by what is at the center of a dish but by how it is cooked and its ingredients and what foods accompany it. Quite a few of the dishes in this book have wine recommendations that represent a kind of vinaceous rainbow coalition. Choose what you think you'll prefer; better still, experiment. And remember that specific suggestions are just that: If you are disinclined to try or can't find a Sauvignon Blanc from New Zealand, drink one you think you'd prefer or that is more readily available.

A very few of the wines (mostly listed third, sometimes second) are not really intended to be drunk young, which is to say in the vintages most likely for sale at the local wine store. This is true primarily of such big tannic red wines as Madiran, Cornas, Barolo, and many fine Bordeaux, though it is also true of such age-worthy whites as Savennières. So if an older vintage is not available, save your money and your tongue, and drink and enjoy something less hermetic. Better yet, consult your wine merchant and do spend your money, but put that bottle down for a decade or more. Modern methods of vinification to the contrary, there are some wines that require and benefit gloriously from age. To drink one of these too young is not quite the vinous equivalent of William Blake's famous dictum—"Better murder an infant in its cradle than nurse an unacted desire"—but for those who love wine, it's close.

In the evening Jack and Jackie would typically

host a dinner for eight—a collection of close friends

with an imported New York artist or writer as a "new face"—

as Italian songs played softly on the Victrola.

—Sally Bedell Smith, Grace and Power:
The Private World of the Kennedy White House

TEN MENUS
FOR SPRING

· · · · · · ·

MENU 7
[PAGE 45]
Aloo Kofta

Spiced Carrot Soup

Kadhai Murgh

Basmati Rice with Saffron

Mango Pudding

MENU 8
[PAGE 52]
Walnut Spread

Moules Marinière

Lamb Chops with Anchovy and Mint Butter

Salt-Crusted New Potatoes

Cheesecake with Blueberry Compote

MENU 9
[PAGE 57]
Mushrooms Sautéed in Vermouth

Pecan-Crusted Crab Cakes with Lime Aioli

Peruvian-Style Pork and Peanut Stew

Braised Collard Greens

Bread Pudding with Lemon Sauce

MENU 10
[PAGE 63]
(VEGETARIAN)

Herbed Pignoli Dolmas

Endive Salad with Toasted Pumpkin Seeds

Penne alla Vodka

Champagne Melon Soup with Raspberry Ice Balls

MENU I

. . . .

Snow Peas with Blue Cheese and Mascarpone

Green peas, also known as English *peas, have tough, inedible pods. In this recipe, tender, crisp snow peas are filled with creamy mascarpone that is mildly flavored with blue cheese. Fresh green peas are inserted in a row on top to make an hors d'oeuvre that is charming to look at and easy to eat.*

> 5 ounces crumbled Roquefort or other blue cheese
> 8 ounces mascarpone cheese
> 8 ounces crisp, fresh snow pea pods
> 1/3 cup (about 4 ounces) raw shelled fresh English (round green) peas

1. Using an electric mixer, blend together the Roquefort and mascarpone until very smooth, light, and fluffy. Cover and refrigerate.

2. Using a small, sharp knife, split open each snow pea by slicing off the thinnest edge possible on the straight side of each pod. Gently pry open the pod so it is shaped like a canoe.

3. Put the cheese mixture into a pastry bag fitted with a 1/2-inch fluted or round tip. (Alternatively, the cheese mixture may be spread in the snow peas with a small blunt knife.)

Fill the snow peas with the cheese mixture. Press a row of evenly spaced peas (4 peas for large pods, 3 for small ones) into each pod, just deep enough for them to stick firmly in the cheese and remain visible.

4. Arrange the stuffed peas on a small platter. Cover loosely with plastic wrap and refrigerate until serving.

WINES: Moscato d'Asti, Vouvray or other Chenin Blanc (demi-sec), Port (White, Ruby, or Tawny, all lightly chilled)

TO MAKE AHEAD
Up to five days before serving: Prepare cheese mixture, cover, and refrigerate.
Three hours before serving: Stuff cheese and peas into snow pea pods and garnish. Cover and refrigerate.

Baked Stuffed Clams

I spent all the summers of my youth in Wellfleet, Massachusetts, on Cape Cod, where my father made this recipe with quahogs we dug ourselves. It freezes beautifully.

24 quahogs, opened by hand, all the juices and half of the shells reserved (ask your fishmonger to do this)
¼ cup finely chopped onions
1 tablespoon finely chopped parsley
1 tablespoon finely chopped green bell pepper
2 teaspoons minced celery
1 small clove garlic, peeled and minced
Olive oil
½ teaspoon Old Bay Seasoning
¼ cup white wine
1 teaspoon Pernod (optional)
Dash of hot sauce
½ cup dry bread crumbs
Finely crushed Saltines or other salted crackers
Paprika
Finely grated Parmesan cheese (optional)

1. By hand or using a food processor or blender, finely chop the clams. In a large mixing bowl, combine the clams with the onions, parsley, bell pepper, celery, and garlic.

2. Place a large sauté pan over medium heat and add 2 tablespoons olive oil. Add the clam mixture and sauté until vegetables are softened, about 2 minutes. Add the Old Bay Seasoning, wine, Pernod, and hot sauce. Sauté another 30 seconds and then remove from the heat. Add the bread crumbs and toss until well combined. Transfer to a bowl and allow to cool. If the mixture seems dry, add a little of the reserved clam juice.

3. Lightly pack equal portions of clam mixture into each shell half. Sprinkle with cracker crumbs and paprika, and drizzle a little olive oil over each. Wrap each filled shell with aluminum foil and place on a baking sheet. Freeze until solid and then transfer to a sealed freezer bag. These may be frozen up to 1 month.

4. Place the frozen clams on a baking sheet and allow to defrost in the refrigerator overnight.

5. Preheat the oven to 400 degrees. Remove the foil from the clams and, if desired, sprinkle with a little Parmesan. Bake until the clams are heated in the center and browned on top, 15 to 20 minutes. To test whether the clams are heated in the center, insert the tip of a knife. The tip should be warm when it is removed. If it is cold, lower the temperature to 350 degrees and allow about 10 more minutes for cooking.

WINES: Cassis (white), Sauvignon Blanc (United States), Riesling (Australia)

TO MAKE AHEAD

Up to one month before serving: Prepare stuffing. Fill clams, cover individually with foil, and freeze.

The day before serving: Transfer clams from freezer to refrigerator to defrost overnight.

To serve: Preheat oven to 400 degrees. Remove foil from clams, place on a baking sheet, and bake until golden brown. Serve hot.

Make-Ahead Risotto
with Sage and Prosciutto

This recipe takes advantage of a trick used by professional chefs: Partially cook the risotto ahead of time and finish the recipe when it is needed. This recipe is finished with sage and prosciutto, but you may wish to substitute other chopped herbs and sautéed vegetables or meats.

FOR THE RISOTTO:

8 cups chicken stock

¼ pound (1 stick) unsalted butter

½ cup extra-virgin olive oil

2 large onions, peeled and minced

4 cups Arborio rice

TO FINISH:

About 6 cups chicken stock

28 leaves fresh sage

4 collard green leaves, trimmed and
   rib removed, torn into small pieces

4 tablespoons unsalted butter

4 thin slices prosciutto, cut into thin
   strips

Salt and freshly ground black pepper

1. *Prepare the risotto:* In a small saucepan, bring the chicken stock to a boil. Lower the heat and keep the stock at a simmer.

2. In a medium saucepan, heat the butter and olive oil over medium heat until the butter has melted. Add the onions and sauté until translucent. Add the rice and stir until it is evenly coated with butter.

3. Reduce the heat to low. Slowly add the hot stock, ⅔ cup at a time, stirring constantly with a wooden spoon until the rice absorbs the liquid, 4 to 5 minutes after each addition. When all the stock has been absorbed, remove the risotto from the heat. Immediately pour onto a baking sheet to stop the cooking and cool as quickly as possible; the rice grains will still be a bit raw in the center. Refrigerate, uncovered, until chilled and then transfer to a covered container. The partially cooked risotto may be refrigerated for up to 2 days.

4. *To finish:* In a small saucepan, combine the chicken stock with the sage and collard greens. Bring to a boil, reduce the heat, and keep at a simmer.

5. In a medium saucepan over medium-low heat, melt the butter and stir in the risotto until it is warm. Add about ½ cup stock (do not include the sage or collard greens), stirring until the stock is absorbed, 4 to 5 minutes. Repeat until all the stock has been absorbed. Add the prosciutto with the final addition of stock. Adjust the amount of stock as needed; the risotto should be very creamy and the rice grains tender but firm. Season to taste with salt and pepper, and serve immediately.

WINES: Beaujolais-Villages, Valpolicella, Nebbiolo d'Alba, Vernaccia di Oristano

TO MAKE AHEAD

Up to two days before serving: Cook risotto until al dente. Chill, cover, and refrigerate.

Thirty minutes before serving: Melt butter, add rice, and reheat stock. Add stock to rice until fully cooked.

Fiddlehead Salad

Fiddleheads are immature ferns. When they first emerge in the spring, they are coiled like the head of a violin. They have a flavor and texture similar to asparagus. In early spring they may be purchased in many greengrocers and supermarkets.

4 cups fiddlehead ferns, trimmed
¼ cup lemon olive oil
2 tablespoons champagne or other white wine vinegar
2 tablespoons chopped fresh dill
1 tablespoon finely chopped shallots
1 large or 2 small heads Boston lettuce, leaves separated
Salt and freshly ground black pepper
⅓ cup toasted chopped pecans

1. Place the ferns in a steamer with 1 inch of water beneath and steam until barely tender, about 5 minutes. Transfer to a bowl. While the fiddleheads are still warm, add the lemon olive oil, vinegar, dill, and shallots. Mix well, cover, and refrigerate.

2. Arrange the leaves of lettuce decoratively on a serving platter or on individual plates. Top with the marinated fiddleheads, drizzling a bit of marinade over the lettuce leaves. Season with salt and pepper to taste and sprinkle with chopped pecans.

TO MAKE AHEAD

The night before serving: Steam fiddleheads and prepare marinade. Dress fiddleheads with marinade, cover, and refrigerate.

To serve: Arrange salad greens on serving platter. Add fiddleheads and garnish.

Bulgarian Baklava

Vasilka Nicolova, an American knitwear designer of Bulgarian descent, was given this recipe by her mother. Her mother made the pastry herself, rolling it out by hand using a cut-off broomstick until it filled the whole kitchen table and was as sheer and transparent as silk—an all day event.

> 5 cups sugar
>
> 1 cup olive oil (not extra-virgin), or as needed
>
> 1 pound box filo (phyllo) pastry (14 × 18-inch sheets, cut in half crosswise)
>
> 2 cups finely ground walnuts
>
> Cinnamon in a shaker
>
> 9 × 14-inch ceramic or glass baking dish

1. In a small saucepan, combine the sugar with 4 cups water. Place over low heat and simmer until the sugar has melted. Allow to cool and then refrigerate until well chilled, about 4 hours.

2. Preheat the oven to 325 degrees. Place the olive oil in a small saucepan over low heat (it will be used after the baklava is assembled and should be hot).

3. Place 2 pastry sheets on the bottom of the casserole. Lightly sprinkle walnuts and a little cinnamon all over. Top with 1 sheet of pastry and again sprinkle with walnuts and cinnamon. Repeat until all the sheets have been used except for 2 unblemished sheets. Place them on top.

4. Cut the baklava into diamond shapes and immediately brush all the cut edges with hot olive oil. Bake until the pastry is lightly browned and fragrant, about 1 hour. Remove from the oven and immediately and carefully pour the cold sugar syrup over it. The entire baklava, including the top, should be saturated.

5. Cover lightly with waxed paper and allow to soak for 1 to 2 hours. Drain and discard the sugar syrup. Cover and store the baklava at room temperature.

WINE: Sweet Muscat (preferably Bulgarian)

TO MAKE AHEAD

Six hours to three days before serving: Assemble baklava. Bake and top with syrup. Drain. Cover and store at room temperature.

MENU 2

. . . .

Tomato Crostini with
Walnut Oil and Shallots

This recipe is the invention of my husband's aunt, Ellen Saltman. Walnut oil is used in the topping and brushed on the crostini before crisping them in the oven, and it's a brilliant touch. The oil can't be detected, yet it enhances the flavor of the tomato, herbs, and spices.

½ cup walnut oil

3 tablespoons butter

½ cup finely chopped shallots

3 cloves garlic, peeled and minced

1½ cups coarsely chopped Italian plum tomatoes

2 tablespoons finely chopped sun-dried tomatoes packed in oil, drained

¼ tablespoon salt

¼ teaspoon red pepper flakes, or to taste

¼ teaspoon oregano

⅓ cup chicken broth

¼ teaspoon onion powder

One baguette, cut into ¼-inch slices

⅓ cup finely grated parmesan cheese

⅓ cup finely shredded fresh basil leaves

1. *Prepare the topping:* In a large skillet, combine ¼ cup of the walnut oil and 1 tablespoon of the butter. Place over medium heat. When the butter has melted, add the shal-

lots and sauté until they begin to soften, about 2 minutes. Add the garlic and sauté 1 more minute. Add the chopped tomatoes, sun-dried tomatoes, salt, red pepper flakes, oregano, and chicken broth. Continue to sauté until all of the liquid has evaporated. Remove from heat and set aside. (If not being used immediately, the tomato mixture may be cooled, covered, and refrigerated for up to two days.)

2. *Prepare the crostini:* Preheat the oven to 350 degrees. In a small saucepan, combine the remaining ¼ cup walnut oil, remaining 2 tablespoons butter, and onion powder. place over low heat until the butter has melted, then remove from heat.

3. Using a pastry brush, brush the walnut oil mixture over both sides of each slice of baguette. Spread in a single layer across a baking sheet, and bake until light golden on top, about 5 minutes. Turn the slices and bake for another 5 minutes. (If not serving immediately, the toasted slices may be cooled and stored in an airtight bag or container for up to two days.)

4. To serve, preheat the oven to 350 degrees. Spread the crostini with topping and sprinkle with parmesan. Place them on a baking sheet and bake until thoroughly heated, about 10 minutes. Sprinkle with shredded basil and serve.

WINES: Brut Rosé, Dolcetto, Barbera, Zinfandel

TO MAKE AHEAD

Up to two days before serving: Make topping. Cool, cover, and refrigerate. Make crostini. Cool and store in an airtight bag or other container.

Cornmeal-Crusted Green Beans
with Spicy Mango Sauce

The dipping sauce for these crispy green beans includes whole Chinese salted black beans, spicy sriracha chili sauce, and fresh mango puree.

FOR THE SAUCE:

3 large, ripe mangoes

1 tablespoon lemon juice, or to taste

1 tablespoon Chinese salted black beans (available in Asian markets),
　　rinsed and dried

½ teaspoon minced jalapeño pepper

Sriracha chili sauce (available bottled in Asian markets; see page 13)

Salt and freshly ground black pepper

1 tablespoon chopped cilantro leaves

Whole cilantro leaves for garnish

FOR THE BEANS:

1 cup cornmeal

2 tablespoons all-purpose flour

1 teaspoon garlic powder

Salt and coarsely ground black pepper

Vegetable oil for frying

1 egg, lightly beaten

1 pound green beans, trimmed and washed (available bagged and
　　ready-to-cook in some supermarkets)

1. *Make the sauce:* Peel the mangoes and cut the flesh into a mixing bowl. Add the lemon juice and mash until the mangoes are pureed. Add the black beans, jalapeño pepper, and about ½ teaspoon sriracha sauce. Season with salt and pepper to taste and, if desired, add more sriracha or lemon juice to taste. The sauce should be both spicy and tangy. Cover and refrigerate until serving.

2. *Prepare the beans:* In a large bowl, combine the cornmeal, flour, garlic powder, and salt and pepper to taste; set aside. Place a large skillet over medium heat and add about 1 inch of vegetable oil. Place the beaten egg in a large bowl, add the beans, and turn them until they are coated with egg. When the oil is hot, dust the beans, a few at a time, in the corn-

meal mixture and then place in the frying pan. When the beans are golden brown, use a slotted spoon to transfer them to paper towels to drain. Continue until all the beans are cooked. Transfer to a serving bowl and pass the sauce separately.

3. To serve, fold the chopped cilantro into the sauce and garnish with a few whole leaves; set aside.

WINES: Viognier, Zinfandel (continued), Chenin Blanc (Mexico or South Africa)

TO MAKE AHEAD
Up to two hours before serving: Make mango sauce. Cover and refrigerate.
Twenty minutes before serving: Add cilantro to sauce, garnish, and set aside. Make cornmeal mixture. Dip beans in egg and cornmeal, and fry.

SRIRACHA SAUCE

Sriracha is a thin red hot sauce made from Thai chili peppers and garlic. It is used as a condiment, marinade, and seasoning.

I first learned about sriracha chili sauce on a visit to a restaurant in California when my husband and I inquired about the flavorful spice in a seafood dish. Our waiter assured us that we could find this marvelous ingredient in a local supermarket, so we headed there directly from the restaurant. We bought several large bottles and hauled them back to the East Coast, only to discover to our chagrin that the same product was easily found at home.

Sriracha is imported from Thailand and is also made in the United States. The heat of the sauce varies, so you may wish to experiment with different brands to see which you prefer.

South Pacific Chowder with Deep-Sea Scallops

Orange juice, coconut milk, and saffron combine to give this chowder remarkable depth of flavor.

FOR THE BROTH:

1/4 cup olive oil

1 Scotch bonnet chili or jalapeño pepper, seeded and minced

6 shallots, peeled and thinly sliced

4 cloves garlic, peeled and thinly sliced

12 small clams, scrubbed

12 mussels, debearded and scrubbed

1 star anise

1 tablespoon cracked black peppercorns

3 cups freshly squeezed orange juice

2 teaspoons saffron threads

4 cups heavy cream

1 cup canned coconut milk

FOR THE VEGETABLES:

6 new potatoes (about 1 pound), scrubbed and diced

1/2 cup olive oil

2 ounces smoked slab bacon, diced (about 1/2 cup)

4 cloves garlic, peeled and thinly sliced

1 poblano chili, seeded and minced

2/3 cup fresh corn kernels (from about 1 ear)

1/2 medium red onion, peeled and diced

2 large carrots, diced

1/2 fennel bulb, cored and diced

2 celery stalks, diced

1 red bell pepper, seeded and diced

1/4 cup roughly chopped cilantro leaves

2 bay leaves, broken into pieces

Salt and freshly ground black pepper

FOR THE SCALLOPS:

24 large sea scallops

Salt and freshly ground black pepper

1/4 cup flour

2 cups panko (available in Asian markets and some supermarkets) or dry, coarse bread crumbs

2 large eggs, lightly beaten

1 1/2 tablespoons half-and-half

3/4 cup peanut oil

1. *Prepare the broth:* In a large heavy-bottomed saucepan, heat the oil over medium-high heat and sauté the chili, shallots, and garlic for 1 minute. Add the clams, mussels, star anise, cracked peppercorns, and orange juice. Stir, then cover the pan. After a few minutes, as the shellfish open, transfer them to a colander set over a bowl to catch the liquid; keep the pan covered as much as possible. Discard any shellfish that don't open after 10 minutes.

2. After all the clams and mussels have been removed, return any liquid in the bowl to the pan. Uncover the pan and reduce the liquid until 1 cup remains, about 10 minutes. Add the saffron, cream, and coconut milk. Bring to a boil, stirring occasionally. Reduce until the mixture just coats the back of a spoon, 15 to 20 minutes. Remove from the heat and strain into a bowl. Discard the solids and set aside the cream. Remove the clam and mussel meat from the shells; set aside.

3. *Prepare the vegetables:* Bring a saucepan of lightly salted water to a boil. Add the potatoes and simmer until just underdone, 8 to 10 minutes. Strain and set aside. In a 6-quart flameproof casserole over medium-high heat, heat the oil and sauté the bacon until half-cooked. Add the garlic and poblano chili, and stir. Add the corn, onion, carrots, fennel, celery, and bell pepper, and stir. Add the cilantro, bay leaves, and salt and pepper to taste. Stir until the vegetables are just tender, about 8 minutes. Add the potatoes, reserved saffron cream, and clam and mussel meat. Allow the chowder to cool, then cover and refrigerate as soon as possible.

4. Place the chowder in a large saucepan over medium-low heat. Heat until steaming and keep warm; do not boil.

5. *Prepare the scallops:* Season the scallops with salt and pepper to taste. Place the flour and panko on separate plates. Whisk the eggs and half-and-half together in a bowl. Dredge the scallops in the flour, then in the egg wash, and finally in the panko. Set aside on a large plate. Place a large skillet over medium-high heat and heat the oil. Working in batches, sauté the scallops until nicely browned on both sides. Drain on paper towels.

6. Ladle the chowder into warm soup plates and place 3 scallops in the center of each plate. Serve immediately.

WINES: Riesling (off-dry, Finger Lakes), Rosé (Provence), Hermitage Blanc

TO MAKE AHEAD
Up to eight hours before serving: Prepare chowder and refrigerate.
Twenty minutes before serving: Reheat chowder. Bread and sauté scallops. Place in chowder.

Soft White Dinner Rolls

[MAKES 30 ROLLS]

Nigella Lawson wrote the recipe for these rolls that have added flavor and aesthetic appeal from two garnishes: sesame seeds and poppy seeds.

FOR THE DOUGH:

3½ to 4 cups all-purpose flour

3 teaspoons rapid-rise, bread machine, or other instant yeast

1 tablespoon salt

1 tablespoon superfine sugar

1½ cups milk

1½ tablespoons butter, softened

Vegetable oil for bowl and baking sheet

FOR THE GLAZE:

1 large egg, lightly beaten

1 tablespoon milk

Pinch of salt

1 teaspoon sesame seeds

1 teaspoon poppy seeds

1. *Prepare the dough:* In a large bowl, combine 3½ cups flour, yeast, salt, and sugar. In a small saucepan, combine the milk and butter, and place over low heat until the milk is lukewarm. Pour into the bowl of dry ingredients and mix with a fork to make a rough dough; add more flour if necessary.

2. By hand or using a mixer with a dough hook attachment, knead the dough until smooth and silky. Place in an oiled bowl, cover with plastic wrap, and set aside to rise in a warm place until doubled in size, about 1 hour.

3. Punch the air out of the dough. Oil a baking sheet. Pull off pieces of dough the size of walnuts and form into balls. Place on the baking sheet about ¼ inch apart, in 6 rows with 5 in each row (a total of 30 balls). Cover with a kitchen towel and allow to rise in a warm place for 30 minutes.

4. *Prepare the glaze:* When the rolls have risen, beat together the egg, milk, and salt. Paint the rolls with the glaze. Sprinkle one row with sesame seeds, the next with poppy

seeds, and leave the third row plain, then repeat the pattern. (A teaspoon of seeds should decorate 2 rows.) Cover the rolls securely with plastic wrap and freeze for up to 1 month.

5. Remove the rolls from the freezer and allow to defrost at room temperature.

6. Preheat the oven to 425 degrees. Bake the frozen or partially defrosted rolls until risen and golden brown, about 15 minutes. Transfer to a cooling rack or serve immediately. To serve, place the entire slab of rolls on a plate so that the rolls can be torn off as they are served.

TO MAKE AHEAD

Up to one month before serving: Prepare dough and shape into rolls. Allow to rise. Garnish and freeze.

One and a half hours before serving: Remove rolls from freezer and allow to defrost at room temperature.

Thirty minutes before serving: Preheat oven. Bake for 15 minutes.

Baked Apples with Amaretto

For a really special presentation, roast these apples in individual apple bakers, small ceramic dishes made expressly for that purpose.

> 8 baking apples, such as Jonathan, JonaGold, Ida Red, Fuji, and Cortland,
> cored (see page 18)
> Vegetable oil for greasing pan
> About 1½ cups dark brown sugar
> About ⅓ cup Amaretto liqueur
> Lightly sweetened whipped cream or vanilla ice cream (optional)

1. Preheat the oven to 350 degrees. Place the apples in a lightly oiled baking pan just large enough to hold them in a single layer. If necessary, trim the bottoms so the apples stand upright.

2. Sprinkle 2 to 3 tablespoons sugar in the center and on the top of each apple. Drizzle 1 or 2 teaspoons of Amaretto in the center and over each apple.

3. Bake until the apples are very tender and the sugar has melted, 45 minutes to 1 hour, depending on the size of the apples. To serve, place the hot apples in individual

bowls and top with some liquid from the pan. If desired, serve with whipped cream or ice cream.

WINES: Amoroso (East India) Sherry or Amaretto

THE BEST APPLES FOR BAKING

Since cooking makes apples sweeter and softer, the best apples for baking are those that are somewhat tart when raw and will retain their shape when cooked.

Granny Smith, Golden Delicious, and Gala apples are often recommended for cooking, and these apples are readily found in most supermarkets. However, Granny Smiths can be starchy if harvested before fully ripe. Golden Delicious and Gala apples are quite sweet and if used in a pie are best mixed with tart apples, cutting the amount of sugar in half. Do not use Red Delicious, which lose both flavor and texture when cooked.

Cortland apples are excellent for baking, as are Melrose, Northern Spy, Winesap, Jonathan, and Ida Red.

JonaGold apples have good flavor for cooking and eating. Their large size makes them convenient for peeling and slicing for pies. They will hold their shape when cooked, but because they tend to be sweet, the amount of sugar in a recipe may need to be cut by as much as half.

One of the newest superstars in the apple market is HoneyCrisp, a large apple similar to JonaGold. It keeps well, can be used for eating or cooking, and has an explosively crisp texture.

MENU 3

. . . .

Lobster Bites

This is essentially the same filling that is found in a classic lobster roll. For even more luxurious flavor, lightly brush the filo cups with melted butter and bake in a 350-degree oven for a few minutes, until lightly browned, before filling with lobster.

4 ounces lobster meat, shredded into small pieces (see page 20)

¼ cup finely diced celery

2 to 3 tablespoons mayonnaise

32 filo cups (available frozen in supermarkets)

1½ tablespoons finely sliced chives or minced green scallions

1. In a mixing bowl, combine the lobster, celery, and mayonnaise. Cover and refrigerate.

2. Fill the filo cups with the lobster mixture. Sprinkle with chives and arrange on a serving platter.

WINES: Sparkling (Australia), Bordeaux (white), Monbazillac (to sip)

TO MAKE AHEAD

One hour to twenty-four hours before serving: Prepare filling. Cover and refrigerate.

To serve: Fill filo cups with lobster mixture. Sprinkle cups with chives.

LOBSTER MEAT

Lobster meat may be purchased, shelled and chilled, from a fishmonger or supermarket. Many markets will allow you to choose your own live lobster and cook it for you on the spot. You can then bring it home and shell it yourself.

The amount of meat in a lobster depends on whether it is hard- or soft-shelled. The meat of hard-shelled lobsters has better flavor and a firmer, drier texture than newly-molted soft-shelled lobsters and is usually a better investment. A 1½-pound lobster of either kind should yield at least 4 ounces of meat, but consult your fishmonger to be sure.

If you would like to cook your own lobster at home, bring a large pot of lightly salted water to a boil. The pot must be large enough to submerge the entire lobster in the water. Put the lobster in headfirst and put the lid on the pot. When the water comes to a boil again, remove the lid and boil for 8 minutes. Remove the lobster and allow to cool until it can be handled. Using a kitchen mallet, lightly smash the claws and "arms," and extract the meat. Twist off the tail and use kitchen shears to cut the length of the underside; remove the meat. Use the meat immediately or cover and refrigerate until needed.

Gnocchi with Caramelized Onions, Sage, and Butter Sauce

Freezing the gnocchi ahead of time makes preparation of this dish easy. To make it even easier, purchased gnocchi may be used. It is available vacuum-packed in supermarkets and specialty food stores.

FOR THE GNOCCHI:

4 large starchy (baking) potatoes

1/2 teaspoon salt

2 large eggs

1 1/2 cups flour, or as needed

FOR THE SAUCE:

2 tablespoons olive oil

3 tablespoons butter

3 large onions, peeled, halved, and very thinly sliced

Salt and ground white pepper

6 to 8 large fresh sage leaves, torn into pieces

Freshly grated Parmigiano-Reggiano cheese

1. *Prepare the gnocchi:* Preheat the oven to 350 degrees. Bake the potatoes until tender in the center when pierced with a knife, about 1 hour. Peel the potatoes and mash or put through a ricer until very smooth. Add the salt, eggs, and flour, and mash or put through a ricer again. The mixture should have the consistency of a smooth, pliable dough.

2. Roll a portion of the dough into a rope about ¾ inch thick. Break off pieces about 1 inch long. Being careful not to squash the gnocchi, use the tines of a fork to lightly imprint lines on one side of each piece. Set the pieces on a baking sheet and continue until all the dough is used. Freeze uncovered. When the gnocchi are firm, transfer them to a sealed plastic freezer bag; freeze for up to 1 month.

3. Remove the gnocchi from the freezer. Place a large pot of lightly salted water over high heat and bring to a boil.

4. *Make the sauce:* Place a large skillet over medium heat and add the olive oil and butter. When the butter has melted, add the onions and sauté until softened, about 5 minutes. Reduce the heat to low and allow to cook, stirring occasionally, until the onions are very soft and caramelized, another 15 to 20 minutes. Season to taste with salt and white

pepper. Add the sage leaves and sauté another 2 minutes. Remove from the heat and keep warm.

5.   Place the gnocchi in boiling water; they will sink and after a few minutes float to the top. As soon as all the gnocchi are floating, drain well and add to the skillet with the sauce. Stir gently to combine. Place in a serving bowl or on individual plates and top each serving with a sprinkling of Parmigiano-Reggiano.

WINES: Pinot Grigio, Soave, Chianti Colli Aretini

TO MAKE AHEAD
Up to one month before serving: Make gnocchi; cover and freeze.
Thirty minutes before serving: Remove gnocchi from freezer. Bring water to a boil. Prepare
    sauce.
To serve: Cook and drain gnocchi and combine with sauce.

Sweet Crusted Leg of Lamb

Debra Tillar has two school-age daughters, teaches elementary school full-time, sings in a women's chorus, cares for her garden and home, and makes beaded jewelry that she sells in boutiques and craft shows. She's a skilled cook who knows how to give a relaxed and entertaining dinner party, and she also happens to be my sister. This recipe of hers results in lamb that is moist, tender, and flavorful.

> 1½ cups fresh bread crumbs
> 4 tablespoons Dijon mustard
> ½ cup orange marmalade
> ½ cup canned jellied cranberry sauce, plus additional for garnish
> 3 cloves garlic, peeled and minced
> 1½ tablespoons chopped fresh rosemary
> 5-pound boneless leg of lamb

1.   Preheat the oven to 350 degrees. In a large mixing bowl, combine the bread crumbs, mustard, marmalade, cranberry sauce, garlic, and rosemary to make a paste.

2.   Unwrap the lamb. If netting has been used, remove it, taking care to keep the

shape of the lamb intact. If the lamb has been tied with string, allow the string to remain. Using your hands, spread the paste so it completely covers the lamb, doing the underside first and then finishing with the top (fat) and sides.

3. Place the lamb in a shallow roasting pan. Cover tightly with foil. Roast until a meat thermometer reads 135 degrees for rare, 140 to 145 degrees for medium-rare, or 160 degrees for medium, 1½ to 2½ hours, removing foil halfway through cooking.

4. Slice the lamb in thick (¾ inch) slices, taking care to keep the flavorful crust together with the meat. Any crust that falls from the sides of the roast can be served as garnish. You may also choose to garnish each serving with a spoonful of cranberry sauce.

WINES: Stay with Chianti Colli Aretini or change to Chianti Classico, Rosé (Bandol), or Chateau Musar (Lebanon)

TO MAKE AHEAD
About 2½ hours before serving: Mix paste in bowl and cover lamb. Roast 1½ to 2½ hours.
To serve: Slice lamb and serve with crust.

Green Beans in Anchovy Butter

To reduce the fat and calories in this recipe, substitute olive oil or butter-flavored spread for half of the butter.

6 to 8 anchovy fillets
4 tablespoons unsalted butter
4 pounds green beans, trimmed

1. Rinse the anchovies, drain well, and chop finely. In a small skillet over low heat, melt the butter. Add the anchovies and stir until they fall apart and the mixture is smooth. Remove from the heat and allow to cool. Cover and refrigerate.

2. Steam the green beans just until tender, 7 to 10 minutes, depending on their size. Drain well, return the beans to the pan, and place over low heat. Add the anchovy butter. Stir for 1 to 2 minutes, until the beans are hot and thoroughly coated with the butter. Transfer to a warmed serving dish and serve immediately.

Up to one week before serving: Prepare anchovy butter. Cover and refrigerate.

Fifteen minutes before serving: Steam beans. Toss with anchovy butter.

Crackling Thin Tarts with Pecans and Sticky Caramel

This dessert looks impressive but is actually very simple to prepare, qualities that make it perfect party fare.

FOR THE CARAMEL SAUCE:

1⅓ cups light brown sugar

¼ cup granulated sugar

⅔ cup light corn syrup

1 cup heavy cream

Pinch of salt

4 tablespoons unsalted butter

FOR THE PASTRY AND ASSEMBLY:

One 1-pound box puff pastry sheets, cut into eight 5 × 5-inch squares

4 cups broken pecan pieces

1. *Prepare the caramel sauce:* In a heavy, medium-sized saucepan, combine the light brown sugar, granulated sugar, corn syrup, heavy cream, and salt. Place over high heat and bring to a boil. Boil for 10 minutes, then remove from the heat and add the butter. Stir well to mix. Allow to cool, then place in a microwave-safe container (such as a glass measuring cup), cover, and refrigerate.

2. *Prepare the puff pastry:* Preheat the oven to 450 degrees. Place 4 puff pastry squares evenly spaced on parchment paper on a baking sheet. Chill in the refrigerator for 15 minutes. Cover with another sheet of parchment paper and weight with another baking sheet on top. Bake for 8 minutes, remove the top baking sheet and top parchment paper, and continue to bake until golden brown, 2 to 3 minutes. Remove from the oven. Repeat with the remaining 4 puff pastry squares. Cover with plastic wrap and store at room temperature.

3. Preheat the oven to 450 degrees. Pour warm caramel sauce over the pastry squares and sprinkle an equal amount of pecans on top of each square. Bake the tarts in the oven until the caramel is bubbly and the pecans are toasted, about 4 minutes. Serve hot, unadorned or as an accompaniment to ice cream.

WINE: Orange Muscat

TO MAKE AHEAD

The day before serving: Prepare caramel sauce; refrigerate. Bake puff pastry, cool, and wrap.

To serve: Preheat oven. Reheat caramel sauce. Drizzle sauce on pastry, sprinkle with nuts, and bake 4 minutes.

MENU 4

. . . .

Marinated Baby Artichokes

Unless you live in California, baby artichokes can sometimes be hard to come by. I buy them whenever I see them in the market and always bring a bag back from a visit to the West Coast. In this recipe either tarragon or mint will work nicely, though the flavors are quite different. Try it both ways to see which you prefer.

2 whole lemons
$\frac{1}{4}$ cup white or cider vinegar
24 small (2 to 3 inches long) artichokes
$\frac{1}{4}$ cup lemon olive oil
3 tablespoons champagne vinegar or other white wine vinegar
2 cloves garlic, peeled and minced
1 shallot, peeled and minced, or 1 tablespoon minced red onion
1 tablespoon chopped fresh tarragon or mint
Pinch of sugar
Salt and white pepper

1. Place a large pot of water over high heat to bring to a boil. Cut the lemons in half and squeeze the juice into the water, then add the squeezed rinds as well.

2. In a large bowl, combine the white or cider vinegar with 4 cups water and set aside. Using a sharp knife, remove a thin slice from the bottom of each artichoke and trim off ¼ to ½ inch from the tip. Pull off any browned or discolored outer leaves to reveal fresh light green leaves beneath. As each artichoke is trimmed, drop it into the vinegar water to prevent discoloration.

3. When all the artichokes are trimmed, add them to the boiling lemon water. Reduce the heat to medium and cook the artichokes at a lively simmer until they are tender in the center when the bottoms are pierced with a knife, 12 to 15 minutes. Drain well and allow to cool.

4. In a mixing bowl, combine the artichokes, lemon olive oil, champagne vinegar, garlic, shallot, tarragon, and sugar. Mix well and season to taste with salt and white pepper. Cover and refrigerate for at least 24 hours or up to 3 days.

5. Remove the artichokes from the refrigerator and bring to room temperature. Halve lengthwise or leave whole and serve with toothpicks for skewering.

WINES: Frascati, Terret (blanc), Sauvignon Blanc (New Zealand); alternative: sparkling water with lemon wedge

TO MAKE AHEAD
One to three days before serving: Boil artichokes and marinate. Cover and refrigerate.
To serve: Bring to room temperature.

Crabmeat and Guacamole Parfait

Many thanks to Brian Engel, a chef working in corporate dining in New York City. Brian was once a chef at a well-known New York seafood restaurant. This layered crabmeat salad, his own creation, looks especially festive when served in transparent goblets.

FOR THE CRABMEAT:
1 pound lump crabmeat, picked over for shells and cartilage
2 tablespoons mayonnaise
2 teaspoons fresh lemon juice
Tabasco sauce
Salt

FOR THE GUACAMOLE:

3 large ripe Hass avocados, halved, pitted, and peeled

2 tablespoons fresh lime juice

$\frac{1}{2}$ teaspoon ground cumin

2 tablespoons finely chopped onion

1 plum tomato, seeded and cut into small dice

1 tablespoon finely chopped cilantro

Tabasco sauce

Salt

Fresh cilantro leaves for garnish

1. *Prepare the crabmeat:* In a mixing bowl, combine the crabmeat, mayonnaise, and lemon juice. Toss to mix. Season to taste with Tabasco sauce and salt. Cover and refrigerate.

2. *Prepare the guacamole:* In a large mixing bowl, combine the avocado flesh, lime juice, and cumin. Mash but do not puree. Add the onion, tomato, and cilantro, and stir gently to mix. Season to taste with Tabasco sauce and salt. Cover with plastic wrap, placing the wrap directly on the surface of the mixture.

3. Spoon about 1 tablespoon guacamole into each of 8 small glasses or goblets. Top loosely with one-eighth of the crabmeat; do not pack the mixture down. Top the crabmeat with another spoonful of guacamole and garnish with a few cilantro leaves. Serve immediately.

WINES: Continue with a wine from the first course (Frascati, Terret, Sauvignon Blanc) or start serving the wine you've chosen for the next (Italian Chardonnay, Tocai Friulano, Gavi).

TO MAKE AHEAD

About 1 hour before serving: Prepare crabmeat. Prepare guacamole. Have eight serving glasses or goblets ready.

To serve: Spoon guacamole and crabmeat into glasses. Garnish and serve.

Mussels with Orechiette

This recipe has a novel garnish: fine strips of fresh collard greens that are fried until crisp and papery. It is from Patrick O'Connell, chef and owner of Inn at Little Washington in Washington, Virginia.

FOR THE MUSSELS AND SAUCE:

3 pounds mussels

4 shallots, peeled and chopped

4 cloves garlic, peeled and minced

6 sprigs thyme

1 bay leaf

6 sprigs parsley

1½ cups dry white wine or vermouth

4 cups heavy cream

½ cup finely grated Parmigiano-Reggiano cheese

Salt and freshly ground white pepper

Freshly ground nutmeg

FOR THE PASTA:

Salt

1 pound orechiette pasta

FOR THE CRISPY COLLARD GREENS:

About 1 quart (or as needed) vegetable oil

1 cup very thin strips of collard green leaves that have been washed, stemmed, and thoroughly dried

Salt

Extra-virgin olive oil

8 pinches finely grated Parmigiano-Reggiano cheese

1. *Prepare the mussels and sauce:* Sort through the mussels, discarding any that have broken or cracked shells. Scrub the mussels with a brush under cold running water and discard any mussels that do not close tightly.

2. In a saucepan large enough to hold the mussels after they open, combine the shallots, garlic, thyme, bay leaf, parsley, and wine. Place over high heat and bring to a rapid boil. Add the mussels and steam about 3 minutes. Check once or twice and transfer open mussels to a bowl; the mussels do not have to be fully cooked because they will be cooked again. Remove the mussels from the shells and set them aside; discard the shells.

3. Strain the liquid and transfer it to a small pan. Place over high heat and bring to a boil. Reduce the liquid by half and set aside. In another small pan, bring the cream to a boil. Reduce by half, until the cream coats the back of a spoon. Add ¼ cup mussel liquid to the cream, adding more as desired for consistency and flavor. The recipe may be prepared up to this point and the mussels, sauce, and any remaining mussel liquid refrigerated for up to 1 day.

4. Place the sauce in a large saucepan. Add the Parmigiano-Reggiano and season to taste with salt, white pepper, and nutmeg. If the sauce has been prepared ahead of time, additional mussel liquid may be desired. Set the pan of sauce aside.

5. *Prepare the pasta:* Bring a large pot of lightly salted water to a boil and add the orechiette. Boil until tender, 8 to 10 minutes. Drain well and set aside.

6. *Prepare the collard greens:* In a deep fryer, wok, or medium saucepan, bring at least 2 inches of oil to 350 degrees. Set aside a large plate or tray covered with absorbent paper. Add the collard greens to the hot oil and fry just long enough to make them curl, about 30 seconds. Transfer them to the absorbent paper to drain. Salt lightly to taste.

7. Bring the sauce to a simmer and add the mussels. When the mussels are warm, add the orechiette and stir to mix well. Sprinkle with olive oil and adjust the seasonings. Spoon onto 8 pasta plates. Top each plate with a pinch of Parmigiano-Reggiano and a mound of crispy collard greens.

WINES: Chardonnay (Italy), Tocai Friulano, Gavi; alternative: Wheat Beer

TO MAKE AHEAD
One day before serving: Prepare mussels and sauce. Cover and refrigerate.
Thirty minutes before serving: Bring a large pot of water to a boil. Reheat mussels. Make crispy collard greens. Cook and drain pasta. Add sauce and garnish.

Vanilla-Roasted Figs with
Wildflower Honey Ice Cream

You can vary the flavor of the ice cream by your choice of honey. Forest honey, acacia honey, tupelo honey—the choices are endless, and each is distinctive and wonderful in its own way.

FOR THE ICE CREAM:

2 cups milk

2 cups heavy cream

½ cup wildflower honey

12 large egg yolks

¼ cup sugar

FOR THE FIGS:

24 whole ripe figs (Black Mission, Brown Turkey, Adriatic Green, or a
  combination), stemmed, washed, and dried

4 vanilla beans, split lengthwise

3 tablespoons unsalted butter

1½ teaspoons sugar

1. *Prepare the ice cream:* In a large saucepan, combine the milk, cream, and honey. Place over medium heat and stir to dissolve the honey. When the honey has completely dissolved, remove the pan from the heat and allow to cool.

2. By hand or using an electric mixer, whisk the egg yolks and sugar in a metal bowl until they have thickened and lightened in color. Gradually whisk in the warm milk mixture. Return the mixture to the saucepan and place over medium-low heat. Stir until the mixture coats the back of a wooden spoon and reaches 175 degrees; do not overheat. Immediately remove from the heat and transfer to a mixing bowl. Chill the bowl by placing it in ice water and allow the mixture to cool to room temperature.

3. Strain the mixture into a container. Cover and refrigerate for at least 5 hours or overnight. Freeze in an ice-cream maker according to the manufacturer's instructions and then transfer to a covered container. Freeze for several hours or until hardened.

4. Preheat the oven to 400 degrees. *Prepare the figs:* Slice off and discard the tops of the figs. Cut the split vanilla beans into 2-inch pieces. Make a small slit in the top of each fig and insert a section of vanilla bean.

5. In an ovenproof pan large enough to hold all the figs upright, melt the butter over

medium heat. Add the sugar to the butter and stir to dissolve. Stand the figs in the butter and add any remaining vanilla bean pieces to the pan. Place the pan in the oven until the figs are thoroughly heated, about 10 minutes. Serve the figs warm or at room temperature.

6. To serve, place a scoop of ice cream into each of 8 bowls. Arrange 3 of the figs (with vanilla bean) around each scoop. Drizzle with a bit of sauce from the fig pan and serve immediately.

WINE: Black Muscat

TO MAKE AHEAD

One day to one week before serving: Prepare ice cream. Chill and freeze in ice-cream maker. Transfer to covered container and store in freezer.

Thirty minutes before serving: Preheat oven. Prepare figs and heat in oven 10 minutes. Serve warm figs with ice cream.

MENU 5

. . . .

Smoked Trout Pâté

This pâté takes only minutes to prepare. It travels well and makes a nice addition to a picnic. To dress it up, garnish with fresh herbs or small edible flowers.

8 ounces cream cheese

$1/3$ cup sour cream

1 tablespoon prepared horseradish

1 tablespoon lemon juice

$1/4$ teaspoon Tabasco sauce

1 pound skinless, boneless smoked trout fillets (available from seafood
markets, specialty food stores, and vacuum-packed in supermarkets)

$1/4$ cup finely chopped scallions (green part only)

1 tablespoon finely chopped parsley

1 tablespoon finely chopped dill

1. In the bowl of a food processor, combine the cream cheese, sour cream, horse-radish, lemon juice, and Tabasco sauce. Process until very smooth. Set aside about one-fourth of the trout fillets and add the remainder to the cream cheese mixture. Process again until almost smooth.

2. Transfer the mixture to a bowl and add the scallions, parsley, and dill. Break the reserved trout into small chunks and stir into the mixture. Cover and refrigerate.

3. Serve chilled with toasted pita bread, crackers, or thin slices of toasted bread.

WINES: Manzanilla, Bianco di Custoza (still or spumante), Riesling (Kabinett)

TO MAKE AHEAD

Up to two days before serving: Make pâté. Cover and refrigerate.

Celery Root and Apple Salad

This dish is commonly found in bistros in France. For a shortcut use jars of imported julienned celery root sold in specialty food markets and cut the apples to julienne of the same size.

2 large celery roots (about 1 pound each)	2 cups crème fraîche (see page 173)
2 Granny Smith apples	¼ cup minced fresh chervil or parsley
¼ cup lemon juice	Salt and white pepper
1½ tablespoons Dijon mustard	8 sprigs chervil or parsley for garnish

1. Peel the celery roots and cut into fine julienne. (This is more easily done by halving each root and using a mandoline.) Place the julienned celery root in a large mixing bowl.

2. Peel and core the apples and cut into julienne. Place in a bowl and add the lemon juice, tossing to make sure all the apples are coated with juice. Add the apples and any juice in the bowl to the bowl of celery root and toss to combine.

3. Add the mustard, crème fraîche, and chervil. Season to taste with salt and white pepper. Cover and refrigerate for 1 to 4 hours. Serve chilled, garnished with chervil or parsley sprigs.

WINES: Continue with selection for first course (Manzanilla, Bianco di Custoza, Riesling)

TO MAKE AHEAD

One to four hours before serving: Prepare salad. Cover and refrigerate.

Braised Short Ribs in
Porcini-Prune Sauce

This recipe was adapted from Laurent Manrique, chef at Gertrude's in New York City. It is worth the trouble of finding duck fat to make this, though vegetable oil will work as well. The combination of flavors—beef, thyme, wine, mushrooms, and the sweetness of prunes—makes this one of my favorite main-course recipes. Make sure you begin this recipe at least one day before serving because the ribs will need to marinate overnight.

6 pounds beef short ribs, cut into 3-inch lengths (ask your butcher to do this)

3 medium carrots, cut into 1-inch pieces

3 stalks celery, cut into 1-inch pieces

1 ounce (about 1 loosely packed cup) fresh thyme sprigs

2 bay leaves

1 tablespoon black peppercorns

10 medium onions, peeled

4 heads garlic

6 cups (about two 750 ml bottles) hearty red wine, such as Cahors or
    Madiran

Salt and freshly ground black pepper

8 tablespoons duck fat, goose fat, or vegetable oil

4 cups canned beef broth

1 pound fresh porcini or sliced shiitake mushrooms

1 pound dried pitted prunes, cut into $1/3$-inch slices

1. In a large nonreactive mixing bowl, combine the short ribs, carrots, celery, thyme, bay leaves, and peppercorns. Cut 4 of the onions into 1-inch chunks and add to the bowl. Cut 2 whole heads of garlic (with peel) in half crosswise and add to the bowl. Pour the wine over all and mix well. Cover and refrigerate overnight.

2. Remove the short ribs from the marinade and drain well. Pat dry with paper towels and season with salt and pepper to taste. Set aside. Strain the marinade into a clean bowl, reserving the vegetables. Remove the thyme, bay leaves, and peppercorns, and reserve. In a large casserole over high heat, heat 4 tablespoons duck fat and add the short ribs. Sear the short ribs until well browned on all sides, about 10 minutes. Remove the short ribs and set aside.

3. Preheat the oven to 375 degrees. Add 2 tablespoons duck fat to the casserole, then add the vegetables. Sauté, stirring constantly, until lightly browned, about 10 minutes. Add

the marinade and stir well. Boil the marinade until reduced by half, about 15 minutes. Add the broth, short ribs, and reserved thyme, bay leaves, peppercorns, and 4 cups water. Cover and braise in the oven until the ribs are very tender, about 2½ hours.

4. Remove the short ribs from the casserole and set aside. Pour the vegetables and liquid through a fine strainer into a large bowl. Discard all the solids and return the liquid to a clean casserole. Bring the liquid to a boil over high heat and reduce by half, about 10 minutes. Remove from the heat and set aside.

5. Cut the remaining 6 onions into large dice. Separate the cloves of the remaining 2 heads of garlic and peel and thinly slice. In a large sauté pan over medium-low heat, add the remaining 2 tablespoons duck fat. Add the mushrooms and sauté until lightly browned. Remove from the pan and set aside. Add the diced onions to the pan and sauté until translucent, about 5 minutes. Add the sliced garlic to the onions and sauté for 1 minute. Add the prunes and mushrooms, and sauté just until heated.

6. Add the sautéed onions, garlic, prunes, and mushrooms to the casserole containing the reduced wine mixture. Adjust the salt and pepper to taste. Add the short ribs and mix gently. Serve hot.

WINES: Cahors, Madiran, Cornas

TO MAKE AHEAD

Two days before serving: Marinate short ribs. Cover and refrigerate.
The day before serving: Sear short ribs. Make sauce. Braise ribs for 2½ hours.
To serve: Reheat short ribs. Serve hot.

Coconut Rice

2 cups basmati rice
1½ cups coconut milk
½ teaspoon salt

1. Place the rice in a fine-meshed strainer and rinse until the water runs clear. Transfer the rice to a bowl and add water to cover. Allow to soak for 25 minutes.

2. Drain the rice and place in a medium saucepan. Add the coconut milk, salt, and 1 cup water. Place over medium heat, and bring to a simmer. Cover, reduce the heat to as low

as possible, and allow to cook without stirring for 15 minutes. Remove from the heat and allow to sit (do not uncover) about 3 minutes.

3. Fluff the rice with a fork and then lightly pack each serving into an ice-cream scoop or half-cup measuring cup. Invert the scoop or cup onto a plate and remove to leave 1 serving of molded rice.

TO MAKE AHEAD

Forty-five minutes before serving: Rinse rice and soak in water. Cook with coconut milk. Remove from heat and set aside.

To serve: Fluff rice. Mold rice on plates.

Meringues with Fresh Fruit

This is an excellent dessert for those on a low-fat diet. Made only with egg whites and sugar, the meringues are light and crunchy, the ideal container for sweet and juicy fresh fruit. While berries are suggested here, any fresh fruit cut into bite-sized pieces will make a suitable filling. And for those who wish to indulge themselves, offer lightly sweetened whipped cream as a topping.

FOR THE MERINGUES:

6 large egg whites

¾ teaspoon cream of tartar

¾ cup superfine sugar

1½ cups confectioners' sugar

FOR THE WHIPPED CREAM:

1 cup heavy cream

1 tablespoon superfine sugar

½ teaspoon vanilla extract

FOR THE FRUIT FILLING:

1 cup fresh blueberries

1 cup fresh red raspberries

1 cup fresh golden raspberries, black raspberries, or blackberries

1 pint strawberries, trimmed and halved or quartered

1. *Prepare the meringues:* Preheat the oven to 200 degrees. Line a large baking sheet with parchment paper. Using a 4-inch plate or other object as a guide, draw 8 equally-spaced circles on the parchment paper.

2. Using an electric mixer at medium-low speed, whisk the whites until foamy, then add the cream of tartar. Continue to whisk, gradually increasing the speed, and very slowly add the superfine sugar. Whisk until stiff, glossy peaks form. Sift the confectioners' sugar into the bowl. Use a large rubber spatula to fold the sugar into the egg whites.

3. Transfer the egg whites to a very large pastry bag with a star or plain tip. Using the outlines on the parchment paper as a guide, first fill in the circles to make disks of meringue, then add a single ring on top of the edge of each one, to make a nest shape. Bake until dry but not browned, about 2 hours. Remove from the oven, allow to cool completely, and transfer to an airtight container. Store at room temperature.

4. *Prepare the whipped cream:* Using an electric mixer, whip the cream, sugar, and vanilla until soft peaks form. Set aside. In a mixing bowl, combine the berries.

5. Place an equal portion of berries in each meringue shell. Garnish the berries with a spoonful of whipped cream for those who wish it or pass the whipped cream separately.

WINE: Moscato d'Asti

TO MAKE AHEAD

Up to one week before serving: Make the meringues. Place in a dry airtight container and store at room temperature.

To serve: Whip cream if using. Immediately before serving, place fruit in meringues.

MENU 6

. . . .

Spiced Rosemary Nuts

Many thanks to Deb Christakos, a former chef at the Union Square Cafe in New York City, for teaching me how to make this addictive treat. The toasted rosemary bits in this recipe are delicious when eaten along with the spicy-sweet nuts. When the nuts come out of the oven, taste them and salt as desired. The large, yet delicate grains of fleur de sel are ideal for salting the mixture. If fleur de sel is not available, substitute another flaky sea salt such as Maldon salt, or simply use ordinary fine-grained table salt. (Do not use kosher salt, which is a bit too coarse for this recipe.)

1 pound mixed unsalted shelled nuts (cashews, pecans, brazil nuts, almonds, pumpkin seeds, etc.)
3 or 4 fresh thin-stemmed rosemary sprigs, broken into 1-inch pieces
4 tablespoons butter
3 tablespoons light brown sugar
½ teaspoon cayenne pepper
Fleur de sel or other salt

1. Preheat the oven to 400 degrees. Place the nuts on a baking sheet, add the rosemary, tossing a bit to mix, and spread out. Bake, tossing once or twice, until toasted, about 5 minutes.

2. Remove the nuts from the oven and set aside. Place a large skillet over medium heat and melt the butter. Add the warm nuts and sprinkle with sugar and cayenne. Toss until the nuts are heated through and the sugar has melted, 1 to 2 minutes.

3. Transfer the mixture to a platter or sheet of waxed paper and sprinkle with salt to taste while the nuts are still warm. Allow the nuts to cool completely. Place the cooled nuts in a covered container and store at room temperature.

WINES: Prosecco, Brut Rosé (Spain), Sparkling (extra dry, sec, or demi)

TO MAKE AHEAD

Up to one week before serving: Prepare nuts and allow to cool. Transfer to an airtight container and store at room temperature.

Sarah Heller's Polenta

Sarah Heller worked for many years in the retail food business and, with her husband, Herb Heller, operated a successful online specialty foods market. This recipe is Sarah's invention, an impressive first course that is made easy by cooking the polenta ahead of time. Sarah garnishes each plate with mixed greens lightly dressed in olive oil and balsamic vinegar; undressed pea shoots or sprouts are a simpler alternative.

Extra-virgin olive oil
1 leek, white and light green parts only, chopped and well rinsed
1 teaspoon fresh thyme leaves
3 cups chicken broth
1 cup polenta (available at specialty food markets and some supermarkets)
¼ cup shredded Asiago or pecorino cheese
¼ cup shredded Parmesan cheese
Salt and freshly ground black pepper
16 thin slices pancetta
½ cup shredded mixed cheeses (preferably a combination of fontina, conte, and Gruyère)
2 whole roasted peppers (bottled roasted peppers are fine), skinned, at room temperature
Pea shoots or other fresh sprouts for garnish

1. Oil an 8 × 4-inch loaf pan and set aside. Place a skillet over medium heat and add 1½ teaspoons olive oil. Add the leek and thyme, and sauté until the leek is tender. Remove from the heat and set aside.

2. In a large saucepan or flameproof casserole, combine the broth and 1½ teaspoons olive oil. Place over medium-high heat and bring to a boil. Pour in the polenta in a thin stream, stirring constantly with a wooden spoon to keep it from clumping. Continue mixing until it has thickened like heavy mashed potatoes; it will lift from the sides of the pan. Add the reserved leek, Asiago, Parmesan, and salt and pepper to taste. Pour into the loaf pan, cover, and refrigerate until solid, at least 4 hours.

3. Preheat the oven to 450 degrees. Cut the polenta into 8 rectangles. Oil a baking sheet. Put a slice of pancetta under each piece of polenta and wrap it up and around the sides. Then place a slice of pancetta on top and wrap the ends down and under. Place each pancetta-wrapped polenta slice on the baking sheet. Brush the tops with olive oil and season to taste with salt and pepper. Bake until the pancetta browns on top, 3 to 5 minutes.

4. Preheat a broiler. Sprinkle the top of each pancetta-wrapped polenta slice with 1 tablespoon shredded mixed cheeses. Broil the slices just until the cheese melts. Remove from the heat. Top each slice with a slice of roasted pepper. Garnish each plate with a small mound of pea shoots or sprouts and serve immediately.

WINES: Sauvignon Blanc, Merlot, Amontillado

TO MAKE AHEAD
Four hours to one day before serving: Make polenta. Pour into a pan and chill.
Thirty minutes before serving: Preheat oven and broiler. Cut polenta and wrap with pancetta.
Bake. Top with cheese and broil. Dress salad. Top polenta with roasted pepper and serve with salad.

Pan-Roasted Chilean Sea Bass with Heirloom Potatoes and Celery Broth

You will need a vegetable juicer (the kind that purees vegetables to extract the juice) to make this recipe because both the potatoes and celery must be juiced to make the accompanying sauce. If you don't have a juicer, you might be able to persuade your local health food store to juice the vegetables for you.

2 Yukon Gold potatoes

4 or 6 celery stalks, as needed

4 cups small heirloom potatoes

8 cups canned low-sodium chicken broth

8 skinless Chilean sea bass fillets (6 ounces each)

Salt and freshly ground black pepper

4 teaspoons grapeseed, canola, or other flavorless oil, or more as needed

6 shallots, peeled and thinly sliced

12 shiitake mushrooms, stems removed, thinly sliced

2 cups diagonally sliced celery

2 tablespoons fresh thyme leaves

1. Using a vegetable extractor (juicer), puree the Yukon Gold potatoes to obtain ½ cup juice; set aside. Clean the extractor and puree 2 or 3 celery stalks to obtain 1⅓ cups celery juice; set aside.

2. Fill a medium saucepan half-full of water and bring to a boil. Add the potatoes and boil until the potatoes are just tender. Drain and set aside. In a medium saucepan over high heat, bring the chicken broth to a boil and reduce to 3 cups. Slowly add the reserved potato juice and stir until the broth thickens slightly. Add additional juice if a thicker broth is desired. Remove the pan from the heat and set aside.

3. Preheat the oven to 450 degrees. Season each fillet with salt and pepper to taste and rub lightly with grapeseed oil. Place a heavy ovenproof sauté pan over medium-high heat. When the pan is hot, add the fillets and sear until the undersides are well browned. Turn the fillets over and transfer the pan to the oven. Roast until the fillets are cooked, about 5 minutes. Remove from the oven and transfer the fillets to a platter; cover with foil, and keep warm.

4. Cut the reserved potatoes in half. Return the sauté pan to medium heat and add the halved potatoes, shallots, and shiitake mushrooms. If necessary, add 1 or 2 teaspoons oil. Sauté until the shallots and mushrooms just begin to wilt. Add the sliced celery and sauté an additional 30 seconds. Add the reserved thickened chicken broth and thyme leaves. Bring to a simmer and then remove from the heat. Add the reserved celery juice and season with salt and pepper to taste.

5. Use a slotted spoon to transfer equal portions of the vegetables to the center of 4 warmed soup plates. Pour the broth over the vegetables and top with the roasted bass. Serve immediately.

WINES: Sémillon (Washington or Australia), Albariño, Meursault

TO MAKE AHEAD

One hour before serving: Juice Yukon Gold potatoes and celery. Boil heirloom potatoes and make celery broth. Sear and bake fillets. Assemble vegetables, fillets, and sauce.

To serve: Place vegetables and broth on plates. Top with fillets.

Braised Fennel

Braising mellows fennel's licorice flavor, and olive oil and lemon juice give it a subtle piquancy.

4 large fennel bulbs including the feathery fronds on top (or substitute ¼ cup chervil leaves for the fronds)
½ cup extra-virgin olive oil
½ teaspoon ground fennel seed, optional
1 teaspoon red pepper flakes
Salt
3 tablespoons fresh lemon juice

1. Clean and trim the fennel bulbs, reserving the feathery fronds. Wash and finely chop the fronds and set aside. Cut the bulbs into eighths and place in a medium saucepan. Add the olive oil and 1½ cups water.

2. Cover the saucepan and bring to a boil over high heat, then immediately lower the heat to medium. Stir the fennel, cover, and cook for 5 minutes. Add the chopped fennel fronds, ground fennel seed, red pepper flakes, and salt to taste.

3. Raise the heat to medium-high. Cook, covered, until the liquid has nearly evaporated and the fennel is thoroughly cooked and soft, about 10 minutes more. (If necessary, simmer uncovered for a few minutes to reduce the liquid.) Remove the pan from the heat and add the lemon juice. Toss to mix well. Serve hot.

Walnut Cake with Frangelico Cream

FOR THE CAKE:

Vegetable oil or nonstick spray

2 tablespoons all-purpose flour

2½ teaspoons baking powder

4 large eggs

¾ cup sugar

1½ cups shelled walnut pieces

FOR THE FROSTING:

2 cups heavy cream

2 teaspoons vanilla extract

½ cup sugar

1 tablespoon Frangelico liqueur

1. *Prepare the cake:* Preheat the oven to 350 degrees. Oil or spray two 8-inch cake pans and set aside. In a small bowl, mix together the flour and baking powder.

2. Put the eggs and sugar in the container of a blender and blend briefly to combine. Add the walnut pieces and blend until the walnuts are finely grated. Add the flour mixture and blend again until thoroughly combined.

3. Divide the batter between the 2 cake pans; there will not be a large quantity of batter. Bake until the layers are lightly golden, about 20 minutes. Remove from the heat and allow to cool completely before frosting.

4. *Frost the cake:* In the bowl of an electric mixer, combine the cream, vanilla, and sugar. Using the whisk attachment, beat until the mixture holds soft peaks. Add the Frangelico liqueur and continue to beat just until the mixture holds stiff peaks.

5. Use half of the frosting on the bottom layer and the remaining frosting on the top layer. Cover with a dome and refrigerate until serving.

WINE: White Port (sweet)

TO MAKE AHEAD

Two to six hours before serving: Make and frost the cake. Cover with a dome and refrigerate.

MENU 7

· · · · · · ·

Aloo Kofta
(Potato Balls)

This savory appetizer is from India. Aloo means potato, and kofta means a ball shape. These kofta, creamy on the inside, are dotted with peas and speckled with cumin seeds and chopped cilantro. They are floured and deep-fried, which gives a thin, slightly crisp surface.

Salt

1 pound (about 3 large) all-purpose
   potatoes

1 tablespoon cornstarch

1 cup cooked peas

1 teaspoon cumin seeds

1 teaspoon garam masala

1 tablespoon lemon juice

Cayenne pepper

1 tablespoon chopped cilantro leaves

¼ cup finely chopped scallions

½ cup all-purpose flour

1 cup ghee (available from Indian
   food markets and specialty food
   stores; see page 46) or vegetable
   oil

1. Bring a large pot of lightly salted water to a boil and add the potatoes. Cook until tender, allow to cool, and peel.

2. In a large mixing bowl, mash the potatoes and add the cornstarch, peas, cumin seeds, garam masala, and lemon juice. Season with cayenne and salt to taste. Mix well, then fold in the cilantro leaves and scallions.

3. Roll the potato mixture into 1½-inch balls. Roll the balls in the flour to coat lightly. Place on a platter, cover, and refrigerate.

4. Place a 5- to 6-inch kadhai (see page 48) or small saucepan over medium-high heat. When the pan is hot, add the ghee and allow it to warm. Working in batches, fry the kofta until golden brown. Drain on paper towels, season with salt to taste, and serve hot.

WINES: Côtes de Gascogne (white), Müller Thurgau, Pinot Blanc (United States)

TO MAKE AHEAD

Up to eight hours before serving: Boil and mash potatoes. Add seasonings and shape into balls. Cover and refrigerate.

To serve: Heat ghee. Fry kofta and drain.

GHEE

The Indian food product known as *ghee* or *usli ghee* is made from butter that has been melted over low heat, allowing the water content to evaporate and the milk solids to settle at the bottom of the pan. The surface is skimmed, the clear fat is poured off, and the residue is discarded. The butter is allowed to simmer until the solids are golden brown, imparting a nutty flavor and a sweet aroma to the ghee.

Vegetable ghee, called *vanaspati ghee*, is made from hydrogenated vegetable oils and resembles shortening.

Either kind of ghee can be heated to high temperatures without burning and is excellent for sautéing and frying.

Spiced Carrot Soup

This light soup, known in India as gaajar *(carrot)* shorba *(soup), is an appetite stimulant. Simply presented and gently spiced without being hot, it is a fine introduction to the remainder of the meal.*

5 medium carrots, trimmed, peeled,
  and cut into chunks
One 2-inch cinnamon stick
3 green or white cardamom pods,
  lightly crushed
5 cloves
1/3 teaspoon crushed black
  peppercorns

2 bay leaves
12 cups (2½ quarts) clear chicken
  stock or broth
1/3 teaspoon cayenne pepper
Salt
Whole fresh cilantro leaves for
  garnish

1. Place the carrots in a food processor and process until they are chopped small; set aside. In a double or triple layer of cheesecloth or a large mesh tea ball, combine the cinnamon stick, cardamom, cloves, peppercorns, and bay leaves. Tie or fasten securely so that the spices are contained and will not fall out; set aside.

2. In a large saucepan or stockpot, combine the chicken stock, carrots, cayenne, and spice mixture. Place over medium heat and bring to a boil. Boil until the liquid is reduced by half. Remove from the heat and allow to cool.

3. Discard the spice mixture. Place a fine-meshed strainer over a large bowl. Transfer one-third of the soup to a blender, puree until smooth, and then pour into the strainer. Stir with a wooden spoon to force the soup through the strainer. Repeat with the remaining soup until it is all pureed and strained. Transfer to a covered container and refrigerate.

4. To serve, place the soup in a saucepan over medium-low heat. Gently reheat until steaming and season with salt to taste. Ladle into bowls and garnish each bowl with a few cilantro leaves. Serve hot.

WINES: Müller Thurgau (continued), Rosé de Loire, Traminer (Australia), or Alto Adage

TO MAKE AHEAD
The day before serving: Prepare soup and allow to cool. Cover and refrigerate.
To serve: Reheat soup. Garnish and serve.

Kadhai Murgh
(Chicken with Tomatoes)

This recipe uses garam masala, an Indian spice mixture that can include cumin, coriander, clove, cardamom, and cinnamon. A kadhai, also known as karahi, is an Indian pan similar to a Chinese wok. Murgh *means chicken.*

    2 tablespoons vegetable oil or light olive oil
    8 cloves garlic, peeled and minced
    2 dried red chili peppers
    4 teaspoons crushed coriander seeds
    Two 28-ounce cans diced tomatoes, drained juices reserved
    2 fresh hot green chilies, minced
    Salt
    4 tablespoons grated fresh ginger
    4 tablespoons fresh cilantro leaves
    10 boneless, skinless chicken breast halves, each cut in half crosswise
    1 tablespoon garam masala
    1½ teaspoons toasted ground fenugreek seeds *or* 2 teaspoons crushed dried
        fenugreek leaves (see Note)

1. Place a large, wide casserole over medium-low heat and add the oil, tilting the pan to cover the surface. When the oil is hot, add the garlic and stir until translucent. Add the chili peppers and coriander seeds, and stir until fragrant, about 30 seconds.

2. Add the tomatoes, fresh hot chilies, and salt to taste. Bring the mixture to a simmer and add 2 tablespoons ginger and 2 tablespoons cilantro. Simmer for 5 minutes.

3. Add the chicken pieces and raise the heat to medium-high. Turn and cook the chicken pieces just until they are opaque, 5 to 6 minutes. If the pan becomes too dry, add a small amount of the reserved tomato juices. Allow to cool. Transfer to a covered container and refrigerate.

4. Remove the chicken mixture from the refrigerator and place in a casserole. Add ¼ to ½ cup reserved tomato juices or water (or a mixture of both). Place over medium-low heat just until reheated, stirring occasionally. Remove from the heat. Add the garam masala, fenugreek, and remaining 2 tablespoons ginger and 2 tablespoons cilantro. Mix well and serve.

NOTE: Fenugreek is also known in Indian markets as *methi*.

WINES: Rosé de Loire (continued), Côtes du Rhône, Beaujolais Cru (preferably Moulin-à-Vent or Morgon, very lightly chilled); alternative: Indian beer

TO MAKE AHEAD

Up to eight hours before serving: Make sauce. Sauté chicken.
To serve: Reheat chicken with tomato juices. Add seasonings.

Basmati Rice
with Saffron

Basmati rice has long, delicate grains and a heady fragrance when cooked. Because the rice is soaked in water before it is placed over heat, it requires only a short cooking time.

2 cups basmati rice
3 tablespoons ghee (available in Indian markets and specialty food markets;
   see page 46) or unsalted butter
2 shallots, peeled and finely chopped
2 teaspoons grated ginger
2 cloves garlic, peeled and minced
One 2-inch piece cinnamon stick
2 cloves
2 cardamom pods (any color)
1 star anise
½ teaspoon crumbled saffron strands

1. Place the rice in a bowl of water, swirl, and then drain off the cloudy water. Repeat as necessary until the water in the bowl remains clear. Allow the rice to soak for 25 minutes. Drain well.

2. Place a large saucepan over medium-low heat and add the ghee. Add the shallots, ginger, garlic, cinnamon, cloves, cardamom, and star anise. Stir until the shallots are softened, about 1 minute. Add the rice and stir until coated with ghee and spices. Add 4 cups water and saffron. Stir, cover, and reduce the heat to as low as possible.

3. Cook for 15 minutes. Remove from the heat and set aside without removing the cover. Allow to sit for 5 minutes. Fluff with a fork before serving.

Forty-five minutes before serving: Rinse rice and soak for 25 minutes. Drain and sauté with
spices. Add water and cook for 15 minutes. Allow to rest 5 minutes.

Mango Pudding

*If fresh mangoes are not available, use bottled mango chunks from the refrigerated section of
your produce department.*

> 3 cups mango chunks (from about 4 mangoes) (see page 51)
> ¼ cup light brown sugar
> 1 teaspoon lemon juice
> 1 cup milk
> ¼ cup heavy cream
> 2 large eggs, lightly beaten
> 8 small pieces candied ginger for garnish

1. In a small saucepan, combine the mango chunks, light brown sugar, and ¾ cup water. Place over low heat and simmer until the mango is very soft. Remove from the heat and mash with a fork or in a food processor until smooth. Mix in the lemon juice and set aside.

2. In the bottom of a double boiler over medium heat, place 1 or 2 inches of water and bring to a simmer. In a small saucepan, combine the milk and cream, and heat until just steaming; do not boil. Whisk 2 tablespoons hot milk into the beaten eggs, then whisk the egg mixture back into the milk. Pour the milk mixture into the top of the double boiler and stir just until the mixture is thick enough to coat the back of a wooden spoon, about 5 minutes; do not boil. Remove from the heat and allow to cool.

3. Add the sweetened mango puree to the cooled milk mixture and stir until blended. Spoon into eight ½-cup glasses. Cover with plastic wrap and refrigerate until chilled, at least 1 hour.

4. To serve, remove the plastic wrap and place a piece of candied ginger on top of each serving.

WINE: Late-Harvest Riesling

TO MAKE AHEAD

One to four hours before serving: Make pudding. Cover and refrigerate.

HOW TO CUT A MANGO

The skin of a mango is easy to peel. First, cut through the skin as if you were going to cut it in half lengthwise. Using your fingers, grasp one edge of the skin and peel it away, removing the skin from one half of the fruit. Use a small knife to cut off as much flesh as possible. The pit of a mango is large and flat, so you will need to work around it. When the flesh is cut away from one side, peel off the remaining skin and remove the flesh from the other side.

MENU 8

· · · · · ·

Walnut Spread

[MAKES 1 CUP]

This is one of my favorite spreads for crusty bread. Serve it with a thinly sliced baguette, coarsely torn chunks of Italian country bread, or thick, crisp crackers. Although the recipe uses only a pinch of marjoram, the fresh herb is essential; dried is not a good substitute here.

> 7 ounces unsalted walnut pieces
> 2 tablespoons plain dry bread crumbs
> 1 clove garlic, peeled
> Sea salt
> 2 tablespoons freshly grated Parmigiano-Reggiano cheese
> Pinch of fresh marjoram
> ¾ cup fresh ricotta cheese
> 4 tablespoons extra-virgin olive oil

1. In the bowl of a food processor, combine the walnuts, bread crumbs, garlic, and salt to taste. Process to form a coarse-textured paste.

2. Add the Parmigiano-Reggiano and marjoram. Process again to blend. Add the ri-

cotta and 2 to 3 teaspoons water. Slowly drizzle in the olive oil, stirring to combine. Taste and adjust the seasonings. Cover and refrigerate.

WINES: Sparkling (Spain), Chardonnay, Tocai Friulano

TO MAKE AHEAD
Up to twenty-four hours before serving: Combine ingredients and process to a paste.

Moules Marinière

This classic French recipe is extremely simple to prepare. Mussels cultivated on ropes suspended above the bottom of the ocean (see page 225) ensure that the shellfish and their broth will not be sandy. If you are not sure whether the mussels have been rope-grown, ask your fishmonger.

3 tablespoons extra-virgin olive oil
4 shallots, peeled and finely chopped
2 cloves garlic, peeled and finely chopped
1 teaspoon fresh thyme leaves or $\frac{1}{2}$ teaspoon dried thyme leaves
$\frac{1}{4}$ teaspoon coarsely ground or cracked black pepper
4 pounds rope-grown mussels, rinsed and debearded
2 cups dry white wine
$\frac{1}{4}$ cup chopped parsley
2 teaspoons freshly squeezed lemon juice, or to taste

1. Place a large, deep casserole over medium heat and add the olive oil. When the oil is hot, add the shallots and sauté until softened, about 2 minutes. Add the garlic, thyme, and pepper, and sauté for 1 minute.

2. Add the mussels and wine. Cover and reduce the heat to medium-low. Simmer until all the mussels have opened, about 12 minutes. Stir in the parsley and lemon juice, tasting and adding more juice if desired.

3. To serve, ladle the mussels into soup plates or bowls and top with a serving of broth from the pan. Serve with crusty country bread.

WINES: Muscadet, Pouilly-Fuissé, Graves or Pessac Léognan (white); alternative: Belgian beer

Lamb Chops with Anchovy and Mint Butter

Amanda Hesser wrote this recipe, lovely for its simplicity of preparation and the surprising complexity of its flavors. Compound butters, like the anchovy and mint butter used here, have flavorings blended into them and are used as both seasoning and garnish.

¼ pound (1 stick) unsalted butter, left out to soften for 20 minutes
¼ cup minced shallots
2 tablespoons finely chopped fresh mint leaves
8 oil-packed anchovy fillets, drained
8 shoulder lamb chops, ½ inch thick
Sea salt and freshly ground black pepper
8 lemon wedges

1. In a small bowl, combine the butter, shallots, mint, and anchovies. Using a fork, mash to a paste. Spoon the paste onto a piece of plastic wrap and roll into a 3-inch log. Twist the ends to seal. Refrigerate up to 1 week or freeze up to 1 month.

2. Cut eight ½-inch slices of anchovy butter and set aside. Save any remaining butter for another purpose. Preheat a broiler with the rack positioned 4 to 6 inches from the flame. Season the lamb generously on both sides with salt and pepper. Place the lamb on a broiling pan and broil about 2 minutes per side for rare, 3 minutes for medium rare.

3. To serve, place 2 chops on each of 8 serving plates and top each with a slice of anchovy butter. Garnish with a wedge of lemon.

WINES: Vino Nobile di Montepulciano, Merlot (Napa), Burgundy (Chambolle-Musigny, Pommard, Gevrey-Chambertin), or try a Pinot Noir from Marlborough, New Zealand

TO MAKE AHEAD

Up to one week (if refrigerating) or one month (if freezing) before serving: Make anchovy
   butter. Wrap and refrigerate or freeze.
To serve: Slice butter and set aside. Preheat broiler. Broil lamb 4 to 6 minutes. Top with
   butter.

Salt-Crusted New Potatoes

When these potatoes are removed from boiling water, they become patterned with a fine salt residue as they dry.

> ¼ cup fine salt
> 2 pounds new (baby) red, white, or yellow potatoes

1. Place 2 quarts of water in a large saucepan and add the salt. Place over high heat and bring to a boil.

2. Add the potatoes to the water and boil, uncovered, until the potatoes are tender in the center when pierced with a knife. Drain and keep warm until serving (may be placed in a 225-degree oven to keep warm).

Cheesecake with Blueberry Compote

Eva Baughman is a professional baker and recipe tester based in New Hampshire. Her recipe for creamy crustless cheesecake is easy enough for a novice baker and has the added bonus of being made with low-fat cream cheese. Serve with Eva's blueberry compote or any fresh berries of your choice.

FOR THE CHEESECAKE:

Butter for greasing pan
4 tablespoons unsalted butter, at
    room temperature
1 pound Neufchâtel (low-fat) cream
    cheese, at room temperature

2 teaspoons vanilla extract
¾ cup sugar
¼ cup cornstarch
3 extra-large eggs
1 cup heavy cream
2 tablespoons fresh lemon juice

FOR THE BLUEBERRY COMPOTE:

2 tablespoons fresh lemon juice
¼ cup sugar
Pinch of salt

2 cups fresh blueberries or 8 ounces
    frozen dry-packed blueberries (do
    not thaw)
2½ teaspoons cornstarch

1. *Prepare the cheesecake:* Preheat the oven to 350 degrees. Place a kettle of water over high heat and bring to a boil. Meanwhile, butter a 9-inch round springform pan and shape a piece of aluminum foil around the outside to make it watertight; set aside.

2. Using an electric mixer, beat together the butter and cream cheese until very smooth. Add the vanilla, sugar, and cornstarch, and beat again until smooth. With the mixer running, add the eggs, 1 at a time. Add the cream and lemon juice, and mix until smooth.

3. Pour the mixture into the pan. Place the pan in a baking dish and pour boiling water into the baking dish so it comes 1 inch up the side of the cake pan. Bake until the cake is set and the top is a light golden brown, about 30 minutes. Remove from the oven and transfer the cake to a wire rack to cool.

4. When the cake is completely cool, place a serving platter over the top and invert the cake so that it is upside down. Leave the cake upside down in the pan and refrigerate until well chilled, at least 4 hours.

5. *Prepare the blueberry compote:* In a medium saucepan, combine the lemon juice, sugar, and salt. Place over medium-low heat and stir until the sugar dissolves. Add the berries and simmer, uncovered, for 3 minutes.

6. In a cup, combine the cornstarch with 2 teaspoons water and stir until smooth. Add to the compote and continue to simmer until thickened, about 3 minutes. Remove from the heat and allow to cool a bit, then transfer to a container. Place a piece of plastic wrap directly on the surface of the compote to prevent a skin from forming. Cover and refrigerate until needed.

7. Remove the pan from the cake and slice the cake with a warm wet knife. Serve slices topped with a spoonful of compote or pass the compote separately.

WINES: Blueberry Wine (Arkansas) or Blueberry beer

TO MAKE AHEAD

Five hours to four days before serving: Bake cake. Cover and refrigerate.
Up to one day before serving: Make compote. Cover and refrigerate.
To serve: Unwrap cake and slice with a warm wet knife. Serve topped with or accompanied by compote.

MENU 9

. . . .

Mushrooms Sautéed
in Vermouth

Although this recipe can be made with white button mushrooms, a mixture of textures, colors, and flavors will make it much more interesting.

    ¼ cup extra-virgin olive oil
    1 shallot, peeled and thinly sliced
    4 cloves garlic, peeled and thinly sliced
    2 pounds mixed mushrooms, such as oyster, cremini, baby Portobello,
       and shiitake, left whole or thickly sliced
    3 tablespoons red vermouth
    Salt and freshly ground black pepper

1. Place a large nonstick skillet over medium heat. Add the olive oil and shallot. Sauté until the shallot is softened, 1 or 2 minutes. Add the garlic and sauté another minute; do not allow to brown.

2. Add the mushrooms and sauté until they are softened and most of the liquid in the pan has evaporated, about 5 minutes. Reduce the heat to low, add the vermouth, and sauté about 1 minute. Season to taste with salt and pepper.

3. Transfer to a serving bowl, cover, and set aside at room temperature. Serve at room temperature with toothpicks for spearing.

WINES: Dão, Fitou, Zinfandel

TO MAKE AHEAD

Up to two hours before serving: Sauté mushrooms, cover, and set aside at room temperature.

Pecan-Crusted Crab Cakes with Lime Aioli

These crab cakes are made ahead of time and take only ten minutes to brown.

FOR THE CRAB CAKES:

1 pound crabmeat, picked over for shells and cartilage

1 large egg

1/2 cup mayonnaise

1 tablespoon finely chopped scallion

1/4 cup finely chopped inner stalks and leaves of celery

1 teaspoon Worcestershire sauce

1 teaspoon dry mustard

1/2 teaspoon salt

Freshly ground black pepper

1 cup fine, dry, unseasoned bread crumbs

1 1/4 cups finely ground pecans

FOR THE LIME AIOLI:

1 slice country bread, crust removed

1/4 cup milk

4 cloves garlic, peeled and minced

2 large egg yolks

2 tablespoons lime juice

1/2 cup extra-virgin olive oil

Salt and finely ground white pepper

1/4 cup vegetable oil

Finely grated lime zest for garnish

1. *Prepare the crab cakes:* In a large mixing bowl, combine the crabmeat, egg, mayonnaise, scallion, and celery. Add the Worcestershire sauce, dry mustard, salt, and pepper to taste. Mix well. Add the bread crumbs and mix again. Shape into 8 balls and lightly coat

with pecans, then place on a baking sheet and pat each ball into a flat oval about ½ inch thick. Cover the baking sheet with plastic wrap and refrigerate.

2. *Prepare the lime aioli:* Crumble the bread into a small bowl and add the milk. Allow to sit for 30 seconds, then squeeze the milk from the bread and place the bread in a blender. Add the garlic, egg yolks, and lime juice. Blend until the mixture is smooth. With the blender running, very slowly add the olive oil in a thin stream; the mixture will thicken. Transfer the aioli to a small bowl and season to taste with salt and white pepper. Cover and refrigerate.

3. Place a large nonstick or well-seasoned skillet over medium-high heat and add the oil. When the oil is hot, add the crab cakes. Allow to brown on the bottom, about 5 minutes. Carefully turn and brown on the other side, about another 5 minutes.

4. To serve, place each crab cake on a small plate, add a dollop of aioli, and garnish with a pinch of lime zest.

WINES: Rosé (Tavel or Garnacha-based Spanish), Riesling (Australia), Châteauneuf-du-Pape (white)

TO MAKE AHEAD

Up to one day before serving: Mix and shape crab cakes. Coat with pecans. Cover and refrigerate. Prepare aioli; cover and refrigerate.

To serve: Sauté crab cakes. Add aioli and garnish with lime zest.

Peruvian-Style Pork and Peanut Stew

¼ cup vegetable oil

3 pounds boneless pork butt, trimmed of excess fat and cut into 1-inch cubes

Salt and freshly cracked black pepper

2 medium yellow onions, peeled and diced

4 tablespoons minced garlic

2 tablespoons paprika

2 teaspoons to 2 tablespoons minced fresh red or green chili pepper

4 teaspoons ground cumin

4 pounds potatoes, peeled and diced

6 cups chicken stock

1 tablespoon sugar

1½ cups roughly chopped shelled, unsalted, roasted peanuts

Lime quarters for garnish (optional)

Cilantro leaves for garnish (optional)

1. In a large flameproof casserole, heat the oil over medium-high heat until hot but not smoking. Sprinkle the pork generously with salt and pepper. Add to the pan and brown well on all sides. Remove and set aside.

2. Drain all but 2 tablespoons fat from the pan. Add the onions and sauté over medium heat, stirring occasionally, until translucent, 5 to 7 minutes. Add the garlic, paprika, chili pepper, and cumin, and cook, stirring, 1 minute more.

3. Add the potatoes, stock, sugar, reserved pork, and salt and pepper to taste. Bring just to a boil. Skim any film off the surface and reduce the heat to very low. Cover and simmer, stirring occasionally, until the pork is quite tender, about 1½ hours. Stir in the peanuts and allow to cool. Cover and refrigerate for up to 24 hours.

4. Place the stew in a large pot over medium heat until reheated. Adjust the seasoning, garnish with lime and cilantro, if desired, and serve with crusty bread.

WINES: Try any of the wines from the first two courses or move on to Sauvignon Blanc (Chile), Chenin Blanc (Steen, South Africa), or Sémillon (Australia).

TO MAKE AHEAD
One and a half to twenty-four hours before serving: Brown pork and add seasonings and vegetables. Simmer 1½ hours.
To serve: Reheat stew. Adjust seasonings and garnish.

Braised Collard Greens

Collard greens are a staple in the American South. I was raised on the traditional recipe that included a chunk of salt pork in the simmering greens. This version without the fat is far healthier, and the flavor is just as good. This recipe is from Army & Lou's restaurant in Chicago.

2 pounds collard greens, trimmed of tough stalks, cut into thin strips,
    and thoroughly washed
1 tablespoon red pepper flakes
1 tablespoon minced garlic
1 tablespoon ground coriander
½ cup red wine vinegar
⅓ cup brown sugar
Salt and freshly ground black pepper to taste

1. In a large stockpot, combine all the ingredients with just enough water to cover. Place over high heat, bring to a boil, and then reduce the heat to low.

2. Simmer, partially covered, until the greens are tender, about 1½ hours. Allow to cool. Cover and refrigerate.

3. Place the greens and liquid in a large pot over medium heat. Simmer until reheated. Use a slotted spoon to serve the greens.

TO MAKE AHEAD

One and a half hours or up to a day before serving: Combine greens and seasonings. Simmer for 1½ hours.

To serve: Reheat greens.

VARIATION: Greens may be served topped with a small amount of the "pot liquor" (broth from the pot). The pot liquor may also be used for dipping corn bread or served separately as a flavorful and highly nutritious soup.

Bread Pudding with Lemon Sauce

Like the preceding recipe, this dish is from Army & Lou's restaurant in Chicago.

FOR THE BREAD PUDDING:

6 large eggs

2 cups sugar

3 cups condensed milk

1 cup whole milk

2 tablespoons vanilla extract

¼ teaspoon nutmeg

¼ teaspoon cinnamon

Butter for baking dish

12 ounces (about 5 cups) cubed French bread

¼ cup golden raisins

½ pound (2 sticks) butter, cut into pats

FOR THE LEMON SAUCE:

½ cup sugar

1 tablespoon cornstarch

1 teaspoon grated lemon zest

1½ tablespoons fresh lemon juice

1. *Prepare the bread pudding:* In a large mixing bowl, combine the eggs and sugar. Mix well. Add the condensed milk, whole milk, vanilla, nutmeg, and cinnamon. Stir to blend well.

2. Butter a shallow 2-quart baking dish. Place the bread cubes in the dish and sprinkle with raisins and butter pats. Pour the egg mixture over the bread, making sure all the cubes are covered or submerged in the liquid. Cover the baking dish with foil.

3. Preheat the oven to 350 degrees. Position the baking dish on the middle rack of the oven and place a pan of water on the lower shelf directly beneath the pudding. Bake until the mixture is browned and set, 1 hour and 15 minutes.

4. *Prepare the lemon sauce:* Place a double boiler (or a saucepan set over a pan of simmering water) over medium heat. In the top half of the pan, combine the sugar, cornstarch, and 1 cup water. Stir with a wooden spoon until thickened. Add the lemon zest and juice, and remove from the heat. Drizzle a spoonful over each serving of bread pudding.

WINE: Barsac

TO MAKE AHEAD

One and three-quarters to three hours before serving: Prepare bread pudding but do not bake.
One and a half hours before serving: Preheat oven. Bake pudding.
To serve: Prepare lemon sauce. Serve warm pudding with warm sauce.

MENU 10

. . . .

Herbed Pignoli Dolmas

These seem to be everyone's favorite finger food. I love this vegetarian version. Dolmas are stuffed grape leaves. Pignoli is the Italian word for pine nuts. Make sure you allow the dolmas to come to room temperature before serving, or the rice will be chilled and hard. This recipe makes about twenty-four dolmas.

FOR THE FILLING:

$2\frac{1}{2}$ tablespoons extra-virgin olive oil

1 cup finely chopped onion

2 cloves garlic, peeled and minced

$\frac{1}{2}$ cup long-grain white rice

$2\frac{1}{2}$ tablespoons toasted pine nuts

1 tablespoon dried currants

$\frac{1}{4}$ cup minced fresh dill

$\frac{1}{4}$ cup minced fresh mint leaves

$\frac{1}{2}$ cup vegetable broth

Salt and freshly ground black pepper

FOR ASSEMBLY:

One 16-ounce jar grape leaves in brine

1½ cups vegetable broth

¼ cup extra-virgin olive oil

4 teaspoons fresh lemon juice, plus additional as desired

Lemon wedges for garnish

1. *Prepare the filling:* Place a large skillet over medium heat and add the olive oil. When the oil is hot, add the onion and garlic, and sauté until the onion is softened, about 3 minutes. Add the rice and mix until coated with oil, about 1 minute. Add the pine nuts, currants, dill, mint leaves, and vegetable broth. Stir and season to taste with salt and pepper. Continue to sauté until the broth is absorbed into the rice, 3 to 4 minutes. Remove from the heat and set aside to cool.

2. *To assemble:* If the grape leaves are rolled up, place them in a bowl of cold water and unroll them carefully so they do not tear. Put them on a kitchen towel to drain. To fill the leaves, place a leaf, smooth side down, on a clean work surface. Place a tablespoon of filling on the leaf near the stem. Roll the stem end up to cover the filling, then fold the sides in and continue to roll. Be sure not to roll too tightly because the filling will expand when the stuffed leaves are cooked.

3. As the leaves are filled, place them in a dry saucepan, seam side down. The dolmas should touch one another but not be packed tightly. When the bottom of the pan is covered in a solid layer, begin a second layer on top of it. When all the grape leaves are rolled, place a small heat-proof plate in the pan to weigh down the leaves. In a small bowl, combine the broth, olive oil, and lemon juice. Pour over the dolmas.

4. Cover the saucepan and place over medium heat. Bring to a boil and reduce the heat to low. Simmer for 30 minutes. Remove the pan from the heat and allow the dolmas to cool in the broth. Transfer the cooled dolmas to a covered container and refrigerate.

5. Remove the dolmas from the refrigerator and arrange on a platter. Garnish the platter with lemon wedges and sprinkle with a bit of lemon juice. Cover lightly with plastic wrap and set aside to come to room temperature.

WINES: Moscato d'Asti, Robola (white), Côtes du Roussillon (white)

TO MAKE AHEAD

Up to three days before serving: Make filling and wrap dolmas. Cover and refrigerate.

One hour before serving: Remove dolmas from refrigerator and allow to come to room temperature.

Endive Salad with
Toasted Pumpkin Seeds

For easy preparation, have all the salad greens except the endive washed and dried ahead of time and stored in separate plastic bags.

FOR THE PUMPKIN SEEDS:

3 tablespoons pumpkin seeds

Kosher salt

FOR THE DRESSING:

2 tablespoons Jerez (sherry) or apple cider vinegar

1/2 teaspoon Dijon mustard

1/4 teaspoon curry powder

6 tablespoons extra-virgin olive oil

Salt and freshly ground black pepper

Pinch of sugar (optional)

FOR THE SALAD:

5 large heads Belgian endive, trimmed and sliced crosswise into
   1/4-inch strips

1/4 cup thinly sliced red radish

2 cups mixed baby lettuce leaves

1 large hard-boiled egg, peeled and coarsely chopped

1. *Prepare the pumpkin seeds:* Place a small skillet over medium heat and add the pumpkin seeds. Stir until lightly browned and fragrant, 1 to 2 minutes. Immediately transfer to a plate to cool. When cool, store in a sealed plastic bag at room temperature.

2. *Prepare the dressing:* In a small mixing bowl, combine the vinegar, mustard, and curry powder. Whisk to blend. Slowly whisk in the olive oil. Season to taste with salt, pepper, and, if desired, the sugar. Cover and refrigerate.

3. *To assemble:* In a large salad bowl, combine the endive, radish, lettuce leaves, and egg. Toss to mix. Add about half of the dressing and mix well. Taste and add more dressing as desired. Add the toasted pumpkin seeds, toss again, and serve.

Up to two days before serving: Toast pumpkin seeds, bag, and store. Prepare dressing; cover and refrigerate.

To serve: Combine salad greens. Toss with dressing, Add pumpkin seeds and toss again.

Penne alla Vodka

This is a favorite recipe of my sons, Jacob and Benjamin. When they were small, we used to go to a New York City restaurant that made this dish. We invariably had to explain to the concerned waitstaff that the dish was neither too alcoholic (the alcohol burns off during cooking) nor too spicy for our children.

Salt

2 pounds imported Italian penne

½ pound (2 sticks) butter

¾ teaspoon hot red pepper flakes, or to taste

2 cups vodka

Two 28-ounce cans imported Italian tomatoes, drained and coarsely chopped

2 cups heavy cream

½ cup finely grated Parmesan cheese (inexpensive is fine)

½ cup finely grated pecorino cheese

2 tablespoons finely chopped Italian parsley

About 2 cups finely grated best-quality Parmigiano-Reggiano cheese, for serving

1. Bring a very large pot of lightly salted water to a boil. Add the penne and cook until al dente, about 8 minutes. While the pasta cooks, prepare the sauce: Place a medium saucepan over low heat and melt the butter. Add the pepper flakes and stir for 1 minute.

2. Add the vodka and tomatoes. (If you wish to burn off the alcohol, use a long match to carefully light the surface of the sauce. Flames will ignite and then quickly die down.) Stir until simmering. Add the cream and bring back to a simmer. Remove the pan from the heat and keep covered and warm.

3. When the pasta is cooked, drain it well and return it to the hot pan. Immediately add the vodka sauce, Parmesan, and pecorino. Add the parsley and toss until combined. Transfer to a warm serving bowl. Pass the Parmigiano-Reggiano separately at the table.

WINES: Gamay (United States), Dolcetto, Alicante Bouchet

Champagne Melon Soup with Raspberry Ice Balls

This dessert is light, elegant, and fun both to serve and to eat. It is adapted from Michel Richard, chef and owner of Citronelle restaurant in Washington, D.C.

4 cups raspberries

Sugar

2 ripe honeydew melons

4 ripe cantaloupes

¼ cup fresh lemon juice, or to taste

24 large mint leaves

3 cups champagne, well chilled

1. In the container of a blender, combine the raspberries with ½ cup water. Puree until smooth. Line a strainer with cheesecloth and set over a bowl. Pour in the puree and twist the cloth to squeeze out the puree. Stir in 8 teaspoons sugar, or to taste. Spoon the mixture into an ice tray that makes round balls or another decorative shape. Freeze until firm.

2. Cut the honeydew melons in half and remove the seeds. Using a melon baller, remove the flesh from the melon to within ¾ inch of the peel. Set aside the melon balls. Using a large spoon, scrape out and reserve the remaining flesh. Discard the peels.

3. Cut the cantaloupes in half, using a straight-cut or sawtooth design. Remove the seeds. Using a melon baller, remove the flesh to within ¼ inch of the peel; reserve any extra flesh. Cut off the bottoms of the cantaloupes so they will stand securely. In a large bowl, mix the honeydew and cantaloupe melon balls with lemon juice. Place an equal amount of melon balls in each melon half. Cover and refrigerate.

4. Using a blender, puree any honeydew or cantaloupe flesh that was not shaped into balls. Press through a fine-meshed strainer and add 2 teaspoons sugar. Refrigerate.

5. Spoon 2 tablespoons melon puree over the melon balls in each cantaloupe half. Allow to sit at room temperature for 30 minutes. Meanwhile, using kitchen shears, cut the mint leaves into very thin strips and dust lightly with sugar.

6. Arrange 4 raspberry balls in each melon half and sprinkle with mint. Set each melon half in a soup bowl and bring to the table. At the table pour champagne directly into the cantaloupe halves and allow to fizz out and over the melon balls.

WINE: Moscato d'Asti

TO MAKE AHEAD

One day to one week before serving: Prepare raspberry ice balls and freeze.

One to four hours before serving: Halve cantaloupes and remove seeds. Scoop melon balls and fill cantaloupe with balls. Cover and refrigerate.

Thirty minutes before serving: Add melon puree to cantaloupe halves and allow to sit at room temperature.

To serve: Add raspberry ice balls to cantaloupe halves. Pour champagne over and serve.

TEN MENUS
FOR SUMMER

. . . .

MENU 1

[PAGE 72]

Tapenade

Mushrooms Stuffed with Spinach and Feta

Braised Chicken with Prunes

Orzo

Tarte Tatin

MENU 2

[PAGE 77]

Shrimp and Mozzarella in Mint Pesto

Bruschetta with Heirloom Tomatoes

Vitello Tonnato

Fresh Peas in Cream

Raspberry-Plum Pie

MENU 3

[PAGE 83]

(VEGETARIAN)

Black-eyed Peas Canapés

Asian Bean Sprout Salad

Vegetarian Lentil Burgers

Fried Baked Potato Wedges with Béarnaise Sauce

Fresh Blueberries in Chocolate

MENU 4

[PAGE 89]

Grilled Vegetable Platter

Eliche with Pine Nuts

Salmon Cakes with Yogurt Chipotle Sauce

Frankie and Johnny's House Salad

Custardy Rhubarb Pie

MENU 5

[PAGE 98]

Shrimp Cocktail with Two Sauces

Vichyssoise

Chicken with Pine Nuts and Sun-dried Tomatoes

Spinach with Garlic Oil

Strawberry Shortcakes

MENU 6

[PAGE 105]

Deviled Eggs with Avocado

Gazpacho

Seafood, Chicken, and Sausage Paella

Rouille

Peppermint Ice Cream

MENU 7
[PAGE 112]
Smoked Salmon Rolls

Crostini with Pesto and Fried Green Tomatoes

Herb-Simmered Leg of Lamb with Sardine Mayonnaise

or Anchovy Vinaigrette

Fire-Roasted Peppers

Poire William Ice Cream

MENU 8
[PAGE 118]
Membrillo with Manchego

Calamari, Watermelon, and Avocado Salad

Grilled Lamb Kebabs with Yogurt Sauce

Israeli Couscous

Greek Rizogalo

MENU 9
[PAGE 123]
Chutney Cheese Ball

Potato and Smoked Mackerel Salad with Creamy Mayonnaise

Jeff's Fast Chicken Mole

Short-Grain Rice

Sticky Toffee Pudding

MENU 10
[PAGE 128]
Cucumber Cups with Roast Pork Filling

Grilled Figs with Fresh Mozzarella

Chilled Baked Salmon with Cucumber-Dill Sauce

Grilled Corn

Carrot Cake with Cream Cheese Frosting

MENU I

· · · · · · ·

Tapenade

Tapenade is an olive spread that originated in the Mediterranean. Tapenade is usually very drab in color, but this version includes sun-dried tomatoes and basil that add brightness to both the flavor and color.

2 cups pitted Kalamata olives

½ cup imported black olives (such as Niçoise), pitted

¼ cup sun-dried tomatoes in olive oil, drained

6 cloves garlic, peeled and minced

1 tablespoon capers

5 anchovy fillets

1 teaspoon lemon juice

¼ cup extra-virgin olive oil

3 or 4 large leaves fresh basil (optional)

1. In the bowl of a food processor, combine the Kalamata olives, black olives, sun-dried tomatoes, garlic, and capers. Process until coarsely chopped.

2. Add the anchovies, lemon juice, and olive oil. Process again until finely chopped; do not puree. Cover and refrigerate.

3. Remove the tapenade from the refrigerator. Finely chop the basil and mix in until blended. Transfer to a decorative bowl and serve with sliced crusty bread.

WINES: Rosé, Rosé, Rosé, but if you must have a white, try one of the southern Frenchettes: Palette, Clairette, or Bellet or Picpoul de Pinet

TO MAKE AHEAD
Up to one week before serving: Prepare tapenade. Cover and refrigerate.
To serve: Add chopped basil to tapenade. Transfer to serving bowl.

Mushrooms Stuffed with Spinach and Feta

These mushrooms can be baked in any kind of shallow baking dish. My favorite way is to bake them in a decorative pie plate that can double as a serving dish.

> 16 large white or cremini stuffing mushrooms
> 8 tablespoons (1 stick) butter
> 2 shallots, peeled and finely chopped
> 1 clove garlic, peeled and minced
> 12 ounces spinach leaves, washed, dried, and coarsely chopped
> ¼ cup fine dry bread crumbs
> 2 ounces feta cheese, crumbled
> Salt and freshly ground black pepper
> ¼ cup finely grated Parmesan cheese

1. Break the stems off the mushrooms and set aside. Use a spoon to scrape out any remaining pieces of stem. By hand or using a food processor, finely chop the stems and pieces, and set aside.

2. Place a large nonstick skillet over medium-low heat and melt 4 tablespoons butter. Place the mushroom caps in the pan with the rounded sides down and sauté until lightly browned, about 1 minute. Turn the caps over and sauté again until the edges are lightly browned, about 30 seconds. Transfer the mushroom caps to a plate and set aside.

3. Add the chopped mushroom stems and pieces to the pan and sauté over medium-low heat just until softened. Transfer to a medium bowl and set aside. Place the remaining 4 tablespoons butter in the pan. Add the shallots and sauté until softened, about 2 minutes.

Add the garlic and sauté for 30 seconds. Add the chopped spinach and sauté just until wilted. Transfer the mixture to the bowl of chopped mushrooms. Add the bread crumbs and feta, and toss to mix. Season with salt and pepper to taste, and allow to cool.

4. Pack equal portions of the stuffing into the mushroom caps. Place the stuffed caps on a baking sheet and sprinkle evenly with Parmesan. Cover and refrigerate.

5. Preheat the oven to 400 degrees. Uncover the mushrooms and bake until heated through and browned on top, 8 to 10 minutes.

WINES: Beaujolais (lightly chilled), Naoussa, Limnio (red or rosé); for white, Sauvignon Blanc (ideally, Pouilly-Fumé)

TO MAKE AHEAD

Up to four hours before serving: Sauté mushrooms. Prepare stuffing. Stuff mushrooms, cover, and refrigerate.

Twenty-five minutes before serving: Preheat oven. Bake mushrooms 8 to 10 minutes.

Braised Chicken with Prunes

This recipe was written by Amanda Hesser. If you are unable to find the plump imported French prunes known as pruneaux d'Agen, *any prunes will give good results.*

> 8 chicken thighs
> 8 chicken drumsticks
> Kosher salt and freshly ground black pepper
> 1 cup flour
> 6 tablespoons olive oil
> ½ cup white wine vinegar
> 2 cups dry white wine
> 24 large, plump prunes, preferably pruneaux d'Agen

1. Season the chicken thighs and drumsticks generously with salt and pepper. Spread flour in a wide, shallow bowl and dredge the chicken pieces until well coated. Shake off any excess flour and set aside.

2. Place a large sauté pan (large enough to hold the chicken pieces in a single layer) over high heat for 1 or 2 minutes. Add the olive oil and heat until the oil shimmers. Arrange the chicken pieces in the pan, skin side down, and sear them without moving them until the undersides are browned, about 3 minutes. Turn and sear again until browned, 3 to 4 minutes more.

3. Add the vinegar, wine, and prunes. Cover and reduce the heat to low. Simmer, basting occasionally, until the chicken is tender and falling off the bone, about 30 minutes.

4. Using a slotted spoon, transfer the chicken to a platter and keep warm. Raise the heat under the pan to high and reduce the pan juices for 1 to 2 minutes. Pour the juices over the chicken and serve.

WINES: Colombard (California), Sémillon/Chardonnay (Australia), Valdepeñas

Orzo

Olive oil
½ small onion, finely chopped
1 clove garlic, peeled and minced
4 cups chicken broth
1 cup dry white wine
2 cups orzo
Salt and freshly ground black pepper
1 tablespoon minced parsley for garnish

1. Place a large saucepan over medium heat and add 2 tablespoons olive oil. When the oil is hot, add the onion and sauté until translucent. Add the garlic and sauté for 1 minute.

2. Add the chicken broth, wine, and 3 cups water. Return to a boil and stir in the orzo. Simmer, uncovered, stirring occasionally until the orzo is cooked al dente (barely tender). Drain the orzo in a fine-meshed strainer and return to the saucepan. Add 1 tablespoon oil and stir until all the orzo is coated. Season to taste with salt and pepper. Garnish with parsley and serve immediately.

Tarte Tatin

No need for a tarte tatin mold. This simple, elegant apple tart by Claude Fouquiau can be baked in an ovenproof nonstick skillet.

> 3 tablespoons butter, at room temperature
> ½ cup sugar
> 6 medium Gala, Golden Delicious, or Granny Smith apples, peeled, cored, and quartered
> 1 thin (⅛ inch) sheet puff pastry, cut into a circle 12 inches in diameter

1. Spread the butter evenly inside a 10-inch tarte tatin mold or 10-inch heavy, ovenproof, nonstick skillet. Sprinkle with the sugar, turning the pan to coat it evenly.

2. Beginning at the edge of the pan, arrange the apples, peeled side down, in concentric circles, fitting the apples closely together without overlapping them. Place the pan over a low flame until the butter melts, then turn the heat to medium-high and cook without stirring until the sugar caramelizes and turns a rich brown color, about 30 minutes. Remove from the heat. Press gently on the apples with a wooden spoon to help fill any spaces between them.

3. Preheat the oven to 350 degrees. Place the puff pastry over the apples, tucking the edge of the dough inside the pan. Bake until the pastry is golden brown, about 30 minutes. Remove and allow to rest for 15 minutes.

4. To unmold, run a thin knife around the inside edge of the pan. Place a serving platter over the pan and invert to release the tarte tatin. If any apples have stuck to the pan, gently remove them and reposition them on the tart. Serve at room temperature.

WINE: Quarts de Chaume

TO MAKE AHEAD
One and a half to eight hours before serving: Prepare and bake tart. Cool, cover, and store at room temperature.

MENU 2

. . . .

Shrimp and Mozzarella
in Mint Pesto

This sumptuous hors d'oeuvre from food writer and radio host Rachel Forrest looks gorgeous spread out on a platter. Though the shrimp and mozzarella are coated with the same pesto, the pesto tastes different with each one.

FOR THE PESTO:

½ cup toasted pine nuts

2 tablespoons feta cheese

2 tablespoons grated Asiago cheese

2 cloves garlic, peeled

1 or 2 tablespoons chopped fresh
   jalapeño chili or other fresh hot chili

2 tablespoons fresh lemon juice

2 cups tightly packed fresh mint leaves

⅓ cup best-quality extra-virgin olive oil

A few drops white truffle oil (optional)

Salt and freshly ground black pepper to
   taste

FOR THE SHRIMP AND MOZZARELLA:

8 ounces small mozzarella balls packed
   in brine, drained

1½ pounds large shrimp, peeled and
   deveined

¼ cup extra-virgin olive oil

2 cloves garlic, peeled and finely
   chopped

2 teaspoons finely chopped fresh mint
   leaves

1 tablespoon finely chopped fresh
   parsley leaves

1. *Prepare the pesto:* In the bowl of a food processor, combine the pine nuts, feta, Asiago, garlic, and jalapeño chili. Process until smooth, stopping to scrape the sides of the bowl as necessary. Add the lemon juice and mint leaves. Process again until smooth. With the motor running, drizzle in the olive oil and truffle oil. Season with salt and pepper to taste.

2. *Prepare the shrimp and mozzarella:* In a small bowl, combine the mozzarella balls with about one-third of the pesto. Toss gently until the mozzarella is well coated. Set aside at room temperature.

3. Preheat a broiler. In a medium bowl, combine the shrimp with the olive oil, garlic, mint, and parsley. Toss until the shrimp are well coated. Place the shrimp in a single layer on a broiling sheet and broil 1 to 2 minutes a side. Transfer the hot shrimp to a bowl and add ¼ cup pesto. Toss until well coated.

4. Mound the shrimp in the center of a serving platter. Surround the shrimp with the mozzarella balls.

WINES: Vinho Verde, Chardonnay (unoaked), Insolia

TO MAKE AHEAD

Up to three days before serving: Make pesto. Cover and refrigerate.

Thirty minutes before serving: Toss mozzarella in pesto to coat. Season shrimp, broil, and toss in pesto. Arrange on platter.

Bruschetta with Heirloom Tomatoes

Multicolored heirloom tomatoes, available in farmers' markets and many greengrocers, will give this dish a striking look. The names of the tomatoes are whimsical and should be shared with your guests: Brandywine, Lemon Plum, Cherokee Purple, and Green Zebra. If you are really lucky, you might be able to find Mortgage Lifter, Pink Ping Pong, Earl of Edgecombe, or fruity Orange Strawberry tomatoes. Whatever the variety, choose tomatoes that are ripe but still firm. Never refrigerate tomatoes; instead, keep them at a cool room temperature.

> 4 ripe heirloom tomatoes, preferably different colors (red, purple, yellow, striped), or ripe red beefsteak tomatoes
> 2 cloves garlic, peeled and finely chopped
> Olive oil
> 1 teaspoon lemon juice
> ¼ cup chopped Italian (flat-leaf) parsley leaves
> ½ cup coarsely chopped fresh basil leaves
> Salt and coarsely ground black pepper
> 8 thick slices crusty country bread
> 2 large cloves garlic, peeled and halved

1. Preheat a grill or broiler. Core the tomatoes and cut into ½-inch chunks. Place in a large bowl with the finely chopped garlic, 2 tablespoons olive oil, lemon juice, parsley, and basil. Mix well and season to taste with salt and pepper.

2. Brush both sides of the bread with olive oil and grill or broil until both sides are lightly browned. Rub 1 side of each toasted slice with a garlic half (1 half should do 2 pieces of bread). Top the garlic-rubbed sides of bread with equal portions of the tomato mixture. Serve immediately.

WINES: Montepulciano d'Abruzzo, Alezio, Regaleali (all either red or rosé)

TO MAKE AHEAD
Thirty minutes before serving: Preheat a grill or broiler. Prepare tomato mixture.
Fifteen minutes before serving: Brush bread with oil and grill. Top with tomato mixture.

Vitello Tonnato

A superb dish for a warm summer evening, Vitello Tonnato may be cooked up to two days ahead of time and needs only to be brought to room temperature before serving. This recipe was adapted from Il Buco restaurant in New York City. The mayonnaise-based sauce was inspired by a recipe by Marcella Hazan.

FOR THE VEAL:

1½ cups dry white wine

1 stalk celery, roughly chopped

1 medium onion, peeled and cut into quarters

1 carrot, roughly chopped

1 leek, white part only, rinsed and chopped

4 sprigs marjoram

4 sprigs thyme

5 cloves garlic, peeled

2½ to 3 pounds top round veal roast, trussed (no thicker than 3 inches in diameter)

FOR THE SAUCE:

2 large egg yolks, at room temperature

Sea salt

2¼ cups extra-virgin olive oil

5 tablespoons freshly squeezed lemon juice

One 6-ounce can tuna, packed in oil

5 anchovy fillets

3 tablespoons capers, drained

Thin slices of lemon, thinly sliced pitted black olives, capers, parsley leaves, and anchovy fillets for garnish

1. *Prepare the veal:* In a pot just large enough to fit the veal, combine the wine, celery, onion, carrot, leek, marjoram, thyme, and garlic. Add 3 inches of water and bring to a boil. Add the veal and bring back to a boil. Immediately turn off the heat, cover the pot, and let the veal cool in its liquid for 2 to 3 hours. When completely cool, cut the veal in slices ¹⁄₁₆ to ⅛ inch thick.

2. *Make the sauce while the veal cools:* In a large bowl, whisk together the egg yolks and ¼ teaspoon salt until pale yellow and the consistency of cream. One drop at a time, add 1¼ cups oil, whisking continually. As the mixture thickens you can add the oil more quickly. When it is quite thick, whisk in 1 tablespoon lemon juice. Continue adding oil until it is all emulsified and the mayonnaise is quite thick and shiny. Whisk in another tablespoon of lemon juice.

3. Drain the tuna and put it in a food processor with the anchovies, remaining 1 cup olive oil, remaining lemon juice, and capers. Process to make a creamy, uniformly blended sauce. Scrape the sauce into the bowl of mayonnaise and fold to combine. Adjust the seasonings if necessary. The sauce should be quite tangy and highly seasoned. Refrigerate until needed.

4. To assemble the dish, reserve ¾ cup sauce, cover, and refrigerate. Smear the bottom of a serving platter with some of the remaining sauce. Place a layer of veal slices on top, meeting edge to edge without overlapping. Cover with sauce, then make another layer of meat and sauce. Repeat until all the meat has been used. Leave enough sauce to blanket the top layer. Cover with plastic wrap and refrigerate at least 24 hours or up to two days.

5. To serve, bring the assembled dish to room temperature. Garnish with some or all of the suggested ingredients. Serve with the reserved sauce on the side.

WINES: Lugana (still or spumante), Orvieto, Chianti Colline Pisane

TO MAKE AHEAD

One to two days before serving: Prepare veal. Prepare sauce. Assemble, cover, and refrigerate.
One hour before serving: Allow to come to room temperature. Garnish.

Fresh Peas in Cream

Though not quite as pretty as when made with fresh ingredients, this recipe is still very good when made with frozen peas and dried mint.

> 2 pounds fresh peas in the pod, shelled, or two 12-ounce packages
>   frozen peas
> Salt
> ½ cup heavy cream
> 2 teaspoons minced fresh mint leaves or 1 teaspoon dried mint leaves

1. Place the peas, 1 cup water, and a pinch of salt in a large saucepan over medium heat. Bring to a simmer and simmer just until the peas are bright green, tender, and thoroughly heated (about 8 minutes for fresh peas, 3 minutes for frozen).

2. Drain the peas and return them to the saucepan. Add the cream and mint, and season with salt to taste. When the cream is bubbling and hot, remove from the heat and transfer to a warm serving bowl.

Raspberry-Plum Pie

1 large egg

½ cup sugar

¼ cup sour cream

1 pound chopped red or black plums (not too sweet), pits
  removed

1½ cups red or black raspberries

2 tablespoons lemon juice

Pinch of salt

Pinch of nutmeg

Pastry for a double-crust 9-inch pie

1. Preheat the oven to 450 degrees. In the bowl of an electric mixer, beat the egg until foamy. Slowly beat in the sugar until the mixture is light. Gently fold in the sour cream until blended. Add the plums, raspberries, lemon juice, salt, and nutmeg. Mix together gently until blended.

2. Pour the mixture into the bottom half of the piecrust. Fit the top crust over the pie and crimp the edges securely. Cut slits in the top of the pie.

3. Place the pie on a baking sheet and bake for 5 minutes. Lower the heat to 375 degrees and bake until the crust is golden brown, about 40 minutes more. Remove from the heat and allow to cool.

WINE: Riesling Auslese

TO MAKE AHEAD

One to four hours before serving: Bake pie and allow to cool.

MENU 3

. . . .

Black-eyed Peas Canapés

My father, Bill Tillar, created this recipe about forty years ago. It has an unusual mixture of ingredients that, when tasted, seem like a stroke of genius.

Two 15.5-ounce cans black-eyed
   peas, drained
½ cup finely chopped celery
¼ cup finely chopped onion
¼ cup diced green or red bell
   pepper
3 tablespoons raisins
2 tablespoons finely chopped Italian
   parsley
1 tablespoon sugar
1 teaspoon paprika

2 tablespoons extra-virgin olive oil
1 teaspoon balsamic vinegar
½ teaspoon Tabasco sauce
½ teaspoon Worcestershire sauce
¼ cup mayonnaise
Salt and freshly ground black pepper
   to taste
¼ teaspoon curry powder (optional)
2 tablespoons chopped cilantro
   leaves

1. Combine all ingredients except the cilantro. Mix well, cover, and refrigerate.

2. Stir the cilantro into the mixture until combined. Spoon onto wheat crackers or toasted baguette slices and serve. Or place in a bowl and serve the crackers on the side.

TO MAKE AHEAD

Up to eight hours before serving: Prepare black-eyed peas mixture. Cover and refrigerate.

To serve: Stir cilantro into mixture. Serve on crackers or toasted baguette slices.

Asian Bean Sprout Salad

A crisp, simple summer salad.

FOR THE DRESSING:

6 fresh red Thai chili peppers, halved, seeded, and very thinly sliced

1 tablespoon finely grated fresh ginger

2 cloves garlic, peeled and minced

¼ cup lime juice or rice wine vinegar

1 tablespoon light brown sugar

1 teaspoon salt

FOR THE SALAD:

4 cups fresh bean sprouts

1 bunch chives, cut into 1-inch lengths

Chopped cilantro for garnish

1. *Prepare the dressing:* In a small bowl, combine the chili peppers, ginger, garlic, lime juice, sugar, and salt. Cover and refrigerate up to 1 week.

2. *Prepare the salad:* In a large bowl, combine the bean sprouts and chives. Toss to mix well. Add the dressing and toss again until everything is well coated. Place equal portions on 8 serving plates and top each with a sprinkling of cilantro.

TO MAKE AHEAD

Up to one week before serving: Prepare dressing.

To serve: Mix salad ingredients in a serving bowl. Add dressing and mix well.

Vegetarian Lentil Burgers

[MAKES 10 BURGERS]

These burgers are known as Palouse Burgers *at Swilley's Cafe in Pullman, Washington. This recipe is from Joan Swensen, the chef at Swilley's.*

½ cup brown lentils

½ cup barley

½ cup brown rice

2 tablespoons olive oil

1⅓ cups minced carrots

¾ cup minced onion

¾ cup minced celery

2 tablespoons toasted or dry-roasted
   sunflower seeds

1 teaspoon oregano

1½ teaspoons salt

Freshly ground black pepper to taste

1 teaspoon minced fresh thyme
   leaves

1 tablespoon dried basil

1½ teaspoons minced garlic

2 large eggs, lightly beaten

½ cup flour

2 tablespoons canola or vegetable oil

1. Place 4 cups water in a large saucepan over medium-low heat and bring to a simmer. Add the lentils, cover, and simmer for 15 minutes. Add the barley, cover, and simmer 15 minutes more. Add the brown rice, cover, and simmer until the water is absorbed and the rice is al dente, about 20 minutes more. Do not let the pan burn dry; if necessary, stir in a small amount of water. Remove from the heat and set aside.

2. In a medium sauté pan, combine the olive oil, carrots, onion, and celery. Place over medium heat and sauté until the vegetables are tender, about 10 minutes. Add the sunflower seeds, oregano, salt, pepper, thyme, basil, and garlic. Sauté for 1 or 2 minutes. Remove from the heat.

3. Combine the grains and vegetables in a large covered container and refrigerate overnight.

4. Add the eggs and flour to the grain-vegetable mixture. Mix well. By hand or using an ice cream scoop, form balls 3½ to 4 inches in diameter. Flatten into disks about ¾ inch thick. Place on a platter, cover, and refrigerate.

5. Place a large nonstick skillet over medium-high heat and add the canola oil. When the oil is hot, add the burgers and cook until golden brown, 3 to 4 minutes per side. Serve immediately.

WINES: Côtes du Ventoux, Rosé (Castel del Monte, Bandol), Greco di Tufo

The day before serving: Cook grains. Cook vegetables. Combine grains and vegetables. Cover and refrigerate.

Up to eight hours before serving: Add eggs and flour to grain mixture. Shape in patties, cover, and refrigerate.

Ten minutes before serving: Heat oil in skillet. Sauté burgers.

Fried Baked Potato Wedges with Béarnaise Sauce

FOR THE POTATOES:

6 large Idaho or other baking potatoes with peels, scrubbed

Salt

FOR THE BÉARNAISE SAUCE:

4 large egg yolks

1/2 teaspoon champagne, or white wine vinegar

Salt and white pepper

1/4 pound (1 stick) unsalted butter, cut into small pieces

2 tablespoons lemon juice, or more to taste

2 1/2 tablespoons finely chopped fresh tarragon

Vegetable oil for frying

1. *Prepare the potatoes:* Preheat the oven to 400 degrees. Bake the potatoes until tender in the center when pierced with a knife, about 1 hour. Remove from the oven and allow to cool. Cover and refrigerate until chilled, at least 1 hour.

2. *Prepare the béarnaise sauce:* Place a few inches of water in the bottom of a double boiler and bring to a boil. (Alternatively, a stainless steel or other heat-proof mixing bowl may be placed over a pan of simmering water.) In the top of the double boiler, combine the egg yolks, vinegar, and a sprinkling of salt and white pepper. Place the mixture over simmering water and whisk to blend. Add pieces of butter slowly, stirring and allowing them to melt and incorporate before adding more. When all the butter is emulsified, add the lemon juice. Remove from the heat and allow to cool. Mix in the tarragon when cool. Cover and refrigerate up to 24 hours.

3. Cut the potatoes lengthwise into eighths to make large wedges; set aside. Place a large skillet over medium-high heat and add enough oil to come about ½ inch up the side of the pan. Meanwhile, reheat the béarnaise sauce in a double boiler, in a pan over simmering water, or in a microwave oven. Be careful to reheat only; do not bring to a boil.

4. When the oil is hot, add a single layer of potato wedges. Turn them with a wooden spoon if necessary to help them brown evenly on all sides. Adjust the heat as necessary so that the potatoes fry quickly without burning. Use a slotted spoon or skimmer to transfer the browned potatoes to paper towels to drain.

5. To serve, place equal portions on serving plates and top with a dollop of béarnaise sauce.

TO MAKE AHEAD

The day before serving: Bake potatoes, cover, and refrigerate. Make sauce, cover, and refrigerate.

Thirty minutes before serving: Cut potatoes into wedges. Heat pan with oil. Fry wedges. Reheat sauce.

Fresh Blueberries in Chocolate

I wrote this recipe after a friend brought me a gift from Canada of fresh blueberries covered in hardened chocolate. These clumps of chocolate-covered fruit are nice to serve with a pot of hot fruity tea and crisp, delicate cookies.

6 ounces best-quality semisweet or bittersweet chocolate, chopped

2 teaspoons corn syrup

3 cups fresh blueberries, washed and thoroughly dried

1. Line 1 large or 2 small baking sheets with waxed paper and set aside. Using a microwave oven, a double boiler, or a bowl set over a pan of simmering water, melt the chocolate and corn syrup together. Stir until very smooth.

2. Add the blueberries to the melted chocolate. Stir gently to make sure they are well coated. Allow the mixture to cool until thickened but still fluid enough to pour. Scoop up heaping tablespoons and drop onto the waxed paper, leaving enough space for any spreading that may occur. (If the mixture spreads too much, let it cool a bit more.) Allow to harden and then cover lightly with plastic wrap. Store in a cool place; do not refrigerate.

WINE: Banyuls

MENU 4

· · · · · · ·

Grilled Vegetable Platter

This platter can be filled with nearly any kind of vegetable. Grill the vegetables and refrigerate this platter hours before your guests arrive but allow the vegetables to come to room temperature before serving.

2 or 3 small eggplants (Japanese or Italian), trimmed and thinly sliced lengthwise

1 Vidalia or other sweet onion, peeled and thickly sliced (keep slices intact)

8 medium mushrooms

1 zucchini, trimmed and sliced lengthwise about 1/3 inch thick

1 summer (yellow) squash, trimmed and sliced lengthwise about 1/3 inch thick

8 scallions, trimmed

1 red bell pepper, cored and cut lengthwise into 8 slices

1 yellow bell pepper, cored and cut lengthwise into 8 slices

Extra-virgin olive oil

Salt and freshly ground black pepper

Whole fresh basil leaves for garnish

About 1 cup small fresh mozzarella balls

1/2 cup good-quality whole Kalamata or other black olives

2 tablespoons red wine vinegar

1 tablespoon finely chopped fresh parsley

1. Preheat a grill or broiler. Brush all the vegetables with olive oil, taking particular care to coat all sides of the eggplant slices. Season to taste with salt and pepper. Grill or broil the vegetables until tender and golden brown. As the vegetables are cooked, transfer them to a baking sheet and allow to cool.

2. Arrange the vegetables decoratively on a serving platter, beginning with the longest pieces arranged like the spokes of a wheel. Build layers of vegetables until all are used. Cover and refrigerate.

3. Garnish the platter with the basil leaves arranged among the vegetables. Dot the platter with mozzarella balls and olives. In a measuring cup, place 3 tablespoons olive oil, the vinegar, and parsley. Beat with a fork until blended, then drizzle over the platter. Cover lightly with plastic wrap and allow to sit at room temperature until serving.

WINES: Trebbiano or Galestro or Lugana, Freisa (still or spumante), Rosé (Les Beaux de Provence, which can be used with the next two courses)

TO MAKE AHEAD

Up to six hours before serving: Grill vegetables and arrange on platter. Cover and refrigerate.
About 1 hour before serving: Garnish platter. Drizzle with oil and vinegar. Cover again and let sit at room temperature until serving.

Eliche with Pine Nuts

There are a lot of reasons to like this first course, and one is that the creamy sauce is made with low-fat yogurt instead of heavy cream. If you have all your ingredients chopped and ready, this pasta dish takes little time to prepare at the last minute.

Salt
½ cup pine nuts
1 pound tricolore (multicolored) eliche
¼ pound (1 stick) butter or low-fat spread
6 ounces white mushrooms, thinly sliced
1 clove garlic, peeled and minced
One 6-ounce package frozen peas (do not thaw)
2 large tomatoes, cored, seeded, and diced
4 ounces prosciutto, chopped

⅓ cup plain low-fat yogurt

⅓ cup finely grated Parmigiano-Reggiano cheese, plus additional
  for garnish

Freshly ground black pepper

1. Place a large pot of lightly salted water over high heat and bring to a boil. Meanwhile, place the pine nuts in a small skillet over medium heat and stir until very lightly browned. Immediately transfer to a plate and set aside.

2. When the water comes to a boil, add the eliche and cook until al dente, about 8 minutes; be careful not to overcook. Meanwhile, place a large wide pan over medium heat and melt the butter. Add the mushrooms and sauté for 1 minute. Add the peas, tomatoes, and prosciutto, and sauté until the peas are bright green and tender, 1 to 2 minutes.

3. Drain the eliche and add it to the pan of vegetables. Stir in the yogurt, Parmigiano-Reggiano, and reserved pine nuts. Season with salt and pepper to taste.

4. To serve, place equal portions on each of 8 small plates. Sprinkle with additional Parmigiano-Reggiano and serve immediately.

WINES: Malvasia, Nebbiolo dei Piemonte, Rosé (Les Beaux de Provence)

TO MAKE AHEAD

Twenty minutes before serving: Bring water to a boil for pasta. Toast pine nuts.

Ten minutes before serving: Add pasta to water. Sauté vegetables. Drain pasta and combine
  with vegetables, yogurt, cheese, and pine nuts.

Salmon Cakes with
Yogurt Chipotle Sauce

These croquettes freeze wonderfully. They are presented here as a main course but can be made smaller to serve as an hors d'oeuvre or first course. They may be prepared and frozen ahead of time or assembled, refrigerated, and cooked on the day they are to be served.

FOR THE SALMON CAKES:

1½ pounds skinless, boneless salmon fillets (with all bones completely
   removed)
1½ tablespoons safflower oil
1 medium onion, finely chopped
1½ teaspoons fresh thyme leaves (no stems)
⅓ cup finely chopped red bell pepper
5 large eggs
1¼ cups mayonnaise
1¼ teaspoons salt
1¼ teaspoons freshly ground pepper
1½ cups dry unflavored bread crumbs, plus more (about 1½ cups) for coating
Vegetable oil spray

FOR THE YOGURT CHIPOTLE SAUCE:

8 ounces plain yogurt
1 or 2 canned chipotle peppers (depending on heat desired)
Salt

1. *Prepare the salmon cakes:* Bring a large pan of water to a simmer, add the salmon, and simmer 3 or 4 minutes, until just cooked through and opaque in the center. Drain, cool, and break into chunks.

2. In a frying pan over low heat, combine the safflower oil, onion, and thyme. Sauté until the onion is translucent, about 5 minutes. Add the red pepper and cook 1 minute more. Allow to cool.

3. In a large bowl, combine the salmon, onion mixture, bell pepper, eggs, mayonnaise, salt, and pepper.

4. To cook the patties immediately, preheat the oven to 450 degrees. In any case, shape into patties: 1 ounce for hors d'oeuvres, 3 ounces for first-course servings, or 6 ounces

for main-course servings. The mixture will be quite loose. First shape one into a ball with your hands, then flatten and dip it in the bread crumbs to coat it. Form it gently into an oval and place on a baking sheet. Finish patting it into shape (about ½ inch thick). Repeat with the remaining mixture, placing the patties on the sheet about ½ inch apart.

5. Cover the sheets with plastic wrap or aluminum foil and freeze until the patties are very solid, a few hours or overnight. They can then be transferred to plastic freezer bags and packed tightly together to save space. To defrost, place them on baking sheets, ½ inch apart, and let sit at room temperature for 2 to 3 hours.

6. *Prepare the sauce:* Place the yogurt in a small strainer lined with cheesecloth or paper towels. Place the strainer over a bowl, cover with plastic wrap, and refrigerate. (Conical yogurt strainers can be purchased at some housewares stores. They look like plastic and nylon mesh coffee filters and do not need to be lined.)

7. Remove the salmon cakes from the freezer and arrange close together on a baking sheet sprayed with vegetable oil. Cover lightly with plastic wrap and set aside at room temperature to defrost. Meanwhile, in the container of a blender, combine the drained yogurt, chipotle peppers, 1 tablespoon water, and salt to taste. Puree until smooth. Transfer to a serving bowl, cover, and refrigerate.

8. Preheat the oven to 450 degrees. Bake the salmon cakes until browned on the bottom, about 5 minutes for 3-ounce patties. Turn over and bake until again lightly browned on the bottom (2 minutes for 3-ounce patties). Serve hot with the Yogurt Chipotle Sauce on the side.

WINES: Gewürztraminer (United States), Zinfandel, Rosé (Les Beaux de Provence)

TO MAKE AHEAD
Several hours to one month before serving: Assemble salmon cakes and freeze or refrigerate.
One day before serving: Drain yogurt for sauce.
Three hours before serving: If salmon cakes have been frozen, defrost. Make yogurt sauce and refrigerate.
To serve: Bake salmon cakes and serve with sauce.

Frankie and Johnny's House Salad

John Shaw is the chef and owner of Frankie and Johnny's in Cape Neddick, Maine. This outstanding salad contains greens, grilled vegetables, nuts, and fruit, and comes with a choice of three different and marvelous vinaigrettes. You may wish to dress the salad with one of the vinaigrettes or allow your guests to choose for themselves.

FOR THE GRILLED VEGETABLES:

4 ounces small mushrooms

1 or 2 carrots, thinly sliced
diagonally

1 small yellow summer squash,
thinly sliced diagonally

1 small zucchini, thinly sliced
diagonally

¼ cup olive oil

2 tablespoons lemon juice

Salt and freshly ground black pepper

FOR THE BLUEBERRY OR RASPBERRY
VINAIGRETTE:

1 clove garlic, peeled and minced

2 tablespoons Dijon mustard

2 tablespoons balsamic vinegar

¼ cup white wine, plus additional as
needed

1 cup fresh or frozen and defrosted
blueberries or raspberries

½ cup canola oil

Salt to taste

Sugar to taste

FOR THE LEMON-DIJON VINAIGRETTE:

1 large egg yolk

1½ tablespoons Dijon mustard

¼ cup balsamic vinegar

2 tablespoons fresh lemon juice, or
more as desired

1 cup canola oil

Salt and freshly ground black pepper

FOR ASSEMBLING SALAD:

5 cups mixed baby lettuces

3 cups torn romaine lettuce
(in bite-sized pieces)

Strawberries, hulled and halved

Blueberries

Small chunks of watermelon or
other melon

Thinly sliced unpeeled apple (such
as Fuji or Granny Smith), brushed
with lemon juice to prevent
browning

Sunflower seeds

Pumpkin seeds

Whole almonds

Pistachio nuts

1. *Prepare the grilled vegetables:* Preheat a grill or broiler. In a large mixing bowl, combine the mushrooms, carrots, squash, and zucchini. Pour on the olive oil and lemon juice, and season with salt and pepper to taste. Mix well so that all the vegetables are coated. Grill or broil the vegetables so that the edges are blackened; they should be somewhat softened but still firm in texture. Remove from the heat and allow to cool. Cover and refrigerate.

2. *Prepare the blueberry or raspberry vinaigrette:* In the container of a blender, combine the garlic, mustard, vinegar, and wine. Add the blueberries or raspberries and puree until smooth. With the motor running, add the canola oil through the feed tube. Stop the motor and taste the dressing. If desired, add a small amount of salt and sugar, and blend again. Adjust the seasonings to taste. Transfer to a covered container and refrigerate.

3. *Prepare the lemon-dijon vinaigrette:* In the container of a blender or in a mixing bowl, combine the egg yolk, mustard, vinegar, and lemon juice. With the motor running or using a whisk, slowly add the canola oil until well blended. Season with salt and pepper to taste. Cover and refrigerate.

4. In a very large bowl, combine the baby lettuces and romaine lettuce. Add the grilled vegetables to taste; you may not wish to use them all. Add the fruit, seeds, and nuts to taste, beginning with very small amounts. If using more than one vinaigrette, pour them into small pitchers to be passed separately. If using one vinaigrette, pour a small amount on the salad and toss lightly to coat. Add a small amount at a time until the salad is dressed to taste. (Be careful not to overdress the salad; the vinaigrette should not overwhelm the greens.) Serve immediately.

TO MAKE AHEAD

Up to one day before serving: Grill vegetables; refrigerate. Make vinaigrette(s); refrigerate.
To serve: Assemble salad. Add dressing and toss.

Custardy Rhubarb Pie

It can be surprisingly difficult to find a recipe for rhubarb pie that doesn't include another fruit. This recipe is adapted from one by Pamalee Reeve, baker for Elderberry Country Foods in Auburn, New York. Don't be put off by the inclusion of nonhydrogenated spread in the piecrust; the dough is easy to handle, nicely flaky, and healthy, too.

FOR THE PIE DOUGH:

2 cups unbleached all-purpose flour

1 teaspoon kosher salt

4 tablespoons cold unsalted butter, cut into small pieces

4 tablespoons Smart Balance or other nonhydrogenated spread

4 tablespoons cold vegetable shortening

2 to 4 tablespoons ice water

FOR THE FILLING:

2 large eggs

1¼ cups sugar

2 tablespoons cornstarch

⅛ teaspoon kosher salt

4 cups (about 1 pound) fresh rhubarb, cut into ¾-inch pieces

1 tablespoon cold unsalted butter

1. *Prepare the pie dough:* Combine the flour and salt in a large mixing bowl or the bowl of a food processor. Add the butter, Smart Balance, and shortening. If working by hand, use a pastry cutter or 2 knives to cut the fat into the flour until the mixture resembles coarse crumbs. If using a food processor, pulse until the fat and flour are combined.

2. Sprinkle 2 tablespoons ice water over the mixture and work in until the dough starts to stick together. Add more water as needed, 1 tablespoon at a time, until the dough forms a ball but is still somewhat crumbly. Turn the dough onto a lightly floured surface and shape into a ball.

3. Cut the dough into 2 pieces, one slightly larger than the other. Wrap each piece in waxed paper and refrigerate for at least 20 minutes and up to 2 days.

4. Preheat the oven to 425 degrees. Roll out the larger piece of dough into an 11-inch disk and place it in a 9-inch pie plate. Roll out the smaller piece on a sheet of waxed paper

into a 9½-inch disk. Place the lined pie plate and top dough in the refrigerator while making the filling.

2. *Prepare the filling:* In a mixing bowl, beat the eggs until frothy. Add the sugar, cornstarch, and salt, and mix to blend. Stir in the rhubarb. Place the filling in the pie shell. Cut the butter into thin chips and dot them over the filling.

3. Cover the pie with the smaller piece of dough, peeling off the waxed paper. Trim and crimp the edges. With a sharp knife, make 4 slits in the center of the top to allow steam to escape while the pie bakes.

4. Bake for 20 minutes. Lower the heat to 350 degrees and continue baking until the crust is golden brown, about 30 minutes more. If necessary, cover the edges of the crust with foil to prevent burning. Cool the pie on a wire rack until lukewarm or room temperature before slicing.

WINE: Late-Harvest Riesling

TO MAKE AHEAD
Three hours to two days before serving: Make pie dough. Cover and refrigerate.
Two to six hours before serving: Roll out dough and fill pie. Bake and cool.

MENU 5

. . . .

Shrimp Cocktail with
Two Sauces

This recipe makes the best shrimp cocktail I've ever had. A bit of gin in the red cocktail sauce gives it special flavor. The recipe was adapted from Rick Moonen, former chef at Oceana in New York City.

FOR THE SHRIMP:

3 pounds shrimp (size 16 to 20 per pound), peeled and deveined,
    shells reserved

5 tablespoons kosher salt

3 cups white wine

1 tablespoon black peppercorns

1 tablespoon coriander seed

2 bay leaves

1 small bunch (about 1 cup) Italian (flat-leaf) parsley

4 sprigs fresh tarragon

2 lemons, halved

FOR THE CHILI SAUCE (MAKES 1½ CUPS):

1 cup prepared chili sauce

2½ teaspoons prepared horseradish, drained

¼ teaspoon kosher salt

Tabasco sauce

Fresh lemon juice

1 teaspoon gin

1 tablespoon chopped Italian (flat-leaf) parsley

Freshly ground black pepper to taste

FOR THE SAUCE VERT (MAKES 1½ CUPS):

1 cup chopped Italian (flat-leaf) parsley

½ cup chopped chervil leaves

½ cup chopped chives

2 cloves garlic, peeled and chopped

1 shallot, peeled and chopped

½ teaspoon chopped anchovy or anchovy paste

¼ cup capers

1 tablespoon fresh lemon juice

1 cup extra-virgin olive oil

Kosher salt

Freshly ground black pepper

1. *Prepare the shrimp:* In a large pot, combine the shrimp shells, 2 quarts water, and 3 tablespoons salt. Bring to a boil over high heat, reduce the heat to low, and simmer for 20 minutes. Remove the pot from the heat and allow the contents to steep until cooled.

2. Strain the shrimp broth into another large pot and bring to a boil over high heat. Add the wine, peppercorns, coriander seed, bay leaves, parsley, tarragon, and lemons. Boil for 2 minutes. Add the shrimp and remove the pot from the heat. Allow the shrimp to steep until they are no longer opaque, about 3 minutes. Fill a large mixing bowl with water, ice, and the remaining 2 tablespoons salt. Transfer the shrimp to the bowl and let cool for 3 minutes, then drain well. Refrigerate with a bag of ice on top until ready to serve.

3. *Prepare the chili sauce:* In a medium mixing bowl, combine the chili sauce, horseradish, salt, 1½ teaspoons Tabasco sauce, 1 tablespoon lemon juice, gin, and parsley. Mix well. Season to taste with additional lemon juice, Tabasco, salt, and pepper. Cover and refrigerate until ready to serve.

4. *Prepare the sauce vert:* In a blender, combine the parsley, chervil, chives, garlic, shallot, anchovy, capers, and lemon juice. Pulse to puree. With the motor running, very slowly add the olive oil until it is thoroughly incorporated. Transfer to a bowl. Season to taste with salt and pepper. Cover and refrigerate until ready to serve.

WINES: Muscadet, Pinot Bianco, Chenin Blanc (demi-sec)

TO MAKE AHEAD

Up to eight hours before serving: Boil and cool shrimp. Make chili sauce. Make sauce vert. Refrigerate.

To serve: Arrange shrimp on plates. Place sauce in bowls.

Vichyssoise

2 medium baking potatoes (such as russets)
4 tablespoons butter
3 medium leeks, white and light green parts only, thinly sliced and well
    washed
1 medium onion, peeled and sliced
4 cups chicken stock or canned broth
1 sprig fresh thyme
Salt and ground white pepper
Freshly ground nutmeg
2 cups heavy cream
2 to 3 tablespoons finely chopped parsley for garnish

1. Peel and thinly slice the potatoes. Put them in a bowl of water to prevent browning.
2. Place a large, wide saucepan over medium-low heat and melt the butter. Add the leeks, onion, and potatoes. Cover the pan and reduce the heat to low. Allow to cook gently without browning, stirring occasionally, until the onions are translucent, 8 to 10 minutes.
3. Add the chicken stock and thyme. Partially cover and cook until the potatoes are very tender, about 15 minutes. Add a pinch of nutmeg and salt and white pepper to taste. Remove from the heat and allow to cool. Remove and discard the thyme.
4. Working in batches, puree the soup in a blender until very smooth. Transfer to a

large container and add the cream. Stir well and adjust the salt, pepper, and nutmeg as desired. Cover and refrigerate.

5. Place the soup in a large chilled soup tureen or in individual serving bowls. Garnish with parsley and serve immediately.

WINES: Continue with the Muscadet or Chenin Blanc, or try a Sercial Madeira

TO MAKE AHEAD

Up to two days before serving: Prepare soup. Cover and refrigerate.
To serve: Transfer soup to a chilled soup tureen or individual bowls. Garnish with parsley.

Chicken with Pine Nuts and Sun-dried Tomatoes

This recipe also makes a wonderful chicken salad. Make the recipe as written and allow to cool. Dice the chicken and roughly chop the tomatoes and peppers. Mix with mayonnaise, diced avocado, and diced red onion, and season to taste with lemon juice, salt, and cayenne pepper. Serve on a bed of buttercrunch lettuce leaves.

  4 whole boneless, skinless chicken breasts, halved and trimmed
  Salt and freshly ground black pepper
  2 tablespoons lemon juice
  Olive or vegetable oil drained from jar of julienned sun-dried tomatoes in oil
  1½ red bell peppers, cored, seeded, and thinly sliced
  ½ cup jarred julienned sun-dried tomatoes in oil, drained
  4 ounces pine nuts

1. Pound the chicken halves flat (see page 102) and season to taste with salt and pepper. Place them in a wide, shallow bowl and add the lemon juice and 2 tablespoons oil from the sun-dried tomatoes. Rub the juice and oil onto both sides of each breast half. Cover and refrigerate.

2. Preheat a large cast-iron ridged skillet or flat skillet. Make sure the kitchen is well ventilated because the seared chicken will create smoke. When the pan is hot, use a pastry or basting brush to coat the surface with oil from the sun-dried tomatoes. (Alternatively,

nonstick vegetable spray may be used.) Spread as many breasts in the pan as will fit in 1 layer. Allow to sit about 30 seconds, then slide a sturdy spatula under the breasts to reposition them slightly in the pan (this prevents sticking). Allow to sit for another 30 seconds, then flip the breasts and cook again until the meat is opaque in the center, about 30 seconds more. Transfer the cooked breasts to a serving platter and cover with foil to keep warm.

3.   When all the chicken is cooked, add the red bell pepper slices to the skillet. Allow them to sit until they begin to sear, then toss them in the pan until slightly softened and charred in places on the edges. Add the sun-dried tomatoes and toss to mix with the peppers. Add the pine nuts and toss quickly for 20 to 30 seconds, until the nuts begin to brown; be careful not to let them burn. As soon as the nuts are lightly browned, uncover the platter of chicken and pour the mixture of peppers, tomatoes, and pine nuts on top. Serve immediately, topping each portion of a chicken breast half with a generous spoonful of vegetables and nuts.

WINES: Côtes de Gascogne (white), Sauvignon Blanc, Riesling

TO MAKE AHEAD

Up to two hours before serving: Pound chicken flat. Rub with lemon juice and oil. Cover and refrigerate.

Thirty minutes before serving: Preheat cast-iron skillet. Sauté chicken; remove from heat. Sauté peppers, tomatoes, and pine nuts.

POUNDING CHICKEN BREASTS

The best way to pound chicken breasts flat is to place them on a clean counter and cover with a large (gallon size or larger) plastic storage bag. Use a wooden kitchen mallet to gently pound the breasts to the desired thickness. Repeat with each breast, remembering to always place the same (sticky) side of the bag down on the chicken. Plastic bags are much sturdier than plastic wrap or foil and will not tear.

Spinach with Garlic Oil

Garlic oil—olive oil or canola oil flavored with garlic—is a useful timesaver in the kitchen, but it is important to find a brand of oil that has true garlic flavor. You can also make your own garlic oil by very gently sautéing sliced or chopped garlic in oil. This recipe takes less than ten minutes to prepare.

¼ cup Tuscan Sun or other garlic-flavored oil
2 pounds spinach leaves, well washed, dried, and stemmed
Salt

1. Place a large skillet or wok over medium heat. When the pan is hot, add the garlic oil, swirling it to cover the bottom. Allow the oil to heat about 1 minute.

2. Add the spinach to the pan and begin tossing it immediately. The spinach will wilt very quickly. As soon as it is thoroughly heated and wilted, remove the pan from the heat. Sprinkle lightly with salt to taste and transfer to a serving dish.

Strawberry Shortcakes

FOR THE SHORTCAKES:

2 cups all-purpose flour
Sugar
1 tablespoon plus ½ teaspoon baking powder
6 tablespoons unsalted butter, chilled and cut into small pieces, plus
    additional for baking sheet
¾ cup heavy cream
1 hard-boiled egg yolk, mashed until smooth
2 tablespoons unsalted butter, melted

FOR THE STRAWBERRIES:

6 cups strawberries, washed, hulled, and halved or quartered
3 tablespoons sugar
1 cup heavy cream

1. *Prepare the shortcakes:* Preheat the oven to 375 degrees. In a large bowl, sift the flour, ¼ cup sugar, and baking powder. Add the unsalted butter pieces. Using your fingertips, quickly work the butter into the flour until it has the texture of very fine crumbs. Add the cream and egg yolk, and stir with a fork until the dough just holds together.

2. Lightly butter a baking sheet. On a lightly floured surface, pat or roll the dough to a thickness of ½ inch. Using a floured 4-inch biscuit cutter, cut into 8 disks, rerolling the dough as necessary. Place on the baking sheet, brush with melted butter, and sprinkle with 1 tablespoon sugar. Bake until golden brown and firm, about 15 minutes. Transfer to a rack and allow to cool for 2 to 3 minutes.

3. *Prepare the strawberries:* In a medium bowl, combine the strawberries and 2 tablespoons sugar. Cover and refrigerate. Whip 1 cup cream with the remaining 1 tablespoon sugar until soft peaks form, cover, and refrigerate.

4. Carefully split the shortcakes in half and set the tops aside. Place the bottoms on dessert plates and heap equal amounts of strawberries on each one. Generously spoon whipped cream on top and replace the tops. Serve immediately, offering any remaining whipped cream separately.

WINES: Sweet Loire (Vouvray Moelleux, Coteaux du Layon, Bonnezeaux, or Quarts de Chaume)

TO MAKE AHEAD

One to twenty-four hours before serving: Make shortcakes. Cover and set aside at room temperature.

Thirty minutes to two hours before serving: Combine berries and sugar; cover and refrigerate. Whip cream; cover and refrigerate.

MENU 6

. . . .

Deviled Eggs with Avocado

8 large eggs, hard-boiled and peeled (see page 106)
¼ cup mayonnaise
½ teaspoon dry mustard
½ large, ripe Hass avocado
½ teaspoon fresh lemon juice
Salt and freshly ground white pepper
Paprika
2 to 3 tablespoons finely sliced fresh chives

1. Cut the eggs in half lengthwise. Set the whites aside and put the yolks in a medium mixing bowl. Add the mayonnaise, mustard, avocado, and lemon juice. Mash until fairly smooth. Season with salt and white pepper to taste and mash again until free of any lumps.

2. Fill the egg whites with the avocado mixture. Arrange on a platter and lightly sprinkle the whites with paprika. Sprinkle the yolks with chives. Cover with plastic wrap and refrigerate until serving.

WINES: Rosé (Valencia, Penedés, Rioja), Pinot Blanc (California), Sangiovese

One hour before serving: Prepare eggs and arrange on platter. Cover lightly with plastic wrap
and refrigerate.

PEELING EGGS

It can be very frustrating to try to peel an egg and have it stick to the shell. It will help if you use eggs that aren't fresh from the supermarket (or hen, if you should be so lucky). Be sure to cook the eggs within the "sell by" date on the carton, but if possible, refrigerate them for a week before hard-boiling and peeling. To hard-boil eggs, submerge them gently in a pan of cold water and place over medium-high heat. As soon as the water comes to a simmer, reduce the heat to low. Simmer, uncovered, for 10 minutes. Drain the eggs and peel immediately under cold running water.

Gazpacho

Prepare this soup twenty-four hours in advance and serve chilled.

1 cup peeled, chopped fresh tomatoes (see page 107)
1 cup peeled, chopped red onions
1 cup chopped green pepper
1 cup peeled, chopped English or other seedless cucumber
1½ teaspoons peeled, chopped garlic
1½ teaspoons kosher salt
¼ teaspoon cayenne pepper
¼ cup tomato paste
1 tablespoon white wine vinegar
¼ cup plus 2 tablespoons extra-virgin olive oil
1 tablespoon fresh lemon juice
3 cups tomato juice
1 sprig thyme

1. In a large nonreactive mixing bowl, combine all the ingredients. Cover and refrigerate overnight.

2. The next day remove the sprig of thyme. Using a blender, puree the remaining ingredients until smooth. For a smoother texture the soup may be strained (this will reduce the quantity of the finished soup). Refrigerate the gazpacho until well chilled. Ladle the soup into bowls and serve cold.

WINES: Sherry (fino, chilled), Rioja (white, red, or the rosé from the first course), Ribera del Duero

TO MAKE AHEAD

The day before serving: Prepare gazpacho. Cover and refrigerate.

PEELING TOMATOES

To peel fresh tomatoes, cut a shallow X on the bottom of each tomato, and submerge in boiling water for 5 to 10 seconds to loosen the skin. Remove and chill under cold water. The skins will slip off easily.

Seafood, Chicken, and
Sausage Paella

This is a recipe for when you are feeling ambitious. It cannot be prepared ahead of time and takes about forty-five minutes of attentive cooking. Although the list of ingredients is long, once they are assembled, the recipe is not hard to execute. You will have plenty of company in the kitchen as you cook. Guests will be enticed by the tantalizing aromas and the sounds of sizzling and bubbling.

1 cup extra-virgin olive oil

1 cup cured ham, diced small

12 ounces chorizo, thinly sliced

1 pound boneless chicken breast, cut into bite-sized pieces

Salt and freshly ground black pepper

1½ pounds large shrimp, shelled

8 ounces squid, cut into rings and small pieces

1 green bell pepper, chopped

1 red bell pepper, chopped

1 medium onion, peeled and chopped

¼ cup chopped parsley

½ teaspoon hot red pepper flakes

3 tomatoes, cored and diced

3 cloves garlic, peeled and finely chopped

1 teaspoon saffron threads

3 tablespoons lemon juice, plus additional as needed

4 cups Valencia or other short-grain Spanish rice

1 pound raw Manila, mahogany, cherrystone, or other small clams

1 pound raw mussels, scrubbed and debearded

One 8-ounce bottle clam broth

4 cups chicken broth

8 ounces cooked lobster meat, in chunks

2 tablespoons nonpareil capers

Chopped parsley leaves for garnish

Lemon wedges for garnish

1. Place a large paella pan (or other very wide, shallow, flameproof pan) over medium heat. Heat the oil and add the ham and chorizo. Sauté until browned, then transfer to a large platter or baking sheet. Season the chicken with salt and pepper, and add to the hot pan. Sauté until lightly browned, then transfer to the platter of ham. Add the shrimp and sauté until seared but not fully cooked, then transfer to the platter. Add the squid, toss until opaque, and then transfer to the platter.

2. Add the green bell pepper, red bell pepper, onion, parsley, and red pepper flakes to the pan. Sauté until softened, about 3 minutes. Add the contents of the platter to the pan and stir in the tomatoes, garlic, saffron, and 3 tablespoons lemon juice. Add the rice and stir well. Add the clams, mussels, clam broth, and chicken broth. Stir again, then cover the pan with a lid or foil. Reduce the heat to low and cook for 10 minutes.

3. Remove the cover from the pan and check to see if the shellfish have opened. If not, cover again and allow to cook a few minutes more. When the shellfish are open, remove the cover and stir in the lobster meat and capers. Simmer, uncovered, until the rice is cooked, another 5 to 10 minutes. If the pan seems dry, add additional broth or water.

4. To serve, sprinkle the paella pan with lemon juice to taste. Garnish with parsley leaves and lemon wedges, and serve immediately.

WINES: Valencia, Penedés, Rioja (all white, red, and rosés from the previous courses)

Rouille

[MAKES 2 CUPS]

This sauce accompaniment to paella takes only ten minutes to prepare. It is traditionally made with a mortar and pestle. It can be made in a small food processor, but pulse just enough to blend the mixture.

4 to 6 cloves garlic, peeled and crushed
Pinch of cayenne pepper
1 medium hunk country bread, crust removed
4 to 6 tablespoons clam broth
4 to 6 cooked potato slices, lightly mashed
½ cup olive oil
Salt and freshly ground black pepper

1. Using a mortar and pestle, mash the garlic and cayenne together. Dunk the bread into the clam broth for a minute, squeeze out the liquid, and add to the mortar. Mash well.

2. Add the potato slices and mash with the pestle into a thick paste. Gradually add the olive oil, drop by drop, mashing the mixture in a circular motion until the mixture is thick and smooth. (If the mixture breaks up, add 1 or 2 teaspoons clam broth or a little more soup-soaked bread.) Season with salt and pepper to taste.

Peppermint Ice Cream

[MAKES ABOUT 2 QUARTS]

Most ice-cream makers make only 1 to 1½ quarts, so you may need to freeze this ice cream in two batches. If necessary, the custard for the second batch can be stored in the refrigerator for up to three days.

6 cups milk
1¾ cups crème de menthe
20 large egg yolks
1½ cups sugar
½ cup packed chopped fresh mint leaves, or more as needed
Fresh mint sprigs for garnish

1. In a medium saucepan, combine the milk and crème de menthe. Bring to a boil and remove from the heat. In the bowl of an electric mixer, combine the egg yolks and sugar. Beat until thick and light. Gradually beat in the milk mixture.

2. Pour the mixture back into the saucepan and place over low heat. Cook gently, stirring with a wooden spoon, until the mixture is thickened enough to coat the back of the spoon; do not allow the mixture to boil or it will curdle. Transfer to a bowl, and add the mint. Cool the mixture by setting the bowl in a bowl of salted ice water (see page 111). Stir until the mixture is at room temperature. Taste and add more mint leaves if necessary. Transfer to the refrigerator until cold, about 1 hour.

3. Strain the mixture and return it to the refrigerator for an additional 2 hours. Freeze in an ice-cream maker, in 2 batches if necessary, according to the manufacturer's instructions. Place the ice cream in the freezer until firm, at least 2 hours. To serve, scoop into bowls or glasses and garnish with mint sprigs.

WINE: Sparkling (sweet) or Crème de Menthe

TO MAKE AHEAD

Up to one week before serving: Prepare ice cream custard. Freeze in an ice-cream maker in two batches. Transfer to a covered container and store in freezer.

To serve: Spoon equal portions into bowls or glasses and garnish with mint sprigs.

MAKING ICE WATER BATH COLDER

Yes, salt lowers the melting temperature of ice. Normally, ice freezes at 32 degrees F. If you add salt to ice or a mixture of ice and water, the ice will liquefy even though the temperature of the salted water is well below freezing. This is why rock salt is mixed with ice in old-fashioned ice-cream machines.

If you have a liquid that you would like to chill quickly, place the food to be chilled in a bowl that will not crack when it comes into contact with the cold water. A stainless steel bowl is ideal for this purpose.

MENU 7

. . . .

Smoked Salmon Rolls

Cut these rolls into pieces small enough to be popped into the mouth in one bite.

1 cup finely chopped lobster or crabmeat
3 tablespoons heavy cream
1 teaspoon finely sliced chives
1 teaspoon minced fresh dill
Salt
8 very thin slices smoked salmon, cut into uniform rectangles
Coarsely ground black pepper

1. In a small mixing bowl, combine the lobster meat, cream, chives, and dill. Season with salt to taste and mix well.

2. Spread the salmon rectangles with an even layer of the lobster mixture. Sprinkle with black pepper to taste. With dampened hands, and using the cutting edge of a table knife for assistance, roll up each rectangle into a tight cylinder. Wrap securely in plastic wrap and refrigerate.

3. Unwrap the cylinders and cut each one crosswise into 3 or 4 pieces. Arrange on a platter. Serve chilled.

WINES: Corbières (white), Pinot Gris (Alsace, Oregon), Burgundy (white), Champagne (blanc de blancs)

TO MAKE AHEAD

Up to one day before serving: Prepare rolls. Cover and refrigerate.

To serve: Unwrap cylinders and cut crosswise into pieces. Arrange on platter.

Crostini with Pesto and Fried Green Tomatoes

1 cup packed fresh basil leaves

2 tablespoons Parmesan cheese

Extra-virgin olive oil

2 cloves garlic, peeled and minced

2 tablespoons pine nuts

2 tablespoons drained and finely chopped sun-dried tomatoes in olive oil

Salt

8 slices sourdough baguette, thinly cut on the diagonal

2 green (unripe) tomatoes, cored and thinly sliced

Thin curls or fine shreds of Parmesan cheese, preferably Parmigiano-Reggiano

1. In the container of a blender or food processor, combine the basil, Parmesan, 2 tablespoons olive oil, garlic, and pine nuts. Process to make a smooth puree. Scrape into a container and mix in the sun-dried tomatoes. Season to taste with salt, cover, and refrigerate.

2. Remove the pesto from the refrigerator and set aside. Place a medium skillet over medium-low heat and add 2 tablespoons olive oil. Add the sliced bread and fry, turning once or twice, until both sides of each slice are golden brown. Transfer to a plate. Add another tablespoon of oil to the skillet and return to medium-high heat. Add the sliced tomatoes in a single layer and allow them to sit until browned on the bottom. Using a spatula, carefully turn to brown the other side. Transfer to a plate. (The tomatoes will be soft and may lose their shape.)

3. Spread each crostini with a thin layer of pesto and top with a slice of fried green tomato. Sprinkle with curls or shreds of Parmesan. Place on serving plates.

TO MAKE AHEAD

Up to one week in advance: Make pesto. Cover and refrigerate.

To serve: Fry bread. Fry tomatoes. Assemble crostini.

Herb-Simmered Leg of Lamb
with Sardine Mayonnaise or
Anchovy Vinaigrette

This recipe by Barbara Kafka offers a choice of two sauces: sardine mayonnaise and anchovy vinaigrette. Either sauce nicely complements the chilled sliced lamb.

FOR THE LAMB:

1 bay leaf

4 medium cloves garlic, unpeeled

2 teaspoons rosemary

2¾ pounds boneless leg of lamb,
  rolled and tied

FOR THE SARDINE MAYONNAISE
  (MAKES 6 CUPS):

3 large eggs

3 cups olive oil

6 cans (3.75 ounces each) oil-
  packed sardines, drained and
  lightly crushed

5 tablespoons green peppercorns,
  packed in brine, rinsed

3 tablespoons tarragon vinegar

1½ teaspoons kosher salt

FOR THE ANCHOVY VINAIGRETTE
  (MAKES 3 CUPS):

10 sprigs Italian (flat-leaf) parsley,
  leaves only, coarsely chopped

4 teaspoons anchovy paste

1 tablespoon Dijon mustard

1 teaspoon kosher salt

1 teaspoon freshly ground black pepper

½ cup red wine vinegar

1 cup olive oil

4 tablespoons coarsely chopped
  capers

2 hard-boiled eggs, finely chopped

1. *Prepare the lamb*: In a 10½-inch-wide braising pan or stockpot, bring 1 gallon water to a boil with the bay leaf, garlic, and rosemary. Add the lamb and return to a boil. Lower the heat and simmer for 1½ hours, turning every 20 minutes.

2. Remove the pot from the stove and allow the meat to cool in the liquid. Remove the meat from the liquid and slice across into ¼-inch slices; there should be 25 to 30 slices. If using sardine mayonnaise, follow the directions below. If using enriched vinaigrette, cover the lamb with plastic wrap and refrigerate until serving.

3. *Prepare the sardine mayonnaise*: In a food processor, pulse the eggs until slightly foamy, about 5 times. With the machine running, pour the olive oil through the feed tube a few drops at a time. When about 1 cup has been added and the sauce starts to thicken, pour a little faster, in a slow, steady stream, until the oil has been incorporated. Add the sardines and 2 tablespoons peppercorns. Pulse to combine, about 10 times. Add the vinegar and salt, and pulse to combine. Scrape into a medium bowl and stir in the remaining 3 peppercorns.

4. Spread 1 cup sardine mayonnaise on a medium platter or on the bottom of a baking dish. Place a layer of lamb slices on top and then spread the slices with more mayonnaise. Continue until all the mayonnaise and meat have been used. Cover with plastic wrap and refrigerate for 1 hour or up to 3 days.

5. *Prepare the anchovy vinaigrette*: In a food processor, pulse the parsley, anchovy paste, mustard, salt, pepper, and vinegar to combine. With the machine running, slowly pour in the olive oil. Remove to a small bowl and stir in the capers and eggs. Cover and refrigerate until serving.

6. If using sardine mayonnaise, uncover the lamb and serve chilled. If using anchovy vinaigrette, uncover the lamb, drizzle with vinaigrette, and serve chilled.

WINES: with sardine mayonnaise: Cahors, Rosé (Bandol), Vino da Tavola/Super Tuscan; with anchovy vinaigrette: Corbières (red, or white continued from the first and/or second course), Chardonnay (oaked), Bordeaux (red, Médoc)

TO MAKE AHEAD
Three hours to three days before serving: Braise lamb, cool, and slice. If using sardine mayonnaise, prepare sauce and spread over lamb. Cover and refrigerate. If using anchovy vinaigrette, cover lamb and refrigerate without sauce.
The day before serving: Prepare vinaigrette if using. Cover and refrigerate.
To serve with sardine mayonnaise: Uncover lamb and serve chilled.
To serve with anchovy vinaigrette: Drizzle vinaigrette over lamb and serve chilled.

Fire-Roasted Peppers

8 bell peppers of mixed colors (preferably 2 each of red, yellow, purple,
    and orange)
Extra-virgin olive oil

1. Preheat a grill or broiler. Quarter the peppers lengthwise and remove the core and seeds. Brush all sides with olive oil.

2. Grill or broil the peppers, turning once or twice, until they are softened and the skins are blackened. Use tongs to transfer them to a plate. When they are cool enough to handle, remove some but not all of the blackened skins. Transfer to a flat covered container and refrigerate.

3. To serve chilled, simply arrange the peppers on a platter. To serve warm, preheat the oven to 400 degrees. Put the peppers on a baking sheet and bake just until heated through, about 3 minutes. Transfer to a platter and serve.

TO MAKE AHEAD

Up to two days before serving: Roast or broil peppers. Cool and peel. Cover and refrigerate.
To serve: Serve chilled or reheat in a preheated 400-degree oven.

Poire William Ice Cream

[MAKES 1½ QUARTS]

This is wonderful accompanied by poached pears, served chilled or warm, and a dollop of whipped cream.

6 large egg yolks
2 cups heavy cream
1 cup half-and-half
⅔ cup sugar
3 tablespoons Poire William eau de vie

1. Whisk the egg yolks just enough to break them up, then set aside. Place the cream in a medium mixing bowl and set aside.

2. In a small saucepan, combine the half-and-half and sugar. Place over medium heat and cook, stirring occasionally, just until steam rises; do not boil. Slowly add about ½ cup of the hot mixture to the egg yolks, whisking vigorously to combine well. Pour the egg yolk mixture into the saucepan and simmer, stirring, over low heat until the custard thickens enough to coat the back of a metal spoon, about 5 minutes.

3. Strain the custard into the bowl of cream. Add the Poire William and stir to mix well. Refrigerate until well chilled, about 30 minutes. Freeze in an ice-cream maker according to the manufacturer's instructions.

WINES: Late-Harvest Riesling or Poire William

TO MAKE AHEAD
Up to one week before serving: Prepare ice cream custard. Freeze in an ice-cream maker. Transfer to a covered container and store in freezer.

MENU 8

. . . .

Membrillo with Manchego

Membrillo, a Spanish specialty, is a thick paste made of quince. It is often served with cheese or, dusted with sugar, as a sweet to nibble with coffee. Here it is paired with Manchego, a Spanish cheese made from sheep's milk. This is a finger food, meant to be eaten without bread or crackers.

8 ounces Manchego cheese
6 ounces membrillo (available in specialty food stores and many cheese stores)

1. Slice the Manchego into thin pieces about 1 inch wide and 1½ inches long. Top with very thin slices of membrillo about the same width and length as the Manchego.

2. Arrange on a serving platter and cover with plastic wrap. Set aside at room temperature until ready to serve.

WINES: Moscato d'Asti, Palo Cortado, Rioja or Cencibel (both red)

TO MAKE AHEAD
Up to three hours before serving: Slice Manchego and top with membrillo. Cover and set aside at room temperature.

Calamari, Watermelon, and Avocado Salad

When this salad is assembled, the shapes and colors make it look like a work of art. The three primary ingredients provide appealing contrasts in texture and flavor.

4 cups fresh cilantro

1/4 cup rice wine, champagne, or white wine vinegar

1 tablespoon grapeseed oil

Salt and freshly ground black pepper

12 ounces cleaned squid, cut into rings, including tentacles

1 egg white, beaten

1/2 tablespoon ground coriander

1 3/4 tablespoons extra-virgin olive oil

1 1/2 teaspoons butter

1 1/2 tablespoons finely chopped shallots

1 tablespoon chopped fines herbes (mixed chervil, tarragon, chives, and parsley)

1 tablespoon lemon juice

1 lemon

2 ounces baby salad greens, washed and dried

16 thin slices of watermelon, cut into 1-inch squares

Eight 1/4-inch-thick slices of avocado

1/2 cup cilantro leaves for garnish

1. *Prepare the cilantro vinaigrette:* Fill a saucepan halfway with water and bring to a boil. Set aside a bowl of ice water. Place the cilantro in the boiling water and immediately transfer to the ice water. Squeeze the cilantro dry. In the container of a blender, combine the cilantro, vinegar, and grapeseed oil. Puree until smooth. Transfer to a bowl and season with salt and pepper to taste.

2. *Prepare the calamari:* Place the squid, egg white, and coriander in a medium bowl and mix well. In a large sauté pan over medium-high heat, heat 1 tablespoon olive oil until it is smoking. Add the squid and sauté until it is translucent, about 2 minutes. Add the butter and stir until melted. Add 1 tablespoon shallots, stir, and remove the pan from the heat. Add the fines herbes and salt and pepper to taste. Toss to mix well.

3. *Prepare the lemon vinaigrette:* In a small bowl, combine the lemon juice, remaining 3/4 tablespoon olive oil, and salt and pepper to taste. Set aside.

4. Grate the zest of the lemon and set aside. Remove the white pith and cut the lemon into segments. In a mixing bowl, combine the lemon zest, lemon segments, salad greens, remaining ½ tablespoon shallots, calamari, and lemon vinaigrette. Toss quickly to blend well.

5. Spread the calamari mixture in the center of a large serving platter. Arrange the watermelon and avocado slices decoratively on top. Pour a ring of cilantro vinaigrette over the salad and around the edge of the platter. Garnish with cilantro leaves.

WINES: Penedés (white), Aligoté, Sauvignon Blanc (New Zealand)

TO MAKE AHEAD

Up to two hours before serving: Prepare cilantro vinaigrette, calamari, and lemon vinaigrette. Cover and refrigerate.

Twenty minutes before serving: Grate lemon zest and cut lemon into segments. Mix salad and lemon vinaigrette.

To serve: Assemble salad and drizzle with cilantro vinaigrette. Garnish.

Grilled Lamb Kebabs with Yogurt Sauce

Serve these kebabs with an attractive platter of tomatoes and greens. If you are using bamboo skewers, you may wish to soak them for up to an hour before using. Do not oversoak, or they will splinter as you thread the meat onto them.

FOR THE LAMB:

2 pounds trimmed boneless lamb leg, cut into 1-inch cubes
¾ cup extra-virgin olive oil
⅓ cup fresh lemon juice
3 cloves garlic, peeled and minced

2 bay leaves
2 tablespoons chopped fresh oregano
½ teaspoon cracked black peppercorns
Salt

FOR THE YOGURT SAUCE:

2 cups Greek or whole-milk yogurt
½ seedless cucumber, peeled and finely chopped

2 tablespoons finely chopped fresh mint leaves
Salt

ACCOMPANIMENTS:

Diced ripe tomatoes

Shredded lettuce

Thinly sliced red onion or sweet
onion

Hummus

Pita bread

1. *Marinate the lamb:* In a heavy-duty plastic storage bag or covered container, combine the lamb cubes, olive oil, lemon juice, garlic, bay leaves, oregano, peppercorns, and salt to taste. Mix well and refrigerate for at least 6 hours and up to 24 hours.

2. Preheat a grill. *Prepare the yogurt sauce:* In a mixing bowl, combine the yogurt, cucumber, and mint. Season with salt to taste. Transfer to a serving bowl and refrigerate until needed.

3. Remove the lamb cubes from the marinade and thread onto 8 or more skewers. Grill the lamb, turning often, until browned on the outside and medium-rare (or to taste) on the inside. Serve with yogurt sauce, tomatoes, lettuce, onion, hummus, and pita bread.

WINES: Minervois, Barbera, Cabernet Sauvignon (United States)

TO MAKE AHEAD

Six to twenty-four hours before serving: Marinate lamb.

Forty minutes before serving: Preheat grill. Prepare yogurt sauce. Grill lamb. Serve with
sauce and accompaniments.

Israeli Couscous

Many people mistakenly assume that couscous is a grain. Israeli couscous, larger than the couscous commonly sold in supermarkets, looks more like the pasta it is. But it still cooks very quickly. Israeli couscous may be found in many specialty food and Middle Eastern food markets.

2 tablespoons olive oil

2 tablespoons finely chopped onion

4 cups beef stock or broth

2½ cups Israeli couscous

Salt and freshly ground black pepper

1 tablespoon minced Italian (flat-
leaf) parsley

1. Place a large saucepan over medium-low heat and add the olive oil. Add the onion and sauté until translucent.

2. Add the stock and allow it to come to a boil. Add the couscous, cover, and reduce the heat to low. Simmer about 10 minutes. Uncover, season with salt and pepper to taste, and stir in the parsley. If all the liquid has not been absorbed, return to low heat for another few minutes. If the liquid has been absorbed, cover the pan and keep warm until serving.

Greek Rizogalo

This traditional Greek dessert takes about 30 minutes to prepare.

2 cups short-grain rice (sushi or Arborio)
8 cups milk
2 cups sugar
Four 2-inch pieces of lemon peel
¼ cup plus 1½ tablespoons heavy cream
Ground cinnamon for sprinkling

1. In a large saucepan (4 to 6 quarts), combine the rice and 2 quarts water. Bring to a boil, then lower the heat and simmer, uncovered, for 10 minutes.

2. Add the milk, sugar, and lemon peel. Bring back to a boil, stirring frequently, and then lower the heat so the milk simmers vigorously without reaching the lip of the pan. Simmer until the liquid has reduced and thickened to a creamy consistency that will coat the back of a spoon, 10 to 15 minutes. Stir frequently to prevent the rice from sticking to the bottom of the pan.

3. Remove and discard the lemon peel. Spoon equal amounts of rice into 8 serving bowls and let set for a minute. Garnish each serving with 2 teaspoons cream and a sprinkling of cinnamon. Serve hot.

WINES: Asyrtiko (sweet) or Sauternes

MENU 9

. . . .

Chutney Cheese Ball

This was an appetizer I learned to make when I was young and employed as an archaeologist in Raleigh, North Carolina. My friend and coworker Rob Worrell taught it to me. It's somewhat sweet and slightly spicy, a nice old-fashioned addition to an hors d'oeuvres table.

8 ounces cream cheese
½ cup Major Grey or other chutney
½ teaspoon mild or hot curry powder
Cayenne pepper
½ cup finely chopped pecans

1. By hand or using an electric mixer, beat together the cream cheese, chutney, curry powder, and cayenne until smooth. Spread the pecans in a thick layer on a sheet of waxed paper or foil. Spoon the cream cheese mixture in a mound on the pecans. Pat the chopped pecans on the top and sides, and turn the cheese mixture to shape it into a ball covered in pecans. Cover the ball snugly in plastic wrap. Cover and refrigerate until firm, at least 2 hours.

2. Uncover and transfer to a decorative plate with a small knife for spreading. Serve with an assortment of crackers.

TO MAKE AHEAD

Two to twenty-four hours before serving: Make cheese ball. Cover and refrigerate.

Potato and Smoked Mackerel Salad with Creamy Mayonnaise

This is one of my husband's favorite recipes. The smoky, slightly oily mackerel pairs wonderfully with potatoes, onions, and piquant mayonnaise.

> 2½ pounds (about 15) baby red-skinned potatoes, washed
> Sea salt
> ½ red onion, peeled and thinly sliced
> 2 stalks celery, thinly sliced on the diagonal
> 2 fillets smoked mackerel, skin discarded
> 2 large egg yolks
> 1 tablespoon Dijon mustard
> 2 tablespoons red wine vinegar, or more to taste
> 2 cups peanut oil
> 6 tablespoons heavy cream

1. Place the potatoes in a medium pan, cover with water, and season generously with salt. Bring to a boil, reduce to a simmer, and cook until tender, about 15 minutes. Drain. When cool enough to handle, slice into ¼-inch rounds. In a large bowl, combine the potatoes, red onion, and celery. By hand, shred the mackerel into pieces no larger than a raspberry; there should be about 2 cups. Add to the salad.

2. *Prepare the mayonnaise:* In a small bowl, whisk together the egg yolks, mustard, vinegar, and large pinches of salt and grains of paradise. Beginning a drop at a time, whisk in the oil. As it emulsifies, add the oil a little faster, in a slow, steady stream. When the mixture is thick, whisk in the cream.

3. Fold ⅔ cup mayonnaise into the potato mixture. There should be just enough mayonnaise to coat the ingredients; add more if necessary. Cover and refrigerate for at least 1 hour. Adjust the seasonings before serving, adding more salt or vinegar as needed.

WINES: Vinho Verde, Ribeiro (white), Tokay d'Alsace

TO MAKE AHEAD

One and a half to eight hours before serving: Prepare salad. Cover and refrigerate.

Jeff's Fast Chicken Mole

This recipe was published in the Sunday Styles column. If you have cooked chicken on hand, it takes about fifteen minutes to assemble and cook the recipe—perfect for a busy day. Just don't tell anyone the mole came from a jar.

> 2 tablespoons peanut oil
> Two 10-ounce jars mole negro (available at Latin American grocery stores
>   and specialty food markets)
> 4 cups chicken stock
> 4 cups canned pureed tomatoes
> 8 boneless, skinless chicken breasts, boiled in lightly salted water until
>   cooked through, or 8 portions of other boneless, skinless cooked chicken
> 3 tablespoons toasted sesame seeds

1. Place a large sauté pan over medium heat and add the oil. When the oil is hot, add the mole and stir with a wooden spoon until the mole is softened.

2. Add the chicken stock and tomatoes, and stir until smooth. Halve the chicken breasts and add to the mole. Simmer for 10 minutes. Transfer to a bowl and sprinkle with sesame seeds.

WINES: Cabernet Sauvignon, Zinfandel, Syrah, Nebbiolo, Grenache (all Mexico, Guadalupe Valley), Malbec (Argentina), Irouléguy

Short-Grain Rice

The flavor of simple white rice complements mole quite well, but if you wish to go one step further to dress up this accompaniment, sauté chopped onion and red and green peppers in olive oil before adding rice to the pan.

> 3 cups imported Spanish or other short-grain rice
> 1 teaspoon salt
> 1 tablespoon light olive oil

1. In a very large saucepan or covered casserole, combine the rice, salt, olive oil, and 6 cups of water. Cover tightly, place over medium heat, and bring to a boil.

2. Reduce the heat to low and simmer for 15 minutes. Remove from the heat but *do not remove the cover from the pot.* Allow the rice to rest in the covered pot for about 15 minutes before serving.

Sticky Toffee Pudding

This is one of those recipes that has traveled the world. Becky Mitchell, who lives in New Hampshire, got it from a neighbor who learned it in a cooking class in Australia. Becky says: "I was told this recipe started life at a Sharrow Bay hotel in England's Lake District." This cake freezes well, and is nice to keep on hand for unexpected company. The cake is served warm with a warm sauce, and goes very nicely with a scoop of vanilla ice cream.

FOR THE PUDDING:

¼ cup butter

1 teaspoon vanilla extract

¾ cup sugar

2 large eggs

1¼ cups self-rising flour, sifted

1½ cups (8 or 9 whole) dates, pitted
    and chopped small

1 teaspoon baking soda

FOR THE SAUCE:

⅓ cup (packed) light brown sugar

5 tablespoons butter

¼ cup heavy cream

½ teaspoon vanilla extract

1. *For the pudding:* Preheat the oven to 350 degrees. Using an electric mixer, beat together the butter and vanilla until creamy. Add the sugar and beat until light and fluffy. Add the eggs one at a time, beating well after each addition.

2. Using a rubber spatula, gently fold in the flour. Bring 1 cup of water to a boil in a saucepan or microwave, and stir in the dates and baking soda. Add to the batter and mix to combine. Transfer the batter to a 9-inch cake pan, and bake until a toothpick inserted into the center comes out clean, 40 to 45 minutes.

3. *For the sauce:* In a small saucepan, combine the light brown sugar, butter, heavy cream, and vanilla. Place over medium-low heat and simmer for about 3 minutes.

4. To serve, cut the cake into squares and pour the sauce over the warm cake. If desired, serve with ice cream.

WINE: Late Bottled Vintage (LBV) Port

TO MAKE AHEAD
Allow cake to cool completely. Wrap airtight and freeze for up to 1 month. After defrosting, reheat gently in a 250-degree oven. Prepare sauce, and serve.

MENU 10

· · · · · · ·

Cucumber Cups with Roast Pork Filling

The roast pork filling can also be put on Belgian endive leaves or served in small lettuce cups.

FOR THE PORK:

1 small (2 pounds) pork tenderloin

1 tablespoon paprika

$\frac{1}{2}$ teaspoon freshly ground black pepper

$\frac{1}{2}$ teaspoon Mexican oregano

$\frac{1}{4}$ teaspoon ground cumin

Pinch of ground allspice

1 clove garlic, peeled and minced

1 tablespoon lime juice

1 tablespoon lemon juice

1 tablespoon fresh grapefruit juice

Vegetable oil

FOR ASSEMBLY:

$1\frac{1}{2}$ tablespoons cider vinegar

1 tablespoon olive oil

1 teaspoon sugar

$\frac{1}{4}$ teaspoon red pepper flakes

2 seedless cucumbers

2 tablespoons finely chopped fresh cilantro for garnish

1. *Prepare the pork:* In a heavy-duty sealable plastic bag, combine the pork, paprika, pepper, oregano, cumin, allspice, and garlic. Add the lime juice, lemon juice, and grapefruit juice. Seal tightly, shake to mix well, and refrigerate for 12 to 24 hours.

2. Preheat the oven to 350 degrees. Remove the meat from the marinade. Place in an oiled baking pan and roast, uncovered, until a meat thermometer inserted in the center registers 180 degrees. Remove from the oven and allow the meat to cool. Cover and refrigerate.

3. *Assemble the cucumber cups:* Remove the pork from the refrigerator and shred or chop coarsely. In a small bowl, whisk together the vinegar, oil, sugar, and red pepper flakes. Toss with the pork and set aside.

4. Trim the ends from the cucumbers and use a vegetable peeler to remove strips from the skin so that the cucumber looks striped. Cut crosswise into 1½-inch pieces. Use a small spoon to hollow out some of the pulp to make the cucumber pieces into cups. Fill the cups with pork and arrange on a platter. Sprinkle with cilantro and refrigerate until ready to serve.

WINES: Riesling (Finger Lakes, off-dry), Pinot Gris (Oregon), Chinon (white or red)

TO MAKE AHEAD
One to four days before serving: Marinate pork 12 to 24 hours. Roast pork.
One hour before serving: Make dressing for pork. Assemble cups and garnish.

Grilled Figs with Fresh Mozzarella

Once the grill is preheated, it takes about ten minutes to prepare and cook the figs.

> 16 ripe, firm, fresh figs
> Extra-virgin olive oil
> 8 small (1 inch in diameter) fresh mozzarella balls, halved
> About 2 tablespoons fresh thyme leaves
> Maldon salt, fleur de sel, or fine sea salt

1. Preheat a grill to medium heat. Halve the figs lengthwise (the stem will stay intact on one half of each fig). Brush the figs on all sides with olive oil and set aside.

2. Place the fig halves cut side down on the grill. Allow to brown for 1 to 2 minutes, just enough to sear the cut side and slightly char the edges. Turn all the figs and top each

with half a mozzarella ball. Sprinkle with thyme and a bit of salt. Cover the grill and allow to cook 1 to 2 minutes more. Serve warm.

WINES: Rueda or continue with Riesling or Pinot Gris or Chinon Blanc

TO MAKE AHEAD
Twenty minutes before serving: Preheat grill. Prepare figs for grilling and set aside.
Five minutes before serving: Grill figs, turn, and top with mozzarella, thyme, and salt. Grill 1
   or 2 minutes more.

Chilled Baked Salmon with Cucumber-Dill Sauce

The salmon can be made the day before serving and doesn't even need to be reheated. Make the sauce and arrange the salmon on a platter several hours before serving, and you couldn't have a simpler or more elegant meal for a hot summer evening.

FOR THE SALMON:
1 whole 8-pound salmon or steelhead trout, head and tail removed
Vegetable oil

FOR THE SAUCE:
2 English (seedless) cucumbers, peeled
¼ cup minced fresh dill
1 cup sour cream
2½ tablespoons cider vinegar
1½ teaspoons salt
⅛ teaspoon ground white pepper
1¼ teaspoons sugar

FOR ASSEMBLY:
1 lemon, sliced paper thin
1 lime, sliced paper thin
½ red bell pepper, julienned
Fresh herb sprigs
Edible flowers and buds (nasturtiums, rose petals, violets, etc.)

1. *Prepare the salmon:* Preheat the oven to 350 degrees. Rinse the salmon well inside and out. Brush the fish with oil and wrap in a double layer of heavy-duty aluminum foil, sealing it so it will not leak. Place the wrapped fish on a large baking sheet and bake for 1 hour. Remove the fish from the oven and allow to cool without unwrapping it. Refrigerate the fish on the baking sheet to prevent leaks.

2. *Prepare the sauce:* Using a food processor, pulse to finely chop the cucumbers; be careful not to overprocess. Transfer them to a fine-meshed strainer and press on them gently with a wooden spoon to help the juices drain. Transfer the cucumber to a mixing bowl. Set aside about 1 teaspoon dill and add the remainder to the cucumbers. Add the sour cream, vinegar, salt, white pepper, and sugar. Mix well and adjust the seasonings as needed. Transfer to a serving bowl and sprinkle with the reserved teaspoon of dill. Cover with plastic wrap and refrigerate.

3. Set aside a large, long platter that will accommodate the salmon. With the salmon still on the baking sheet (to catch drips), carefully open the top of the foil to expose the whole fish. Starting at one end of the fish, gently peel off the skin; it should lift away easily. Pull away the foil so that the fish rolls over onto the baking sheet. Remove the skin from the other side.

5. Transfer the fish to the platter. Decorate the platter with alternating slices of lemon and lime around the edge of the plate. Place the julienned bell pepper diagonally across the top of the salmon. Decorate the fish and the plate with the herb sprigs and edible flowers. Cover with plastic wrap and refrigerate.

6. Cut each portion through the top fillet only as far as the bone, then slide a spatula under the fillet to remove a boneless section of fish. When the entire top fillet is gone, re-move the platter from the table and lift and discard the bone from the fish. Return the plat-ter and the remaining fillet to the table and continue to serve. Pass the sauce separately.

WINES: Continue with any of the wines from the first two courses or try a Menetou-Salon or Chardonnay (California, Chablis, Corton-Charlemagne). All three courses can be served with sparkling wine: Brut, Brut Rosé, or vintage Champagne.

TO MAKE AHEAD

The day before serving: Bake salmon; cool and refrigerate.

Three hours to shortly before serving: Make sauce; cover and refrigerate. Remove skin from salmon. Arrange on platter; cover and refrigerate until serving time, with the sauce passed separately.

Grilled Corn

As always when cooking corn on the cob, use the freshest corn possible.

8 to 16 ears of fresh corn, with husks attached but folded back,
   corn silk removed
¼ pound (1 stick) butter, melted
Salt and freshly ground black pepper

1. Preheat a grill. With the husks of the corn folded back, brush the ears with butter and season to taste with salt and pepper. (You may wish to leave a few ears unbuttered and unseasoned for guests who prefer it plain.) Close the husks and twist the ends to help them stay closed, or tie with a bit of husk.

2. Place the ears on the hot grill. Cook the ears, turning them constantly, for 1 to 3 minutes. They should be thoroughly heated (beginning to steam) with charring on the husks and some of the kernels, and the husks may open somewhat. Be careful not to overcook, or they will lose their sweetness and be tough and chewy. Transfer to a platter and serve immediately.

TO MAKE AHEAD

As necessary before serving: Preheat a grill. Allow 15 minutes for preparation and grilling. Serve immediately.

Carrot Cake with
Cream Cheese Frosting

I sometimes order carrot cake in restaurants, just to see how it compares with mine. I always think mine is better.

FOR THE CAKE:

Vegetable oil or nonstick spray for greasing pan

2 cups all-purpose flour

2 teaspoons baking soda

2 teaspoons cinnamon

1/2 teaspoon salt

3 large eggs

3/4 cup unsweetened applesauce

3/4 cup buttermilk

1 1/2 cups light brown sugar

2 teaspoons vanilla extract

8 ounces crushed pineapple, drained

2 cups grated carrots

1/2 cup shredded coconut

1 cup chopped walnuts

FOR THE FROSTING:

One 8-ounce package cream cheese, at room temperature

1/4 pound (1 stick) butter, at room temperature

2 teaspoons orange juice

1 1/2 teaspoons finely grated orange zest

1 teaspoon vanilla extract

2 cups confectioners' sugar

1. *Prepare cake:* Preheat the oven to 350 degrees. Oil or spray a 13 × 9-inch cake pan and set aside. In a large mixing bowl, sift the flour, baking soda, cinnamon, and salt; set aside.

2. In a separate bowl, beat the eggs until well blended. Add the applesauce, buttermilk, light brown sugar, and vanilla, and mix well. Add the flour mixture, pineapple, carrots,

coconut, and walnuts; mix well. Pour into the baking pan. Bake until a toothpick inserted in the center of the cake comes out dry, 50 minutes to 1 hour. Cool completely.

3. *Prepare the frosting:* In the bowl of an electric mixer, combine the cream cheese and butter. Beat until thoroughly blended and smooth. Add the orange juice, orange zest, and vanilla, and beat again until mixed. Add the confectioners' sugar and beat until very smooth and fluffy.

4. Use an icing spatula to cover the cake evenly with frosting. Place the cake in an air-tight container and refrigerate. If a container is not available, the cake may be refrigerated, uncovered, until the icing sets, about 2 hours. Cover lightly with plastic wrap, tucking the edges under the plate to make an airtight seal. Refrigerate.

5. Remove from the refrigerator and allow to sit at room temperature long enough to take the chill off the cake, about 45 minutes. Slice and serve.

WINE: Late-Harvest Gewürztraminer

TO MAKE AHEAD
Up to three days before serving: Make the cake. Cool completely. Frost, cover, and refrigerate.
To serve: Remove from the refrigerator thirty minutes before serving.

TEN MENUS
FOR FALL

· · · · · · ·

MENU 1
[PAGE 138]
Hummus with Toasted Pita Triangles
Eggplant with Chopped Tomato Vinaigrette and Spiced Chèvre
Bourbon-Marinated Roast Pork
Savory Mashed Potatoes
Florida Apple Pie

MENU 2
[PAGE 144]
Filo Cups with Roast Pork and Scallions
Arugula Salad with Walnuts, Pears, and Blue Cheese
Scotian Lobster Chowder
High-Rise Biscuits
Black Magic Cake with Chocolate Glaze

MENU 3
[PAGE 150]

Mushroom Triangles
Potato Pancakes with Caviar and Sour Cream
Pistachio-Crusted Steelhead Trout with Red Currant Sauce
Cucumber Gratin
Bananas Flambé with Ice Cream

MENU 4
[PAGE 158]

Caponata Toasts
Broccoli Salad
Southern Italian Meatballs in Tomato Sauce
Spaghettini
Buttered Orange Cream

MENU 5
[PAGE 165]

(VEGETARIAN)
Bagna Cauda
Mushroom Tart
Roasted Squash with Corn Bread, Sage, and Chestnut Stuffing and
Smoked Tempeh-Root Vegetable Ragout
Shaker Lemon Pie

MENU 6
[PAGE 172]

Plantain Crisps with Smoked Salmon, Wasabi, and Crème Fraîche
Crusted Chèvre with Balsamic Vinaigrette
Grilled Duck Breast with Pepper Jelly Glaze
Wheat Berry Cucumber Salad
Brown Sugar Pumpkin Pie with Cinnamon Whipped Cream

MENU 7

[PAGE 179]

Gouda, Chutney, and Apple Bites

Baby Vegetables with Lemon-Dill Sauce and Crispy Noodles

Kalbi-Chim

Parsnip and Potato Puree

Pear Pecan Tart

MENU 8

[PAGE 186]

Boursin Spinach Triangles

Melon with Prosciutto

Marinated Chicken with Chickpeas and Ham

Broth-Cooked Rice

Panna Cotta with Pomegranate

MENU 9

[PAGE 192]

Cherry Tomatoes Stuffed with Roasted Eggplant

Cockles with Smoked Paprika Butter

Latin-Style Beef Stew with Corn and Sweet Potatoes

Chocolate Banana Cream Pie

MENU 10

[PAGE 197]

Clam Dip

Oyster Soup

Turkey Breast Roasted Like a Leg of Lamb

Roasted Potatoes

Lemon-Ginger Crepes

MENU 1

· · · · · · ·

Hummus with Toasted Pita Triangles

Hummus, a Middle Eastern specialty, is a thick spread made with pureed chickpeas. This garlicky recipe uses six cloves of garlic in the puree. If you prefer a milder flavor, use four or five.

One 16-ounce can chickpeas, drained
1 cup extra-virgin olive oil
6 cloves garlic, peeled
¼ cup fresh lemon juice
Three 6-inch pita breads, each cut into 8 wedges (like a pizza)

1. In a blender or food processor, combine the chickpeas, ⅔ cup olive oil, 5 cloves garlic, and lemon juice. Puree until very smooth. Cover and refrigerate.

2. Preheat the oven to 350 degrees. Remove the hummus from the refrigerator and place in a decorative bowl; set aside. Pour ⅓ cup olive oil into a small bowl. Mince the remaining clove of garlic and mix with the oil.

3. Slide a small knife horizontally through each pita wedge to split it into 2 thin slices. Lightly brush the rough side of each slice with oil and place on a baking sheet. Bake

just until lightly browned, about 6 minutes. Cool and place in an airtight container until serving.

    4. Pile the pita triangles in a bowl and serve with the hummus for dipping.

WINES: Asyrtiko Strofilia, Gewürztraminer, Vidal Blanc (United States, Canada)

TO MAKE AHEAD
The day before serving: Make hummus.
Two hours before serving: Remove hummus from refrigerator. Make pita triangles.

Eggplant with
Chopped Tomato Vinaigrette
and Spiced Chèvre

I had something similar to this in a bistro in Paris. I liked the combination of warm fried eggplant, piquant chilled tomato, and creamy cheese. With that in mind, I created this recipe.

FOR THE EGGPLANT:
1 large eggplant
Olive oil (not extra-virgin)

FOR THE CHÈVRE:
8 ounces creamy chèvre cheese
Pinch of allspice
2 teaspoons finely chopped fresh oregano leaves
Salt and freshly ground black pepper

FOR THE TOMATO VINAIGRETTE:
3 large, firm, ripe tomatoes
2 tablespoons extra-virgin olive oil
½ teaspoon minced garlic
2 teaspoons minced shallot
1 tablespoon red wine vinegar
1 tablespoon minced fresh parsley

1. *Prepare the eggplant:* Trim the ends from the eggplant and cut the eggplant into ½-inch dice. Place a large nonstick or well-seasoned skillet over medium-high heat and add ¼ cup olive oil. When the oil is hot, add the eggplant and cook, tossing frequently, until the cubes are well browned on all sides. Use additional oil as needed if the pan becomes dry. Drain the eggplant on paper towels and allow to cool, then transfer to a covered container and set aside at room temperature.

2. *Prepare the chèvre:* In a small mixing bowl, combine the chèvre and allspice. Use a fork or wooden spoon to blend together until well mixed and creamy. Add the oregano and salt and pepper to taste, and mix again. Cover and refrigerate.

3. *Prepare the tomato vinaigrette:* Core and halve the tomatoes, discarding the pulp and seeds. Chop or dice into ⅓-inch pieces and place in a small mixing bowl. Add the olive oil, garlic, shallot, vinegar, and parsley, and toss to mix. Cover and refrigerate.

4. Remove the tomato vinaigrette and spiced chèvre from the refrigerator. Gently reheat the eggplant mixture by putting it in a small skillet or saucepan over low heat just until well warmed. Divide the eggplant mixture among 8 small plates. Use 2 spoons to place a dollop of spiced chèvre on the eggplant. Top each plate with an equal portion of tomato vinaigrette and serve.

WINES: Continue with the Gewürztraminer; or Chenin Blanc, Riesling Spätlese, Cabernet Franc (Loire, Napa)

TO MAKE AHEAD

Up to one hour before serving: Prepare eggplant mixture; set aside. Prepare tomato mixture; refrigerate. Prepare spiced chèvre; refrigerate.

To serve: Reheat eggplant and assemble mixtures on plates.

Bourbon-Marinated Roast Pork "Not for the Common People"

This recipe is for utterly delicious marinated roast pork which is accompanied by a tangy, creamy, chilled white sauce. It is one of my favorite recipes for entertaining and is almost certain to become one of yours. It was given to me by fashion designer Vasilka Nicolova, who had received it from her mother-in-law, Lorna Barnett. I was given a photocopy of the recipe and was amused to see that across the top of the recipe Lorna had written "Not for the Common

People." Once I made the recipe, I agreed: Although it's very simple to prepare, I like to save this recipe for the most special of friends.

FOR THE MARINADE:

¼ cup bourbon

¼ cup soy sauce

3 tablespoons light brown
   sugar

1 boneless pork roast loin (5 or
   6 pounds)

FOR THE SAUCE:

⅓ cup mayonnaise

⅓ cup sour cream

¼ cup finely chopped onion

1 tablespoon dry mustard

1 teaspoon white or red wine
   vinegar

Vegetable oil for greasing pan

1. *Prepare the marinade:* In a small bowl, combine the bourbon, soy sauce, and sugar. Mix well. Place the pork loin in a heavy-duty zippered plastic bag. Pour the marinade over the pork, close the bag securely, and turn the bag so that the pork is well coated in the marinade. Place the bag (with the sealed opening up to prevent leaks) in the refrigerator.

2. *Prepare the sauce:* In a small decorative bowl, combine the mayonnaise, sour cream, chopped onion, dry mustard, and vinegar. Mix well. Cover and refrigerate.

3. Preheat the oven to 350 degrees. Lightly oil a baking pan. Remove the loin from the marinade and place it in the pan. Bake until an instant-read thermometer inserted in the center reaches 180 degrees, about 50 minutes.

4. To serve, transfer the meat to a carving board and cut diagonally into thin slices; keep warm. Add ½ cup water to the pan, return to medium heat, and stir to deglaze the pan. Arrange the sliced pork on a serving platter and drizzle the liquid from the pan on top. Serve with the sauce passed separately.

WINES: Continue with the Gewürztraminer, Riesling Spätlese, or Cabernet Franc, or try a Pommard

TO MAKE AHEAD

The day before serving: Marinate pork and refrigerate.

One to eight hours before serving: Combine ingredients for sauce. Cover and refrigerate.

One hour before serving: Roast pork.

Savory Mashed Potatoes

The use of a yogurt-based spread, low-fat milk, and chicken broth reduces the calories and fat in these lightly herbed potatoes.

4 pounds (8 to 10) Yukon Gold potatoes, peeled and halved
3 tablespoons yogurt-based spread (such as Brummel and Brown)
¾ cup low-fat milk
½ cup chicken broth
2 tablespoons minced parsley
1 tablespoon finely sliced garlic chives or plain chives
Salt and freshly ground black pepper

1. Bring a large pot of water to a boil and add the potatoes. Boil until tender in the center. Drain well and allow to cool. Cover and refrigerate.

2. Place a large saucepan over low heat. Add the yogurt-based spread, milk, and broth. When the mixture is heated, add the potatoes and mash until the potatoes are smooth, fluffy, and hot. Add the parsley, chives, and salt and pepper to taste. Serve hot.

TO MAKE AHEAD

The day before serving: Boil potatoes. Cover and refrigerate.

To serve: Add yogurt spread and liquid to potatoes, reheat, and mash. Season with herbs and spices.

Florida Apple Pie

As with most recipes, the origins of this pie are hard to trace. Although it was a specialty of Floridian Bernie Oldham, the recipe was given to him by his Kentucky mother. Bernie gave the recipe to his good friend Margaret Gram, who brought it with her when she moved from Florida to New Hampshire apple country. Since a key ingredient in this pie is freshly squeezed orange juice, I always think of it as Florida *apple pie.*

> 8 Granny Smith or other tart apples, peeled, cored, and very thinly sliced
> 1 cup freshly squeezed orange juice
> 1¾ cups sugar, or as needed
> 2 tablespoons flour
> Double piecrust for 9-inch deep-dish pie
> 1 large egg white, lightly beaten
> ¼ pound (1 stick) butter, thinly sliced

1. In a large saucepan, combine the apples, orange juice, and 1 cup sugar. Cook over low heat until crisp-tender; do not overcook. Taste and add ⅓ to ½ cup sugar depending on the tartness desired. (The tartness depends on the kind of apples and orange juice. Florida oranges are not as sweet as California Sunkist; fresh orange juice is not as sweet as bottled.) Allow the apple mixture to cool, and drain off the liquid. Add flour and toss to mix.

2. Preheat the oven to 325 degrees. Place the bottom crust in the pan and brush with some of the egg white. Sprinkle with 1½ tablespoons sugar. Add the apple mix and top with the butter. Place the top crust on the pie and crimp the edges. Brush the top with the remaining egg white and sprinkle with an additional 1½ tablespoons sugar.

3. Slice several small holes in the top of pie to vent the crust. Place the pie on the bottom rack of the oven and bake for 30 minutes. Transfer the pie to the middle rack of the oven and bake until golden brown, 30 minutes more. Cool completely, cover, and set aside at room temperature.

WINE: Vidal Blanc (from first course) or Ice Wine (Canada)

TO MAKE AHEAD
Up to four hours before serving: Assemble and bake pie. Cool completely. Cover lightly and set aside at room temperature.

Filo Cups with Roast Pork and Scallions

The pork in these cups requires only fifteen minutes of marinating, but the meat tastes as if it has marinated for hours.

$\frac{1}{4}$ cup soy sauce

$\frac{1}{4}$ cup fish sauce

$\frac{1}{2}$ teaspoon five-spice powder

2 teaspoons sesame oil

$\frac{1}{4}$ cup sugar

2 cloves garlic, minced

2 tablespoons minced cilantro

1 tablespoon rice wine

1 pound lean boneless pork, cut into small ($\frac{1}{2}$ inch) dice

Vegetable oil for greasing baking sheet

2 tablespoons finely diced seedless, skinless cucumber

2 scallions, white and green parts, finely sliced

36 small filo (phyllo) cups (available frozen in supermarkets)

Sesame seeds for garnish

1. Preheat the oven to 400 degrees. In a mixing bowl, combine the soy sauce, fish sauce, five-spice powder, sesame oil, sugar, garlic, cilantro, and rice wine. Stir well until blended. Add the pork and stir until well coated. Allow to marinate for 15 minutes.

2. Lightly oil a shallow baking pan. Remove the pork from the marinade (reserving marinade) and spread in an even layer across the pan. Bake, stirring occasionally, until well browned, about 20 minutes. Remove from the heat and allow to cool.

3. Place ⅓ cup of the reserved marinade in a small saucepan over medium-low heat. Simmer for 5 minutes, and add flour, whisking until thickened.

4. Preheat the oven to 400 degrees. In a mixing bowl, combine the pork, cucumber, and scallions. Fill the filo cups and place them on an ungreased baking sheet. Drizzle with thickened marinade and sprinkle with sesame seeds. Bake just until heated, about 5 minutes. Serve warm or at room temperature.

WINES: Riesling Spätlese, Savennières, Puligny-Montrachet

TO MAKE AHEAD
The day before serving: Preheat oven. Marinate pork. Sauté until browned. Cool, cover, and
　　refrigerate.
Twenty minutes before serving: Preheat oven. Mix filling and place in cups. Bake until lightly
　　browned. Garnish and serve warm.

Arugula Salad with Walnuts, Pears, and Blue Cheese

A satisfying combination of flavors to whet the appetite for the next course.

　　12 ounces washed-and-ready-to-eat baby arugula leaves (available bagged
　　　　in supermarkets)
　　½ cup toasted walnut pieces
　　½ cup crumbled Stilton cheese
　　2 firm, ripe Anjou pears
　　⅓ cup hazelnut or walnut oil
　　¼ cup tarragon, champagne, or white wine vinegar

1. In a serving bowl, combine the arugula, walnuts, and Stilton. Toss to blend. Cover and refrigerate.

2. Core and slice the pears into thin wedges. Add to the salad. Add the oil and toss to blend. Add the vinegar, toss again, and serve.

Scotian Lobster Chowder

This recipe is from a New York Times *Chef column by Sam Hayward, chef at Fore Street in Portland, Maine. Shoepeg corn, used here, has long, firm bicolored kernels. It can be found in the frozen foods department of many supermarkets.*

> 3 ounces slab bacon, cut into ¼-inch dice
> 4 tablespoons unsalted butter
> 2½ pounds (about 5 medium) russet potatoes, peeled, quartered lengthwise,
>   and sliced
> 2 medium leeks, white and light green parts only, cut into ¼-inch dice
>   and rinsed well
> 6 live lobsters (1¼ pounds each)
> 8 ounces frozen shoepeg corn kernels
> 2 cups heavy cream
> Salt and freshly ground black pepper

1. Place a large, heavy stockpot or soup kettle over medium-low heat and add the bacon and 1 teaspoon butter. Sauté until the bacon yields its fat and is crisp on the edges. Add the potatoes, leeks, and 1¼ cups water. Cover and allow to simmer until the potatoes are barely tender, about 10 minutes, then remove from the heat.

2. In a separate kettle large enough to hold all the lobsters, put about 2 inches of water. Place over high heat and bring to a rapid boil. Add the lobsters, return to a boil, and boil for 4 minutes. Immediately add some cold water to the pan to stop the cooking, then drain. Immerse the lobsters in cold water until cool enough to handle.

3. Place a fine-meshed sieve over a large bowl and break the lobsters open over the sieve, draining and reserving all the body liquids. Break the claws and tails from the bodies and pull apart the body sections. Break open the carapace and remove any red coral or green tomalley. Push this through the sieve using a wooden spoon. Add the liquid from the bowl to the potato mixture and place over low heat to bring to a gentle simmer.

4. Extract the lobster meat from the claws and tails and cut into chunks. Put in a skillet with the remaining butter (2 tablespoons plus 2 teaspoons) and place over medium-low heat, stirring until the lobster meat becomes opaque. Scrape the lobster meat and butter into the chowder pot. Cover and continue to simmer gently for 20 minutes. (At this point, if desired, the chowder may be removed from the heat and cooled to room temperature, then covered and refrigerated for up to 8 hours.)

5. Bring the chowder to a simmer. Add the corn and simmer about 2 minutes. In a small saucepan over medium-low heat, simmer the cream for 2 to 3 minutes, then add it to the chowder. Season to taste with salt and pepper, and ladle into warm bowls. Serve hot.

WINES: Manzanilla or continue with any wine from the first course: Riesling Spätlese, Savennières, Puligny-Montrachet

TO MAKE AHEAD

Up to eight hours before serving: Prepare chowder, cover, and refrigerate.
To serve: Reheat chowder. Simmer cream and add to chowder.

High-Rise Biscuits

These biscuits were meant to be served at breakfast, but I think they make a fine accompaniment to lobster chowder. The recipe is adapted from Hominy Grill, Charleston, South Carolina.

4 cups all-purpose flour, plus additional for dusting
2 tablespoons baking powder
1 teaspoon salt
2 teaspoons sugar
4 tablespoons chilled butter
4 tablespoons chilled vegetable shortening
2 tablespoons chilled lard
1½ cups milk

1. In a large bowl, sift together the flour, baking powder, salt, and sugar.
2. Using a pastry cutter or 2 knives held scissors-fashion, cut the butter, shortening, and lard into the dry flour until slightly crumbly. Add the milk and stir gently until the mixture is cohesive.

3. Turn the dough onto a lightly floured surface. Knead lightly (less than 10 strokes) and loosely shape into a ball. With floured hands pat into a large disk about 1¼ inches thick. Using a floured 3-inch biscuit or cookie cutter, cut 12 biscuits. Place on a baking sheet about 2 inches apart.

4. Preheat the oven to 425 degrees. Bake the biscuits until golden brown, 10 to 12 minutes.

TO MAKE AHEAD

One hour before serving: Make dough. Shape and cut out biscuits. Cover with plastic wrap and set aside at room temperature.

Thirty minutes before serving: Preheat oven. Bake biscuits.

Black Magic Cake with Chocolate Glaze

This recipe comes from the Germain-Robin family, makers of fine brandy. The original recipe called for an exceedingly expensive aged brandy, but even made with cheap stuff the cake has marvelous flavor and texture. Allowing it to sit for a day or two actually improves the flavor.

¼ cup blanched slivered almonds

12 ounces semisweet chocolate

14 tablespoons (1¾ sticks) unsalted butter

Butter and flour for the baking pan

8 large eggs, separated

1 cup sugar

2½ tablespoons brandy

2 tablespoons heavy cream

1. Using a food processor or blender, chop the almonds very finely, but do not allow them to form a paste; set aside. In a microwave-safe bowl or the top half of a double boiler, combine 8 ounces of the chocolate and 10 tablespoons of the butter. Use a microwave oven or double boiler to melt the chocolate mixture, then set aside.

2. Butter a 9-inch springform pan, dust it with flour, and tap out the excess flour. Preheat oven to 400 degrees.

3. In the bowl of an electric mixer, combine the egg yolks and sugar. Mix well until very smooth. Add the melted chocolate mixture to the yolk and sugar mixture, and mix to blend. Add the ground almonds and brandy, and set aside.

4. In the bowl of an electric mixer, whisk the egg whites until stiff but not dry. Add about ½ cup beaten whites to the chocolate batter and stir to thin and loosen the batter. Carefully fold in the remaining whites until smooth. Pour the batter into the prepared springform pan. Bake until a toothpick inserted in the center of the cake is dry when removed, 35 to 40 minutes. Transfer to a rack and allow to cool in the pan; the center of the cake will sink slightly when cooled.

5. When the cake is cool, remove from the pan and transfer to a serving platter. In a small pan over low heat, combine the remaining 4 ounces of chocolate, remaining 4 tablespoons butter, and cream. Stir with a wooden spoon until smooth and glossy. Slowly pour the mixture onto the cake and let it run down the sides. Allow to cool and then put it in the refrigerator.

6. Remove the cake from the refrigerator and set aside at room temperature. To serve, cut slices with a knife warmed in hot water.

WINE: Vintage Port or Alembic Brandy (California)

TO MAKE AHEAD
One to two days before serving: Bake and ice cake. Cover and refrigerate.
Twenty minutes before serving: Remove cake from refrigerator and set aside at room temperature.

MENU 3

· · · · · · ·

Mushroom Triangles

This recipe by Eva Baughman is the perfect hot appetizer, combining mushrooms, walnuts, and cheese to make a savory filling in flaky filo dough. The pastry is made healthy and tasty by using olive oil instead of butter. And assembly, which can be done as long as a month in advance, is made astonishingly easy by using spray-on oil.

FOR THE FILLING:

¼ ounce (½ cup loosely filled) dried porcini or other dried mushrooms

10 ounces button mushrooms

⅓ cup grated Parmesan cheese

3 tablespoons grated fontina cheese

Pinch of grated nutmeg

¼ cup chopped Italian (flat-leaf) parsley

½ cup finely chopped walnuts

2 tablespoons butter

2 shallots, peeled and minced

2 cloves garlic, peeled and minced

1 tablespoon Jerez (sherry)

1 large egg, lightly beaten

½ teaspoon dried thyme
Salt and freshly ground black pepper

FOR ASSEMBLY:
1 pound package filo dough
Olive oil spray (available in supermarkets)

1. *Prepare the filling*: Place the dried mushrooms in a microwave-safe cup and cover with water. Microwave just until the water is boiling, about 45 seconds. Drain the mushrooms, finely chop, and set aside.

2. In a large bowl, combine the Parmesan and fontina cheeses, nutmeg, and parsley; set aside. Place a large skillet over medium heat and add the walnuts. Toss until the walnuts are toasted, about 2 minutes. Add to the bowl of cheeses.

3. Return the skillet to medium-low heat and melt the butter. Add the shallots and garlic, and sauté until the shallots are translucent. Add the button mushrooms and sauté until they release their liquid and it has nearly evaporated. Add the sherry and reserved dried mushrooms, and sauté for 1 minute. Remove from the heat and allow to cool for a few minutes.

4. Stir the mushroom mixture into the cheese mixture. Add the egg and thyme, and season to taste with salt and pepper. Set aside.

5. *To assemble*: Remove the filo dough from the box. Using a sharp knife, cut the roll of filo dough in half by cutting right through the plastic or paper covering. (The width of the halved sheet should be about 4 inches.) Put the dough that is not to be used immediately in a plastic bag in the refrigerator. Unfold the remaining dough and place it on a countertop covered by a sheet of plastic wrap topped by a dampened kitchen towel.

6. Remove a single sheet of dough and cover the remainder again. Spray the sheet lightly with olive oil, fold in half lengthwise, and spray again. Place a spoonful of filling (about 1½ teaspoons) at the top left-hand corner of the dough and fold it over to make a triangle. Fold the triangle down again and again, as if folding a flag. When the packet cannot be folded any more, spray again with olive oil and press lightly on the seams to seal them. Place on a baking sheet and continue with the remaining filling and dough. (The amount of dough needed will vary depending on the amount of filling used in each triangle and whether any sheets of dough tear and have to be discarded.) Put the baking sheet of triangles in the freezer, uncovered, until solidly frozen. Transfer to a freezer bag, gently squeeze out the air, and store in the freezer.

7. Remove the triangles from the freezer and arrange on baking sheets. Cover loosely and set aside at room temperature to defrost.

8. Preheat the oven to 375 degrees. Bake until golden brown, 15 to 20 minutes.

WINES: Salice Salentino, Naoussa, Saumur-Champigny (red), Pinot Noir (Oregon), or open some Champagne on the way to the next course

TO MAKE AHEAD

Four hours or up to one month (if freezing) before serving: Prepare filling. Fill and fold triangles. Cover and freeze or refrigerate.

Several hours before baking (if frozen): Remove triangles from freezer and arrange on baking sheets. Cover loosely and set aside at room temperature to defrost.

About thirty minutes before serving: Preheat oven and bake.

Potato Pancakes with
Caviar and Sour Cream

These pancakes may be made and frozen up to one month before serving.

2 large potatoes (about 1½ pounds total), peeled and cut into chunks
1 small onion, peeled and quartered
1 large egg plus 1 large egg white
½ teaspoon salt
2½ tablespoons flour
Freshly ground black pepper
Vegetable oil for frying
8 sprigs fresh dill
About ½ cup sour cream
Caviar of your choice

1. Place the potatoes in the bowl of a food processor and add the onion. Process until the potatoes are finely grated. Transfer the mixture to a fine-meshed strainer and gently press to squeeze out any excess moisture.

2. Place the mixture in a large mixing bowl and add the egg, egg white, salt, flour, and pepper to taste. Mix well.

3. Place a large nonstick or well-seasoned cast-iron skillet over medium heat. Add enough oil to come ¼ inch up the side of the pan. When the oil is hot, test it by adding a heaping tablespoon of the potato batter. Press lightly on the batter to make a flat disk. When it is golden brown on one side, flip it to brown the other side, adjusting the heat as neces-

sary. Transfer to a paper-towel-lined plate to drain and cool. Continue with the remaining batter, filling the pan but not crowding it, to make a total of 16 pancakes. Allow to cool, then place on a baking sheet and freeze until solid. Transfer the frozen pancakes to a freezer bag and store in the freezer.

4. Preheat the oven to 400 degrees. Place the frozen pancakes on a baking sheet and bake until thoroughly heated, 10 to 15 minutes. Place 2 pancakes on each of 8 plates. Garnish each plate with a dill sprig and top each pancake with about ¾ teaspoon sour cream and a spoonful of caviar. Serve immediately.

WINES: Chenin Blanc (New Zealand or Vouvray, sec), Chardonnay (light oak or no oak), Champagne; alternative: Vodka (chilled, neat)

TO MAKE AHEAD

Up to one month before serving: Prepare potato pancakes. Freeze.

About twenty-five minutes before serving: Preheat oven. Reheat potato pancakes. Top with sour cream and caviar.

Pistachio-Crusted Steelhead Trout
with Red Currant Sauce

This recipe is equally good prepared with salmon and could even be made with fresh whole rainbow trout.

8 center-cut pieces of steelhead trout fillet (4 to 6 ounces each)
Salt and freshly ground black pepper
3 tablespoons unsalted butter
1 tablespoon vegetable oil
¾ cup finely chopped pistachio nuts

FOR THE SAUCE:
4 tablespoons unsalted butter
2 shallots, peeled and finely chopped
3 tablespoons Grand Marnier
¼ cup red currant jelly
8 ounces fresh red currants (optional)
⅛ teaspoon cayenne pepper
Salt and freshly ground black pepper
1 teaspoon finely chopped fresh mint leaves

1. Season the fillets with salt and pepper to taste and set aside. Place a small skillet over medium-low heat and add the butter and oil. Add the pistachios and toss until the nuts are lightly browned. Press the flesh side of each fillet into the nuts, patting lightly so they adhere. Transfer the coated fillets to a small baking sheet or pan where they will fit in a single layer. When all the fillets are coated, cover them tightly with plastic wrap and refrigerate.

2. Preheat the oven to 400 degrees. Remove the plastic wrap from the fillets and place them in the oven until barely opaque in the center, about 12 minutes.

3. *Meanwhile, prepare the sauce:* Place a large skillet over medium heat and melt the butter. Add the shallots and sauté until tender, about 2 minutes. Add the Grand Marnier and stir until reduced to a glaze.

4. Add the currant jelly and fresh currants, if using, and stir until the jelly has dissolved. Add ¾ cup water, cayenne, and salt and pepper to taste. Stir until the currants are tender. To serve, place a fillet on each plate and garnish with a tablespoon of currant sauce.

WINES: Chardonnay (continue from the second course), Saumur-Champigny (red; continue from the first course), Pinot Noir (Oregon; continue from the first course)

TO MAKE AHEAD

Up to eight hours before serving: Season trout and coat with pistachios. Cover and refrigerate. *Thirty minutes before serving:* Panfry trout. Make sauce. Garnish.

Cucumber Gratin

Hot sliced cucumbers in a creamy sauce make a nice accompaniment to seared steelhead trout or salmon. This recipe is adapted from Colvin Run Tavern in Vienna, Virginia.

> 2 seedless cucumbers
> 2 lemons
> 2 cups crème fraîche (see page 173; available in specialty food markets)
> 2 cups heavy cream
> 2 teaspoons red wine vinegar
> Kosher salt and freshly ground black pepper
> Nonstick vegetable spray
> 6 tablespoons unsalted butter
> 4 tablespoons chopped fresh chives

1. Peel the cucumbers and cut them in half lengthwise. Using a teaspoon, remove the core and small seeds by running the spoon from one end to the other. Cut the cucumber halves crosswise into ¼-inch slices and set aside. Finely grate the zest of the lemons and set aside. Juice the lemons and reserve the juice.

2. In a medium saucepan, combine the crème fraîche and cream. Place over medium-low heat and simmer until reduced to 2 cups, 30 to 40 minutes. Using a blender or immersion blender, puree the reduced cream mixture while it is still hot. Add the lemon zest, lemon juice, and vinegar. Season with salt and pepper to taste. Allow to cool, cover, and refrigerate.

3. Preheat a broiler. Coat a 4-cup (about 8 × 8 inches) broiler-safe baking dish with the vegetable spray. Place a medium pan over medium-low heat and add the butter. As the butter foams, add the cucumber slices and toss about 45 seconds. Use a slotted spoon to

transfer the cucumber slices to the cream mixture, and toss to coat the cucumbers. Using the slotted spoon, place the cucumbers in the baking dish. Top with the cream. Cover with plastic wrap and refrigerate.

4. Place the baking dish under the broiler until reheated and bubbly and brown on top, 5 to 10 minutes. Garnish with the chives and serve.

TO MAKE AHEAD

The day before serving: Make the cream sauce and refrigerate.

Two hours before serving: Slice and cook cucumber. Combine with sauce in baking dish and refrigerate.

To serve: Preheat broiler. Brown gratin.

Bananas Flambé with Ice Cream

I am very fond of this classic recipe. I invented this version on a rainy day on vacation, with ingredients we happened to have in our beachfront cottage. It takes only 15 minutes to prepare even for a crowd.

> 4 large medium-ripe (with unspotted peels) bananas
> 8 tablespoons (1 stick) unsalted butter
> ½ cup light brown sugar
> ½ cup dark rum, plus additional for flaming
> 8 scoops vanilla ice cream
> Lightly sweetened whipped cream

1. Peel the bananas and halve each one crosswise, then lengthwise. Set aside.

2. Place a large nonstick skillet over medium-low heat. Add the butter and stir with a wooden spoon until melted. Add the sugar and stir until melted and starting to caramelize, about 1 minute.

3. Add the banana pieces, rounded sides down. Stir gently to coat the rounded sides with melted sugar. Turn the pieces over (flat sides down) and allow to cook until lightly browned underneath and caramelized along the edges; do not overcook. Working quickly, place 2 banana pieces on each of 8 small plates. Add the rum to the hot pan and stir to make a smooth sauce. Place a scoop of ice cream on each plate and drizzle each scoop with a spoonful of rum sauce. Garnish each plate with whipped cream.

4. To serve, drizzle ½ teaspoon rum on each plate. Carefully light the rum using a kitchen lighter or long match. Serve immediately.

WINE: Marsala or Rum (Jamaica)

MENU 4

. . . .

Caponata Toasts

Olive oil

1 large eggplant (with peel), trimmed and cut into 1/2-inch dice

1 red onion, peeled and diced

1 clove garlic, peeled and minced

1/4 cup diced green Italian frying pepper or green bell pepper

1/2 cup diced red bell pepper

1 tablespoon nonpareil capers

3 anchovy fillets, finely chopped

1/3 cup light brown sugar

1/4 cup balsamic vinegar

1/4 cup red wine vinegar

1 tablespoon tomato paste

1 tablespoon chopped fresh oregano leaves

1/2 cup (loosely packed) roughly chopped fresh basil leaves

Salt and freshly ground black pepper

4 to 8 slices 1/2-inch-thick bakery white bread such as peasant white
    or other light fine-grained bread

1. Place a large nonstick skillet over medium-high heat and add ¼ cup olive oil. When the oil is hot, add the eggplant. Sauté, turning often with a spatula, until the cubes are golden brown. Transfer to a platter or baking sheet lined with paper towels.

2. Add the onions and garlic to the skillet and sauté until the onions are tender, about 2 minutes. Remove and discard paper towels that are under the eggplant and add the onions and garlic to the platter. Sauté the green pepper and red bell pepper until tender, and add to the platter. Remove the pan from the heat and add the capers, anchovies, brown sugar, balsamic vinegar, wine vinegar, tomato paste, and oregano. Stir until blended.

3. Add the contents of the platter to the warm skillet (do not return it to the heat). Toss to mix well. Add the basil and season with salt and pepper to taste. Allow to cool in the skillet, then transfer to a covered container and refrigerate.

4. Remove the caponata from the refrigerator and allow to come to room temperature.

5. Trim the crusts from the bread and cut the bread into neat squares. Halve each slice into triangles (or quarter if the slices are large). Place a large skillet over medium heat and coat the bottom with 1 tablespoon olive oil. Add the bread and cook on each side until lightly browned. Place on a platter, top each slice with a spoonful of caponata, and serve. Or serve the caponata in a bowl accompanied by toasted pita triangles or crackers.

WINES: Rosé (Lagrein), Sparkling (Spain, Brut Rosé; or Lambrusco DOC, dry), Falerno (red), Cerasuolo di Vittoria

TO MAKE AHEAD
The day before serving: Prepare caponata. Cover and refrigerate.
About 1 hour before serving: Remove caponata from refrigerator and allow to come to room temperature.
To serve: Trim and toast bread. Spread with caponata.

Broccoli Salad

Many thanks to Margaret Gram for this unusual and delicious salad recipe.

FOR THE SALAD DRESSING:

1 cup mayonnaise

⅓ cup sugar

2½ tablespoons red wine vinegar

Salt and freshly ground black pepper

FOR THE SALAD:

1 head fresh broccoli, all stems removed and cut into tiny
   (½ to 1 inch) florets

6 slices bacon, fried until crisp, crumbled

½ cup shelled sunflower seeds

1 small red onion, finely chopped

1. *Prepare the salad dressing:* In a small container, stir together the mayonnaise, sugar, and red wine vinegar. Season with salt and pepper to taste. Cover and refrigerate.

2. In a large mixing bowl, combine the broccoli, bacon, sunflower seeds, and onion. Toss until well mixed. Stir the salad dressing and pour about half on the salad. Toss to mix and gradually add more to taste. All the dressing may not be needed.

TO MAKE AHEAD

Up to two days before serving: Prepare salad dressing. Cover and refrigerate.

To serve: Combine salad ingredients and toss with dressing.

Southern Italian Meatballs in Tomato Sauce

Grandmothers have in their possession some of the best recipes in the world. This old family recipe is from Grace Amore's southern Italian nonna, Girolama Bosco, who was born in Castellammare del Golfo, Sicily. Grace describes her relationship with her grandmother in this way: "Although she never learned to speak English very well, and I never learned to speak Italian, we did manage to communicate. One of the ways was by cooking together. She never used measur-

ing cups and such. It was always a pinch of this and a handful of that. I followed her around with the measuring spoons and cups, and so forth, when we cooked Sunday family dinners together. Eventually I got to the point where things felt right, smelled right, and definitely tasted great."

FOR THE TOMATO SAUCE:

¼ cup olive oil

4 cloves garlic, peeled and minced

Two 28-ounce cans San Marzano or other whole tomatoes with added puree

Two 28-ounce cans crushed tomatoes with basil

1½ tablespoons sugar

½ cup finely grated Parmesan cheese

½ cup finely grated pecorino Romano cheese

⅓ cup chopped fresh basil

1 teaspoon dried oregano

2 bay leaves

Salt and freshly ground black pepper

FOR THE MEATBALLS:

3 pounds lean ground beef

1 small onion, minced

2 cloves garlic, peeled and minced

½ cup seasoned Italian bread crumbs

½ cup finely grated Parmesan cheese

½ cup finely grated pecorino Romano cheese

½ cup raisins, roughly chopped

2 ounces toasted pine nuts

3 large eggs, lightly beaten

½ cup finely chopped Italian (flat-leaf) parsley

1 teaspoon Italian seasoning

Salt and freshly ground black pepper

3 tablespoons olive oil

    1. *Prepare the sauce:* Place a large saucepan over medium-low heat and add the olive oil. When the oil is hot, add the garlic and sauté until translucent. Add the whole tomatoes and puree, crushed tomatoes, sugar, Parmesan, pecorino Romano, basil, oregano, and bay leaves. Using 2 knives, coarsely cut up the whole tomatoes while they are in the pan. Mix

well and season with salt and pepper to taste. Reduce the heat to low and simmer for 45 minutes to 1 hour. The mixture should be thick, but it may be thinned with a little water if desired.

2. *Prepare the meatballs while the sauce is simmering:* In a large bowl, combine the ground beef, onion, garlic, bread crumbs, Parmesan, pecorino Romano, raisins, and pine nuts. Toss lightly to mix. Add the beaten eggs, parsley, Italian seasoning, and salt and pepper to taste. Toss again to combine the ingredients thoroughly, but try not compress the meat more than necessary.

3. With moistened hands, shape the mixture into balls about 1½ inches in diameter. Place a large nonstick or well-seasoned skillet over medium-high heat and add the olive oil. When the oil is simmering, add the meatballs in batches; avoid crowding the pan. Brown the meatballs on all sides and use a slotted spoon to transfer them to the pot of simmering sauce. Continue until all the meatballs are in the sauce. Simmer the meatballs in the sauce about 1 hour.

4. Remove the pot from the heat and allow to cool to room temperature. Transfer to a covered container and refrigerate. To freeze, transfer to one or more freezer containers, leaving about 1½ inches of air space at the top of each one. Seal well and place in the freezer. To defrost, place the containers in the refrigerator overnight.

5. To serve, place the meatballs and sauce in a large saucepan over medium-low heat until the sauce is bubbling and the meatballs are thoroughly reheated.

WINES: Continue with two red wines from the first course (Falerno, Cerasuolo di Vittoria) or move on to Leverano, Cannonau di Sardegna, Aglianico del Vulture

TO MAKE AHEAD

One month before serving, if frozen, or two days before serving: Prepare tomato sauce. Prepare meatballs. Combine meatballs and sauce; refrigerate or freeze.

Spaghettini

Salt

2 pounds spaghettini (thin spaghetti), preferably imported bronze-cut (see below)

2 tablespoons garlic-infused oil or extra-virgin olive oil

1. Fill a very large stockpot with lightly salted water. Cover and place over high heat and bring to a boil.

2. When the water is boiling, add the spaghettini and stir constantly until the water comes to a boil again. Boil the pasta just until al dente (barely tender); begin tasting when it has cooked for 6 minutes.

3. Drain the pasta in a large colander and immediately return it to the hot pot. Pour the oil over the pasta and toss to coat all the strands. Serve immediately.

HOW TO BUY AND COOK PASTA

Most supermarkets now carry an array of high-quality pastas. Old-fashioned bronze dies are used to shape "bronze-cut" pasta, which gives the exterior of the pasta a faintly rough texture. Most bronze-cut pasta is labeled as such on the package. If you do not have a favorite brand, choose a pasta imported from Italy; these tend to have a slightly chewy texture and better flavor than some (though not all) American brands. Most important, do not overcook the pasta. The only way to know if pasta is properly cooked is by tasting it. Drain it as soon as it is no longer crunchy in the center. It should still have some resistance when chewed—hence the Italian term *al dente*, literally "to the tooth."

Buttered Orange Cream

This refreshing dessert is adapted from a recipe by Clarissa Dickson Wright, who formerly costarred in the successful BBC cooking show Two Fat Ladies.

Grated zest and juice from 2 large, juicy navel oranges
¼ cup superfine sugar
5 large egg yolks
1 teaspoon rose water
¼ pound (1 stick) unsalted butter, softened, cut into large cubes
½ cup heavy cream
8 teaspoons finely chopped soft candied orange rind

1. Place 2 inches of water in the bottom half of a double boiler and bring to a simmer. In the top half of the double boiler, mix together the orange zest and juice, sugar, and egg yolks.

2. Place the orange mixture over the simmering water. Stir slowly and constantly with a balloon whisk, scraping the sides of the pan, until the mixture is thick and custardy, about 5 minutes. Remove the orange mixture from the heat and place the pan in a shallow bowl of ice water. Stir in the rose water. Quickly whisk in the butter, 1 cube at a time, allowing each cube to emulsify before adding the next. Allow the mixture to cool to room temperature. Cover and refrigerate.

3. Whip the cream until it holds soft peaks, then gently fold it into the orange mixture until blended.

4. To serve, place an equal portion of the orange cream in each of 8 stemmed glasses. Sprinkle a teaspoon of candied orange rind on each one and carefully fold it in so that the rind is suspended throughout the cream. Serve immediately.

WINES: Sparkling Wine from the first course or Late-Harvest Sémillon

TO MAKE AHEAD
The day before serving: Prepare orange custard. Cover and refrigerate.
Fifteen minutes before serving: Whip cream and fold into custard. Spoon into glasses and garnish.

MENU 5

. . . .

Bagna Cauda

A salty, garlicky dip for bread and vegetables, served warm. Wonderful for a chilly evening.

Two 2-ounce cans flat anchovy fillets in oil
1/2 cup extra-virgin olive oil
6 cloves garlic, peeled: 4 minced and 2 thinly sliced
4 tablespoons butter
1 tablespoon lemon juice
1/2 teaspoon coarsely ground black peppercorns
Crusty bread, cut into chunks for dipping, and a selection of: carrot sticks;
    celery sticks; fennel wedges; cherry tomatoes; red, yellow, and orange
    bell pepper strips; sugar snap peas; cauliflower florets; zucchini sticks;
    summer squash sticks; steamed, chilled asparagus spears

1. Drain the anchovies, reserving the oil. Using a mortar and pestle or a fork and a small bowl, mash the anchovies and set aside.

2. Place a medium saucepan over low heat and add the olive oil and anchovy oil. Add the minced garlic and sliced garlic, and sauté until the garlic is softened but not browned. Add the mashed anchovies, butter, lemon juice, and peppercorns. Stir until the butter has

melted, then remove from the heat and allow to cool. Transfer to a covered container and re-frigerate.

3. Prepare a small chafing dish or heat a small bowl by submerging it in a large bowl of hot water. Scrape the bagna cauda into a small saucepan. Place over low heat and stir until melted and thoroughly heated; do not boil. Transfer to the heated chafing dish or dried warmed bowl. Serve with crusty bread and a selection of fresh vegetables for dipping.

WINES: Albariño, Gavi, Barbera d'Asti

TO MAKE AHEAD

Up to twenty-four hours before serving: Make bagna cauda and allow to cool. Cover and re-frigerate. Cut up vegetables, cover, and refrigerate.

To serve: Reheat bagna cauda. Transfer to a small chafing dish or warm serving bowl.

Mushroom Tart

FOR THE CRUST:

1 cup all-purpose flour
1/4 pound (1 stick) chilled butter, cut into small pieces
1 teaspoon white vinegar
3 or 4 tablespoons ice water, as needed

FOR THE TOPPING:

2 tablespoons extra-virgin olive oil
3 shallots, peeled and chopped
1 clove garlic, peeled and minced
8 ounces shiitake mushrooms, trimmed and sliced
8 ounces crimini mushrooms, trimmed and sliced
2 large eggs
1 tablespoon sour cream
1/4 cup shredded Gruyère cheese
Salt and freshly ground black pepper
1/4 cup grated Parmesan cheese

1. *Prepare the crust:* Preheat the oven to 400 degrees. Place the flour in a large mixing bowl and scatter the butter over it. Using a pastry blender or 2 knives, cut the butter into the flour until the flour resembles coarse crumbs. Mix the vinegar with about 3 tablespoons ice water and sprinkle on top. Stir with a fork until the mixture comes together to make a dough. If necessary, add an additional tablespoon of water, but be careful not to make the dough too wet. Shape the dough into a ball.

2. On a lightly floured surface, roll the dough into an 11-inch disk. Lift the disk (this is most easily done by folding the dough in half and in half again, then unfolding it after it is moved) and place in a 10-inch tart pan with a removable bottom. Fold and press the edges of the dough to fit neatly into the pan. (If the dough tears when it is moved, simply moisten the edges of the tear with a bit of water and press together while it is in the pan.) Prick the dough all over with a fork. Bake until the dough is light golden brown, about 15 minutes. Remove from the heat and set aside.

3. *Prepare the topping:* Lower the oven to 350 degrees. Place a large sauté pan over medium-low heat and add the olive oil. When the oil is hot, add the shallots and sauté until tender, 1 to 2 minutes. Add the garlic, stir, and add the mushrooms. Continue to sauté until the mushrooms are tender and have released their juices, 5 to 7 minutes. Remove from the heat and set aside.

4. In a mixing bowl, whisk together the eggs and sour cream. Stir in the Gruyère and sautéed mushrooms, and season generously with salt and pepper to taste. Pour the mixture into the prepared pie shell and spread evenly. Sprinkle with the Parmesan. Bake until the filling is set and beginning to brown, 15 to 20 minutes. Remove from the heat and allow to cool. Cover lightly and store at room temperature until serving.

WINES: Barbera d'Asti (continued), Brouilly, Zinfandel, Shiraz (Australia)

TO MAKE AHEAD
One to four hours before serving: Prepare and bake tart. Cover and set aside at room temperature.

Roasted Squash with Corn Bread, Sage, and Chestnut Stuffing and Smoked Tempeh-Root Vegetable Ragout

This savory recipe comes from Eric Tucker, chef at the vegan Millennium Restaurant in San Francisco. Celebrating the flavors of fall, stuffed roasted squash makes a perfect vegetarian Thanksgiving meal. Although the recipe is a bit complicated, all the work can be done the day before serving.

FOR THE SQUASH:

8 round, medium-sized winter squash such as gold, white, or green acorn,
   carnival, red kuri, or sweet dumpling
Salt and freshly ground black pepper
2 cups vegetable stock

FOR THE STUFFING:

2 tablespoons extra-virgin olive oil
1 cup diced yellow onion
½ cup finely diced celery
1½ cups finely diced carrots
6 cloves garlic, peeled and minced
⅓ teaspoon celery seed
½ teaspoon caraway seed
⅓ teaspoon nutmeg
2 tablespoons dry sherry
1 cup vegetable stock
4 cups crumbled toasted corn bread
1 cup crumbled (into large pieces), shelled, roasted chestnuts, fresh or
   from a jar
2 tablespoons minced fresh sage
Salt and freshly ground black pepper

FOR THE VEGETABLE RAGOUT:

2 tablespoons olive oil
2 leeks, white and light green parts only, cleaned and cut into ½-inch-thick
   slices

4 cloves garlic

1 cup coarsely chopped mushrooms

8 ounces smoked tempeh or tofu, cut into small cubes

½ teaspoon dried thyme

1 teaspoon minced fresh rosemary

¼ teaspoon ground juniper berries

2 bay leaves

1 cup apple cider

1½ cups finely diced parsnips

2 cups finely diced butternut or other winter squash

1½ cups finely diced carrots

2 cups vegetable stock

2 tablespoons Dijon mustard

Salt and freshly ground black pepper to taste

1. *Prepare the squash:* Preheat the oven to 400 degrees. Slice 1½ inches off the tops of the squash and set the tops aside. Scoop out and discard the seeds and pith. Sprinkle the cavities with salt and pepper to taste. Place the squash, cut sides down, in a baking pan. Pour in the stock and enough water so the liquid is ⅓ to ½ inch deep. Cover the pan tightly with foil. Place the squash tops, cut-side down, on a baking sheet and add just enough water to cover the bottom of the pan. Bake until the squash are slightly soft when squeezed and the flesh is fork-tender, 30 to 40 minutes; the tops can be baked for the same length of time or until very lightly browned. Remove from the heat and allow to cool. Cover and refrigerate up to 24 hours.

2. *Prepare the stuffing:* Place a large skillet over medium heat and heat the oil. Add the onion, celery, carrots, and garlic. Sauté until lightly browned. Add the celery seed, caraway seed, and nutmeg, and sauté 1 minute. Add the sherry and vegetable stock, stirring and scraping the bottom of the pan. Simmer until reduced by one-third, then remove from the heat. In a large bowl, combine the corn bread, chestnuts, and sage. Add the carrot mixture and mix well. Season with salt and pepper to taste. Set aside and allow to cool. Cover and refrigerate up to 24 hours.

3. *Prepare the vegetable ragout:* Place a deep skillet over medium heat and add the olive oil. Add the leeks and garlic, and sauté until softened. Add the mushrooms and tempeh, and sauté until the mushrooms are softened. Add the thyme, rosemary, juniper berries, and bay leaves, and sauté for 1 minute. Stir in the apple cider, scraping the bottom of the pan. Add the parsnips, diced squash, carrots, and stock. Bring to a boil, then reduce the heat to low. Cover and simmer until the vegetables are just fork-tender, about 30 minutes.

Stir in the mustard and adjust the salt and pepper to taste. Set aside and allow to cool. Cover and refrigerate up to 24 hours.

4. Preheat the oven to 350 degrees. Fill the squash loosely with equal portions of stuffing. (The stuffing will not fill the squash, leaving room for the ragout.) Place the squash and tops on a baking sheet and bake just until reheated, about 15 minutes. Meanwhile, place the ragout in a small saucepan over medium-low heat just until thoroughly reheated.

5. When the squash are reheated, place each squash in the center of a warm serving plate. Top with a portion of ragout, heaping it over the top of the squash. Lean the squash's top decoratively against it. Serve immediately.

WINES: Continue with any of the wines from the last course: Barbera d'Asti, Brouilly, Zinfandel, Shiraz

TO MAKE AHEAD
The day before serving: Roast squash. Prepare stuffing. Prepare ragout. Cover and refrigerate.

Thirty minutes before serving: Preheat oven. Reheat vegetable ragout. Fill squash with stuffing and bake until reheated. Top with ragout and serve.

Shaker Lemon Pie

This recipe is adapted from the Pleasant Hill Shaker Community in Harrodsburg, Kentucky.

> 2 large, thin-skinned, seedless lemons, sliced paper-thin
> 2 cups sugar
> 4 eggs, well beaten
> Pastry for a double-crust 9-inch pie

1. In a medium bowl, combine the lemons and sugar. Allow to stand at room temperature, mixing occasionally, for at least 2 hours or overnight.

2. Preheat the oven to 450 degrees. Add the beaten eggs to the lemon mixture and stir well. Pour into the bottom half of the pie crust, arranging the lemon slices evenly. Cover with the top crust and crimp the edges. Cut several slits near the center of the crust.

3. Bake the pie for 15 minutes, then lower the heat to 375 degrees. Continue to bake until a knife inserted near the edge of the pie comes out clean, 20 to 25 minutes. Allow to cool at least 30 minutes; the center of the pie will continue to set as it cools. Serve at room temperature or chilled.

WINE: Muscat Blanc

TO MAKE AHEAD

One to two days before serving: Combine lemon slices and sugar; set aside.
Two to eight hours before serving: Finish making filling and place in crust. Bake and allow to cool.

MENU 6

· · · · · · ·

Plantain Crisps with Smoked Salmon, Wasabi, and Crème Fraîche

4 large green plantains

Vegetable oil for frying

½ firm, ripe Hass avocado

1 tablespoon lemon juice

Prepared wasabi paste

6 ounces smoked salmon, thinly sliced

½ cup crème fraîche (see page 173)

1. Trim the ends of the plantains and then cut each plantain crosswise into 4 chunks about 1½ inches long. To remove the hard green skin, cut a slit through the skin of each chunk and use a knife to help peel it off.

2. Place about ¼ inch of oil in a deep skillet or wide saucepan. Place over medium-high heat. When the oil is moderately hot, add the plantains and allow to sizzle until the bottom half of the chunks are browned. Turn the chunks to brown the other sides. Remove the plantains from the oil, drain on paper towels, and allow to cool. Set the pan of oil aside.

3. Place the cooled chunks of plantain on their cut sides. Smash the chunks by using the oiled bottom of another heavy skillet or an oiled kitchen mallet. The flattened chunks

should be about ¼ inch thick and have an irregular edge. Return the pan of oil to medium heat. When the oil is hot, fry the flattened chunks again until golden brown. Remove the plantains from the oil, drain on paper towels, and allow to cool. Discard the oil. When completely cool, transfer the plantain crisps to an airtight container and set aside at room temperature.

4. Finely dice the avocado and mix with the lemon juice. Set aside. Very lightly smear a plantain crisp with about ⅛ teaspoon wasabi paste. Cut a piece of salmon about the width of the crisp and twice as long. Double it and place on the wasabi. Top with about 1 teaspoon crème fraîche and garnish with a small dollop of avocado. Repeat with the remaining plantain crisps.

WINES: Sparkling (Australia), Sauvignon Blanc Vin de Pays d'Oc, Riesling (Kabinett), Pinot Noir

TO MAKE AHEAD
Up to four hours before serving: Fry plantains. Cover and set aside.
To serve: Spread crisps with wasabi paste, salmon, and crème fraîche. Garnish.

CRÈME FRAÎCHE

Crème fraîche is a thick, tangy cream often used in French cooking. It has a taste and texture somewhere between heavy cream and sour cream, and in a pinch you can substitute lightly whipped cream mixed with a small amount of sour cream. But crème fraîche can be purchased in many markets and is easily made at home.

To make it yourself you will need to plan a bit ahead because the mixture will need most of a day to thicken. To make about 1 cup, mix together 1 cup of heavy cream with 2 to 3 tablespoons buttermilk or yogurt. Set aside at room temperature just until thickened, about eight hours, or refrigerate overnight. Crème fraîche can be stored refrigerated for about two weeks. If you wish, when you are down to the last few tablespoons, you may add another cup of heavy cream to develop a fresh batch.

Crusted Chèvre with Balsamic Vinaigrette

John Shaw, owner of Frankie and Johnny's in Cape Neddick, Maine, is one of the most talented chefs I know. Though sophisticated and elegant, his food is created with ingredients and techniques accessible to the home cook. This recipe is a study in contrasts: soft tangy goat cheese with a thin, crisp crust, drizzled with balsamic vinegar that has been simmered until mellow and syrupy.

1 cup balsamic vinegar
2 teaspoons light brown sugar
½ cup flour
1 cup heavy cream
1 cup panko (Japanese bread crumbs)
8 ounces log-shaped chèvre, chilled
Extra-virgin olive oil
4 cups (loosely packed) mixed baby salad greens
Salt and freshly ground black pepper
8 slices large ripe tomato
16 to 24 pitted Kalamata or other olives

1. In a small saucepan, combine the vinegar and brown sugar. Place over medium heat and bring to a boil. Cook until the mixture is reduced by about half; it should be thick and syrupy. Remove from the heat and set aside.

2. Place the flour, cream, and panko in three separate bowls. Using a warm knife, cut the chilled chèvre into slices ⅓-inch thick. (If the chèvre crumbles a bit, just press it back into place. The coating will help hide imperfections.)

3. Dust the slices with flour, then dip into the cream, turning to coat all sides. Coat with panko, and set aside on a plate.

4. Place a nonstick skillet over medium heat and pour in enough oil to come about ¼ inch up the side of the pan. When the oil is shimmering, slip in the coated chèvre slices. Allow them to sit undisturbed until they are golden brown on the bottom, about 1 minute. Carefully turn and brown the other sides, about 1 more minute. Transfer to a plate lined with paper towels, and set aside.

5. Place the salad greens in a mixing bowl, and toss with 1 to 2 tablespoons olive oil. Add 2 teaspoons of the balsamic reduction. Season with salt and pepper to taste, and add more balsamic reduction as desired. Toss again to mix well.

6. Place a tomato slice on one side of each of 8 small plates. Add a serving of salad greens slightly overlapping the tomato. Top the salad with 2 or 3 olives. Place a serving of crusted chèvre on each plate, and drizzle the plate (not the chèvre) with a teaspoon or two of olive oil and some of the remaining balsamic reduction.

Grilled Duck Breast with Pepper Jelly Glaze

Use a top-quality flavorful pepper jelly for this recipe, adapted from Susan Spicer of Bayona in New Orleans.

8 boneless duck breasts (about 6 ounces each), skin on, trimmed of fat
Coarse salt
1 teaspoon freshly ground black pepper
2 teaspoons chopped fresh thyme
2 teaspoons chopped fresh rosemary

FOR THE PEPPER JELLY GLAZE:
2 tablespoons chopped shallots
¾ cup sherry vinegar
3 cups well-seasoned chicken or beef stock
3 tablespoons hot pepper jelly
2 tablespoons unsalted butter
Salt and freshly ground black pepper
1 jalapeño pepper, seeded and finely minced (optional)

1. Wash and dry the duck breasts. Mix together the salt, pepper, thyme, and rosemary. Sprinkle the mixture over the skin side of the breasts and refrigerate for several hours or let stand about 30 minutes before cooking.

2. *Make the glaze:* Combine the shallots, vinegar, and stock in a small pot and bring to a boil. Reduce the heat and simmer until the liquid is reduced to about 1 cup. Whisk in the pepper jelly and then the butter. Season to taste with salt and pepper. Add the jalapeño if using. Add more vinegar if the sauce is too sweet.

3. Grill or sauté the duck breasts, skin side down, about 6 minutes, then turn and cook about 2 minutes more depending on how rare you want the breasts. Remove from the

heat and let stand about 2 minutes. Slice each duck breast on the diagonal into 5 or 6 pieces and arrange on a plate, skin side up. Spoon the glaze over the top.

WINES: Gewürztraminer (Alsace), Châteauneuf du Pape (red), Burgundy (red, in order of cost: Bourgogne Côte Chalonnaise, Gevrey-Chambertin, Clos Saint-Denis, Bonnes Mares; also New Zealand Pinot Noir)

TO MAKE AHEAD

Thirty minutes to three hours before serving: Season duck breasts and set aside.
Thirty minutes before serving: Make glaze. Grill or sauté duck breasts.

Wheat Berry Cucumber Salad

This recipe from Laurie Zwaan, whose family owns and runs Champlain Valley Apiaries in Middlebury, Vermont, has just a hint of sweetness from honey in the dressing. A food processor makes preparation of the vegetables quick and easy, but an old-fashioned knife will work just as well.

FOR THE SALAD:

2 cups uncooked wheat berries

½ cup dark raisins or currants

1 bunch parsley (about ½ cup, packed)

3 stalks celery, trimmed

2 large seedless cucumbers (or 4 small cucumbers, seeds removed), peeled and cut into chunks

FOR THE DRESSING:

3 shallots, peeled

½ teaspoon honey

2 tablespoons fresh orange juice

1 tablespoon finely grated orange zest

1½ tablespoons champagne vinegar or apple cider vinegar

¼ cup extra-virgin olive oil

Salt and freshly ground black pepper

1. *Prepare the salad:* Place a large pot (2 to 3 quarts) of water over high heat and bring to a boil. When the water is boiling, add the wheat berries and reduce the heat to low. Partially cover and simmer until the berries are just tender, about 1 hour. Drain, rinse with cold water, and drain again. Transfer to a large mixing bowl.

2. Put the raisins in a small bowl and cover with hot water; set aside. Using a food processor, finely chop the parsley, then transfer it to the bowl of wheat berries. Add the cel-

ery to the unwashed food processor and process until finely chopped. Add to the bowl of wheat berries.

3. Add the cucumbers to the processor. Being careful not to overprocess, pulse the cucumbers only until chopped small. Transfer the chopped cucumbers to a fine-meshed strainer and press gently to extract the excess liquid. Add the cucumbers to the bowl of wheat berries and toss to mix.

4. *Prepare the dressing:* Put the shallots in the still-unwashed food processor and finely chop. Transfer to a medium mixing bowl. Add the honey, orange juice, orange zest, and vinegar. Whisk to blend. Slowly whisk in the olive oil. Season with salt and pepper to taste and whisk again.

5. Pour the dressing over the salad and toss gently to mix well. Transfer to a decorative serving bowl, cover, and refrigerate until ready to serve.

TO MAKE AHEAD

Up to two hours before serving: Prepare salad, cover, and refrigerate.

Brown Sugar Pumpkin Pie with Cinnamon Whipped Cream

If you prefer to use fresh pumpkin, peel it, cut the flesh into chunks, and bake or steam them until tender. Puree and measure out 2 cups for the pie. Otherwise, canned puree makes this recipe so simple that a child can prepare it.

FOR THE PIE:

3 large eggs

One 15- or 16-ounce can pumpkin
   puree

¾ cup firmly packed light brown
   sugar

⅛ teaspoon salt

½ teaspoon ground ginger

1 teaspoon ground cinnamon

1 cup heavy cream

1 lightly baked piecrust

FOR THE WHIPPED CREAM:

1 cup heavy cream

2 tablespoons sugar

⅛ teaspoon ground cinnamon

1. *Prepare the pie:* Preheat the oven to 375 degrees. In a mixing bowl, beat the eggs just until frothy. Add the pumpkin puree, brown sugar, salt, ginger, cinnamon, and cream. Mix until blended.

2. Pour the pumpkin mixture into the baked pie shell and bake for 45 minutes. The pie will be soft in the center and will solidify as it cools. Place the pie on a rack to cool. Cover the cooled pie and refrigerate.

3. *Prepare the cream:* By hand or using an electric mixer, whisk together the cream, sugar, and cinnamon until thick enough to hold peaks. Cover and refrigerate until serving.

4. To serve, cut wedges of pie and top each with a dollop of cinnamon whipped cream.

WINE: Pedro Ximénez

TO MAKE AHEAD

One to eight hours before serving: Bake pie. Cool, cover, and refrigerate.

Up to one hour before serving: Whip cream, cover, and refrigerate.

MENU 7

· · · · · · ·

Gouda, Chutney, and Apple Bites

The name of this recipe says it all. It's a delicious combination that takes just a few minutes to prepare. The name Gouda is properly pronounced "how-da" after the town where it is made in the Netherlands.

3 large, seasonal, fresh eating apples, such as McIntosh, Cortland,
    Yellow Delicious, and Granny Smith
About 4 ounces smoked Gouda cheese
About ½ cup mild or hot chutney

1. Halve the apples, core them, and cut them into slices about ¼ inch thick. Thinly slice the Gouda into pieces about the same size as the apple slices.

2. Spread 1 side of each apple slice with a thin layer of chutney. Top with a slice of Gouda. Arrange on a serving platter.

WINES: Apple cider, but, if you must, try Beaujolais or Chenin Blanc

Baby Vegetables with Lemon-Dill Sauce and Crispy Noodles

FOR THE SAUCE:

1 cup sour cream

$\frac{1}{2}$ cup plain yogurt

1 teaspoon sugar

1 teaspoon Dijon mustard

$\frac{1}{4}$ cup minced fresh dill

1 tablespoon finely grated lemon zest

1 clove garlic, peeled and minced

$\frac{1}{2}$ teaspoon salt

Generous grating of black pepper

FOR THE NOODLES:

8 ounces very thin rice noodles (also called rice sticks; available in Asian
   markets and many supermarkets)

Vegetable oil for frying

FOR THE VEGETABLES:

8 cherry tomatoes

8 baby (1- to $1\frac{1}{2}$-inch) pattypan or crookneck yellow squash

8 baby (2-inch-long) zucchini

8 pearl onions, trimmed and peeled

2 to 4 small Japanese eggplants, trimmed and sliced lengthwise into
   a total of 8 pieces

$\frac{1}{4}$ cup olive oil

Salt and freshly ground black pepper

1. *Prepare the sauce:* In a mixing bowl, combine the sour cream, yogurt, sugar, mustard, dill, and lemon zest. Add the garlic, salt, and pepper to taste. Mix well and transfer to a covered container. Refrigerate.

2. *Prepare the noodles:* Place about 2 inches of oil in a large saucepan. Have ready a wire-meshed ladle and a baking sheet lined with paper towels. Place the pan over high heat. When the oil is hot, test it by dropping in a few pieces of rice noodle. The oil should foam

and the noodles instantly expand and turn white. Remove them immediately with the ladle and transfer to the paper towels to drain. If necessary, adjust the heat.

3. Working in batches, break off small amounts of rice noodles and drop them in the hot oil, removing them as soon as they foam up. Allow the cooked noodles to cool completely, then transfer to a covered container. Store at room temperature.

4. *Prepare the vegetables:* Preheat a broiler. Place all the vegetables in a large bowl. Drizzle with oil and season to taste with salt and pepper. Toss the vegetables with a wooden spoon to make sure they are well coated. Put the vegetables in a broiling pan and broil, turning often, until they are tender and slightly charred in places. Remove from the heat and allow to cool. Place in a covered container and refrigerate until chilled.

5. Place a mound of crispy noodles on each plate, making a small well in the center. Divide the chilled vegetables among the plates, making sure that each plate has some of each vegetable. The plates may be set aside at room temperature for about 30 minutes if desired. When ready to serve, stir the dressing and drizzle some over each portion of vegetables.

WINES: Chenin Blanc from the previous course or try a Grüner-Veltliner or Sylvaner

TO MAKE AHEAD

The day before serving: Make the lemon-dill sauce; cover and refrigerate. Make the crispy noodles; store in an airtight container at room temperature.

One to six hours before serving: Broil vegetables. Cool, cover, and refrigerate.

To serve: Arrange noodles and vegetables on plates. Top with dressing.

Kalbi-Chim

This beef stew with Asian flavors is adapted from Gordon Churchwell.

6 pounds beef short ribs or other meaty ribs, cross-cut into 2 strips
3 tablespoons sugar
2 tablespoons sesame oil
8 large cloves garlic, minced
12 scallions, chopped
4 tablespoons minced fresh ginger
6 tablespoons dry sherry
½ cup tamari (Japanese soy sauce)
6 tablespoons mirin (sweet rice wine)
¼ cup peanut oil
2 onions, chopped
4 carrots, 2 minced and 2 cut into 1-inch chunks
1½ cups chicken or beef broth
2 cups red wine
20 to 24 dried shiitake mushrooms
24 peeled chestnuts: fresh; or dried and soaked in water for 2 hours;
   or jarred
2 pears or apples, peeled, cored, and chopped

1. Score the ribs diagonally on the fatty side and place in a large bowl. Add the sugar and rub into the meat. Rub the sesame oil into the meat and let rest for 15 minutes. Add the garlic, scallions, ginger, sherry, tamari, and mirin. Rub into the meat, then refrigerate. Allow to marinate, for 2 to 3 hours.

2. Preheat the oven to 350 degrees. In a Dutch oven or other covered pan large enough to hold the ribs in 1 layer, heat 2 tablespoons peanut oil over medium heat. Add the onions and carrot, and sauté until the vegetables are tender, 5 minutes. Place the ribs on the vegetables, fat side up. Add the marinade, broth, and wine. Bring to a boil on top of the stove, cover, and place in the oven for 1 hour.

3. While the meat is in the oven, reconstitute the mushrooms by adding boiling water to cover and soaking until tender, about 20 minutes. Drain, pat dry with paper towels, and slice thinly. In a small skillet over medium-low heat, heat the remaining 2 tablespoons peanut oil, and add the mushroom slices. Sauté until lightly browned, about 3 minutes.

When the meat is cooked, remove from the oven, add the mushrooms, and mix into the hot broth. Allow the mixture to cool. Cover and refrigerate.

4. Preheat the oven to 350 degrees. Skim the fat from the meat mixture and turn the ribs fat side down. Add the chestnuts and pears. Partially cover and place in the oven for 1½ to 2 hours, until the liquid has almost evaporated.

WINES: Côtes du Rhône, Zinfandel, Shiraz, Barolo

TO MAKE AHEAD

The day before serving: Marinate meat. Prepare stew. Cool, cover, and refrigerate.
Two hours before serving: Skim fat from pan. Bake stew.

Parsnip and Potato Puree

10 potatoes, peeled and quartered
8 medium parsnips, peeled and cut into equal-sized chunks
2 cups milk, or as needed
4 tablespoons butter, or as desired
Salt and freshly ground black pepper

1. Place the potatoes in a large saucepan and cover with cold water. Bring to a boil over high heat, then reduce to a simmer. Simmer until the potatoes are very tender, about 20 minutes.

2. While the potatoes are cooking, place the parsnips in a medium saucepan and cover with a mixture of half water and half milk. Bring to a boil, reduce the heat, and simmer until the parsnips are tender, about 15 minutes. Drain the potatoes and parsnips, and allow to cool. Combine in a covered container and refrigerate.

3. Remove the potatoes and parsnips from the refrigerator. In a large saucepan, heat about 1 cup milk until simmering. Add the potatoes and parsnips and mash together until well pureed and thoroughly heated. Thin to taste with additional milk if desired. Season with butter, salt, and pepper to taste. Serve hot.

TO MAKE AHEAD

The day before serving: Cook potatoes and parsnips until tender. Cool and refrigerate.
Fifteen minutes before serving: Heat milk. Add potatoes and and parsnips. Reheat and puree.

Pear Pecan Tart

This recipe is adapted from Michael Romano, chef at the Union Square Cafe in Manhattan.

2 cups granulated sugar

2 teaspoons vanilla extract

2 Anjou or Comice pears, peeled and halved lengthwise (do not core)

6 tablespoons butter, at room temperature

1/3 cup plus 2 tablespoons brown sugar

3/4 cup plus 2 tablespoons flour

Pinch of salt

3 large eggs

1 1/2 cups coarsely chopped pecans

1/3 cup grated sweetened coconut

1. In a medium saucepan, combine the granulated sugar, 2 cups water, and 1 teaspoon vanilla. Bring to a boil, reduce the heat to low, and simmer, stirring, until the sugar dissolves. Add the pears and simmer until tender, about 15 minutes. Remove the pears with a slotted spoon and allow to cool.

2. Using an electric mixer fitted with a whisk attachment, cream the butter and 1/3 cup brown sugar. Add 3/4 cup flour, salt, and remaining 1 teaspoon vanilla extract. Knead briefly to form a smooth dough and press into a ball. Cover with plastic wrap and refrigerate 15 minutes.

3. Preheat the oven to 350 degrees. On a lightly floured surface, roll the dough into a 10-inch disk. Press into a 10-inch tart pan with a removeable bottom. Bake until the tart shell begins to color, about 5 minutes. Remove from the oven and set aside.

4. In a medium bowl, combine the eggs, pecans, coconut, remaining 2 tablespoons flour, and remaining 2 tablespoons brown sugar. Whisk until blended. Remove the cores from the pear halves with a melon baller or knife. Slice each pear into thin wedges but leave the narrow end attached, or simply slice the pears and fan them out in the pan.

5. Pour the pecan mixture into the tart shell. Place the pears on top, with the narrow ends in the center of the tart. Fan the slices so that they lie nearly flat, covering the surface of the tart. Bake until the tart is set and golden brown, about 35 minutes. Transfer to a rack and allow to cool to room temperature. Cover with a glass dome or plastic wrap and set aside at room temperature until serving.

WINE: Trockenbeerenauslese

TO MAKE AHEAD

Two to eight hours before serving: Prepare tart. Cool, cover, and set aside at room temperature.

MENU 8

- - - - - - -

Boursin Spinach Triangles

Boursin is the brand name of a soft herbed cheese that is available in several different varieties, any of which would be suitable for this recipe. If you wish, you may make your own herbed cheese by mixing softened cream cheese with finely chopped herbs (parsley, chives, tarragon, marjoram) and spices such as crushed pink, green, and black peppercorns, allspice, cayenne pepper, and smoked paprika.

Two 5⅓-ounce packages Boursin
    cheese
1 large egg
¼ teaspoon nutmeg
2 tablespoons olive oil
2 tablespoons finely chopped
    onion

One 10-ounce package washed-
    and-ready-to-eat baby spinach
    leaves
Salt and freshly ground black pepper
One 8-ounce package filo (phyllo)
    dough, halved crosswise
Olive oil or vegetable oil spray

    1. In a mixing bowl, combine the Boursin, egg, and nutmeg. Mix until smooth and set aside.

    2. Place a large skillet over medium-low heat. Add the olive oil and onion, and sauté until the onion is softened, about 2 minutes. Add the spinach and sauté until wilted. Re-

move from the pan and chop coarsely. Add to the Boursin mixture, season with salt and pepper to taste, and mix until well blended.

3. Place a half sheet of filo dough on a counter with the shortest end toward you. Spray the dough lightly with oil. Fold in half lengthwise and spray again. Place a heaping tablespoon of filling in the upper right-hand corner and fold down the filled corner to make a neat triangle. Continue folding to make a compact filled triangle. Continue with the remaining dough and filling.

4. Place the triangles on a baking sheet lined with waxed paper. Freeze uncovered. When the triangles are frozen, transfer them to an airtight freezer bag, squeezing out as much air as possible. Store in the freezer for up to 1 month.

5. Remove the triangles from the freezer. Place on a baking sheet and allow to defrost at room temperature.

6. Preheat the oven to 375 degrees. Bake the triangles until light golden brown, about 15 minutes. Serve hot.

WINES: Beaujolais-Villages (lightly chilled), Saint-Véran, Sancerre

TO MAKE AHEAD
Up to one month before serving: Prepare filling. Assemble triangles. Freeze uncovered.
     Transfer to airtight bags.
About two hours before serving: Remove triangles from freezer and allow to defrost at room
     temperature.
To serve: Preheat oven. Bake until golden brown.

FILO DOUGH

Filo dough (also known as phyllo dough) comes to us from Greek and Middle Eastern cuisines. It consists of paper-thin sheets that are traditionally brushed with butter and stacked, often interspersed with layers of sweet or savory filling.

The dough can be found in the frozen foods section of most supermarkets and should be defrosted before using. It can be tricky to work with because the delicate, flexible sheets become brittle when exposed to dry air. To prevent the dough from drying, cover it with a sheet of plastic wrap topped with a large dampened kitchen towel. The towel should overlap the edges of the plastic, keeping dry air from reaching the dough.

Fold back the plastic and towel just long enough to remove and set aside a sheet of dough, then replace them immediately. This should keep the dough moist and pliable for as long as you need it.

Melon with Prosciutto

The large flaky grains of English Maldon salt add a nice finish to this recipe. Maldon salt may be found in specialty food markets or may be ordered by mail from spice traders such as Adrianna's Bazaar (see Resources, page 267).

  1 small to medium ripe melon (such as cantaloupe, honeydew, or crenshaw)
  8 ounces very thinly sliced prosciutto
  Maldon salt or sel de fleur

  1. Halve the melon and scoop out the seeds. Cut 16 thin slices and remove the rind from each one. Cover and refrigerate.
  2. Arrange 2 slices of melon on each plate. Place a slice or two of prosciutto across the middle of the melon slices, draping slightly on the plate. Sprinkle the melon and the plate with 1 or 2 pinches of salt. Serve immediately.

WINES: Vernaccia di San Gimignano, Malvasia dei Colli Piacentini, Chardonnay (Alto Adige), or Beaujolais (from the first course)

Marinated Chicken with Chickpeas and Ham

This is one of the first recipes I used successfully for entertaining. It was given to me about thirty years ago by Elaine Wiesenfeld, the mother of my then-boyfriend, who was adept at throwing large dinner parties. This dish is easy enough for the most inexperienced cook to prepare, and the entire recipe can be assembled ahead of time and popped in the oven when guests arrive. It makes a sumptuous feast and yet is low in carbs and fat.

  8 leaves napa cabbage, diced
  2 red onions, peeled and diced
  Three 16-ounce cans chickpeas, drained and rinsed
  8 ounces baked ham, cut into ½-inch dice
  1 pepperoni sausage, cut into ½-inch dice
  2 tablespoons extra-virgin olive oil

¾ cup vegetable oil

⅓ cup red wine vinegar

1½ teaspoons Italian herb seasoning

Salt and freshly ground black pepper

3½ pounds skinless, boneless chicken breasts, trimmed and halved

1. In a large mixing bowl, combine the napa cabbage, onions, chickpeas, ham, and pepperoni. In a small bowl, combine the olive oil, vegetable oil, vinegar, and Italian seasoning. Mix well and season to taste with salt and pepper. Pour the oil mixture over the cabbage mixture and toss well to mix. Cover and refrigerate overnight.

2. Spread the chicken in an even layer in a ceramic or glass 9 × 13-inch baking dish. Spread the cabbage mixture and its liquid evenly over the chicken. Cover and refrigerate.

3. Remove the baking dish from the refrigerator and allow it to sit at room temperature for about 30 minutes. Meanwhile, preheat the oven to 350 degrees.

4. Bake the chicken, uncovered, just until the chicken is opaque in the center, 45 to 50 minutes. While the chicken is baking, baste occasionally with pan juices. If necessary, add a little water to the pan to prevent it from drying out. Serve hot.

WINES: Beaujolais (from the first course), Rosé (Jumilla, from Monastrell or Syrah; or Provence), Taurasi

TO MAKE AHEAD

The day before serving: Prepare vegetable-ham mixture. Cover and refrigerate.

Three to six hours before serving: Spread chicken in baking dish and top with vegetable-ham mixture. Cover and refrigerate.

One and a half hours before serving: Remove baking dish from refrigerator and allow to sit at room temperature for 30 minutes. Preheat oven.

Forty-five minutes to one hour before serving: Bake for 45 to 50 minutes.

Broth-Cooked Rice

2 tablespoons olive oil

1 small onion, peeled and finely chopped

3 cups long-grain white rice

$\frac{1}{4}$ teaspoon salt

6 cups chicken or vegetable broth

$1\frac{1}{2}$ tablespoons minced fresh Italian (flat-leaf) parsley

1. Place a large saucepan over medium heat and add the olive oil. When the oil is hot, add the onion and sauté until translucent, 1 to 2 minutes. Add the rice and sauté until translucent and coated with oil, about 1 minute.

2. Add the salt and broth. Stir well and cover. Reduce the heat to very low and simmer for 15 minutes. Remove from the heat but do not lift the cover. Allow to sit undisturbed for 5 to 10 minutes. Stir in the parsley and serve.

Panna Cotta with Pomegranate

$1\frac{1}{2}$ cups milk

Zest of 2 lemons, finely grated

3 cups heavy cream

3 vanilla pods, halved lengthwise

3 teaspoons unflavored gelatin

1 cup confectioners' sugar

$\frac{2}{3}$ cup pomegranate seeds

6 tablespoons grappa

2 teaspoons granulated sugar

1. In a small saucepan, combine the milk, lemon zest, and $1\frac{1}{2}$ cups cream. Scrape the pulp from the vanilla pods into the mixture and add the pods as well. Place over low heat and simmer gently until reduced by one-third, about 15 minutes.

2. Remove from the heat and sprinkle the gelatin over the hot liquid. When the gelatin looks spongy, about 2 minutes, stir until the gelatin dissolves. Allow the mixture to cool

a bit, then transfer to a bowl. Refrigerate, stirring occasionally, until the mixture is thick enough to coat the back of a spoon, about 15 minutes.

3. In a small mixing bowl, mix the remaining 1½ cups cream and confectioners' sugar until smooth. Add to the gelatin mixture, stir, and then strain into 8 half-cup molds or ceramic coffee cups. Cover and refrigerate overnight.

4. In a small bowl, mix the pomegranate seeds, grappa, and granulated sugar. Dip each of the molds into hot water to loosen the panna cotta, then invert onto a small serving plate. Sprinkle the pomegranate mixture on top of and around the panna cotta, and serve.

WINES: Asti Spumante or Grappa

TO MAKE AHEAD

The day before serving: Make custard. Strain into molds.

To serve: Combine pomegranate, grappa, and sugar. Unmold panna cotta. Garnish with pomegranate mixture.

MENU 9

· · · · · · ·

Cherry Tomatoes Stuffed
with Roasted Eggplant

I learned this method of cooking eggplant from my friend Lavanya Joshi, who is from Ahmed-abad, India. It is superb as a stuffing for small, sweet tomatoes. Lavanya also taught me that siz-zling a spice in a bit of oil is a clever way to bring out its flavor and make an oil for seasoning the dish.

1 large eggplant
1½ tablespoons olive oil
1 teaspoon cumin seeds
1½ tablespoons finely chopped cilantro, plus additional for garnish
Salt and freshly ground black pepper
2½ pints cherry tomatoes

1. Place the eggplant on a preheated grill, under a broiler, or directly over a gas flame. Cook, turning often, until well charred on the outside and collapsed and soft in the middle. Remove from the heat and allow to cool on a baking sheet (to catch any juices).

2. When the eggplant is cool, scrape the interior pulp into a bowl. In a small pan (or even in a metal spoon; wear an oven mitt), combine the olive oil and cumin seeds. Place

over medium heat until the oil is sizzling. Immediately add to the eggplant and mix well. Add the cilantro and season with salt and pepper to taste. Cover and refrigerate.

3. Using a small, sharp knife, cut off the top third of each tomato. Use a small spoon to remove as much pulp as possible. Fill the tomatoes with the eggplant mixture and arrange on a plate. Sprinkle with cilantro, cover, and refrigerate until serving.

WINES: Rosé (Navarra), Côtes du Languedoc or Côtes de Roussillon (both red), Alentejo (red)

TO MAKE AHEAD

Up to eight hours before serving: Prepare eggplant. Cover and refrigerate.
Up to two hours before serving: Hollow out tomatoes. Fill with eggplant. Cover and refrigerate until serving.

Cockles with
Smoked Paprika Butter

Smoked paprika has a very different flavor from sweet or hot paprika. It has a rich, smoky flavor that can't be duplicated with any other seasoning.

> ½ pound (2 sticks) butter, at room temperature
> ¼ cup Spanish smoked paprika (available at specialty food markets and spice markets)
> ¼ cup paprika
> 2 teaspoons kosher salt
> 3 pounds fresh cockles or very small clams
> 2 cups dry white wine
> ⅓ cup Jerez (sherry)
> ⅓ cup finely chopped Italian (flat-leaf) parsley

1. *Prepare the paprika butter:* In a mixer fitted with a paddle, cream the butter. Add the paprikas and salt, and mix thoroughly. Transfer to a sheet of plastic wrap. Shape into a log and chill until needed.

2. Heat a large sauté pan over high heat until very hot. Add the cockles and wine. Cover and cook until the cockles open, 2 to 3 minutes. Transfer the cockles to a plate, cover, and keep warm.

3. Return the sauté pan to the stove and reduce the liquid by half. Swirl in the cold paprika butter, 1 tablespoon at a time, until the sauce has thickened. Sprinkle on the sherry.

4. Place an equal portion of cockles on 8 serving plates and top with the sauce. Sprinkle with parsley and serve immediately.

WINES: Seyval Blanc (Michigan or New York), Muscadet, Amontillado, or Oloroso

TO MAKE AHEAD
Up to one week before serving: Prepare paprika butter. Wrap and refrigerate.
To serve: Steam cockles. Add paprika butter and sherry.

Latin-Style Beef Stew with Corn and Sweet Potatoes

This was inspired by a recipe from chefs John Willoughby and Chris Schlesinger.

2 pounds blade roast, chuck-eye
   roast, or other boneless chuck,
   cut into 1-inch cubes
Salt and freshly ground black pepper
¼ cup cumin seeds
3 tablespoons vegetable oil
3 medium red onions, 2 diced and
   1 sliced very thin
¼ cup minced garlic
2 to 3 tablespoons pureed chipotle
   peppers or minced fresh chili
   peppers

3 tablespoons ground coriander
2 plum tomatoes, roughly chopped
Two 12-ounce bottles dark beer
2 cups dry red wine
1 cup beef stock
2 medium sweet potatoes, peeled
   and cut into 1-inch cubes
1 cup fresh or frozen corn kernels
1 cup roughly chopped fresh cilantro
¼ cup fresh lime juice (about
   2 limes)

1. Place the chuck cubes in a large bowl. Add salt and pepper to taste and cumin, and mix well to coat the meat. In a large Dutch oven or flameproof casserole, heat the oil over medium-high heat until hot but not smoking. Add the seasoned meat in small batches and brown on all sides, about 5 minutes. Remove and set aside.

2. Pour off all but 2 tablespoons fat from the pan. Add the 2 diced onions and sauté, stirring frequently, until limp and shiny, 7 to 9 minutes. Add the garlic, chipotle peppers, coriander, and tomatoes, and sauté, stirring, for 2 minutes.

3. Add the beer, wine, and stock, and bring just to a boil, stirring once or twice and scraping any browned bits from the bottom of the pan. Add the reserved meat, bring the mixture back to a boil, and then reduce the heat and simmer, uncovered, for 35 minutes. Allow to cool, cover, and refrigerate until chilled, preferably overnight.

4. Skim the fat from the surface of the mixture and place the mixture over medium-low heat until simmering. Add the sweet potatoes and corn, season to taste with salt and pepper, and continue to simmer 25 minutes more, until the sweet potatoes are easily pierced by a fork but still offer a bit of resistance.

5. In a small bowl, mix together the cilantro, lime juice, and very thinly sliced red onion. Remove the stew from the heat and serve, topping each serving with some of this mixture.

WINES: Malbec (Argentina), Cabernet Sauvignon (Argentina or Chile), Petite Sirah

TO MAKE AHEAD

One to three days before serving: Make stew. Cool and refrigerate.

Thirty minutes before serving: Reheat stew. Add sweet potatoes and corn, and simmer 30 minutes. Prepare garnish.

Chocolate Banana Cream Pie

An old-fashioned dessert.

FOR THE FILLING:

2 ounces bittersweet chocolate,
    chopped

1 tablespoon unsalted butter

1 tablespoon cornstarch

2 tablespoons unsweetened Dutch-
    process cocoa

1/4 cup sugar

1 1/4 cups milk

2 large egg yolks

FOR THE PIE:

1 prebaked 9-inch pie shell or
    9 1/2-inch tart shell

2 ripe bananas, peeled and sliced
    1/4 inch thick

1/2 cup confectioners' sugar

1/4 cup unsweetened cocoa

2 cups heavy cream

1. *Prepare the filling:* Using a microwave oven or double boiler, melt together the chocolate and butter. In a medium bowl, combine the cornstarch, cocoa, and 2 tablespoons sugar. Add 2 tablespoons milk and stir to blend. Add the egg yolks and whisk until smooth.

2. In a medium saucepan, combine the remaining 1 1/8 cups milk and remaining 2 tablespoons sugar. Place over medium heat until scalded. Slowly drizzle into the cocoa mixture, stirring gently with a whisk to blend without aerating the mixture.

3. Return the mixture to the saucepan and cook over medium heat just until tiny bubbles appear. Remove from the heat and strain into a clean bowl. Add the melted chocolate and stir until thoroughly blended. Place waxed paper directly on the surface of the pudding and let cool for 1 hour, then refrigerate until completely chilled.

4. *Prepare the pie:* Spoon the pudding into the baked pie shell. Arrange the banana slices on top. Sift the confectioners' sugar and cocoa together into a bowl, add the cream, and mix well. Whip until the cream is the consistency of shaving cream. Spoon over the bananas in the pie shell. Refrigerate until serving.

WINE: Madeira

TO MAKE AHEAD

The day before serving: Prepare pie filling. Cool and refrigerate.

Up to two hours before serving: Spoon filling into pie shell. Top with sliced bananas. Mix
    cream topping and beat until stiff. Mound over bananas. Refrigerate until serving.

MENU 10

. . . .

Clam Dip

This is not a fancy dip, but it is easy to make at the last minute. If you want to dress it up, serve it alongside a bowl of multicolored root-vegetable chips, available in supermarkets and health food stores.

½ small onion (to make 2 to 3 tablespoons when minced)
One 8-ounce package cream cheese
Two 6½-ounce cans minced clams, drained and liquid reserved
Salt and freshly ground black pepper

1. Place the onion in the bowl of a food processor and process until minced. Add the cream cheese, clams, and about 2 tablespoons of the clam liquid. Season with salt and pepper to taste. Process until well blended.

2. Adjust the consistency of the dip by adding more clam juice if desired. Add more salt and pepper if needed. Cover and refrigerate. Serve with crackers, chips, or crudités.

WINES: Chardonnay (California), Sémillon (Australia), Riesling (Alsace)

TO MAKE AHEAD
Up to twenty-four hours before serving: Prepare dip. Cover and refrigerate.

Oyster Soup

This soup is so simple to prepare that it can be made shortly before serving. Allow about fifteen minutes for preparation. Ask your fishmonger to shuck the oysters for you and save the liquid.

    2 quarts milk
    1 quart heavy cream
    ½ pound (2 sticks) butter plus ¼ pound (1 stick) for garnish
        (optional)
    1 cup chicken broth
    1 teaspoon white pepper, or to taste
    2 teaspoons celery salt
    1 teaspoon paprika
    2 tablespoons Worcestershire sauce
    2 quarts shucked fresh oysters and their liquor
    Salt

1. In a medium saucepan, combine the milk and cream. Cook over low heat just until steam rises from the surface; do not boil. Remove from the heat and set aside.

2. In a large soup pot, combine the ½ pound butter, chicken broth, white pepper, celery salt, paprika, and Worcestershire sauce. Bring to a simmer.

3. Add the oysters and their liquor to the soup pot. Simmer until the edges of the oysters begin to curl, 2 to 3 minutes. Add the hot milk mixture and season with salt to taste. Heat gently. Do not boil, or the oysters will toughen and the broth may curdle.

4. To serve, ladle equal portions into warmed bowls. If desired, float 1 tablespoon butter in each bowl as garnish. Serve with oyster crackers.

WINES: Continue with Chardonnay, Sémillon, Riesling

Turkey Breast Roasted
Like a Leg of Lamb

1 large (about 6 pounds) turkey breast
6 cloves garlic, peeled and slivered, plus 2 unpeeled heads garlic, halved
    crosswise
4 cloves
Salt and freshly ground black pepper
¼ cup corn or peanut oil
2 large onions, peeled and quartered
2 large carrots, thickly sliced
Bouquet garni (1 sprig each fresh rosemary, sage, and thyme, and 2 bay leaves
    tied together with kitchen string or wrapped and tied in cheesecloth)
1 cup low-salt chicken broth

1. Preheat the oven to 400 degrees. Pierce the turkey all over with a fork and insert the garlic slivers, poking them in with the point of a knife. Insert 2 cloves near the middle and 2 near the end of the breast. Sprinkle with salt and pepper to taste.

2. In a large roasting pan over medium-high heat, heat the oil until very hot but not smoking. Add the turkey and brown it, skin side down, for 8 to 10 minutes. Turn and brown the other side for 8 to 10 minutes. Add to the pan the onions, carrots, heads of garlic, and bouquet garni. Cook 5 minutes, then put in the oven for 20 minutes. Add the broth and bake until browned, shiny, and firm, another 20 to 25 minutes. To serve, slice the roast thinly and moisten with a few tablespoons sauce.

WINES: Riesling (from earlier courses or substitute Idaho), Rioja (red), Chianti Classico, Bordeaux (red, Pomerol or St.-Émilion)

TO MAKE AHEAD
One and a half hours before serving: Preheat oven. Season and brown turkey. Roast about 45 minutes.

Roasted Potatoes

If you wish, fresh or dried rosemary may be added to these potatoes. Rub the rosemary all over the potatoes along with the oil. Allow about forty-five minutes for roasting.

>   4 large baking potatoes
>   Garlic-infused olive oil or a mixture of olive oil and minced garlic to taste
>   Salt and freshly ground black pepper

1. Preheat the oven to 400 degrees. Peel the potatoes and cut lengthwise into 6 or 8 pieces depending on the size of the potatoes. Dry thoroughly on paper towels and rub with oil. Season with salt and pepper to taste.

2. Place the potatoes in a heavy metal baking pan or add to a pan with a roast already cooking in it. Roast until well browned on the outside and tender on the inside, about 40 minutes. Turn occasionally. If the potatoes are done before the roast, use a spatula to transfer them to a plate; cover and keep warm.

Lemon-Ginger Crepes

These lemon curd–filled crepes are adapted from a recipe by Susan Spicer of Bayona in New Orleans.

FOR THE LEMON CURD:

3 large eggs

½ cup sugar

⅛ cup orange juice

⅓ cup plus 1 tablespoon lemon juice

2 teaspoons peeled, minced fresh ginger

4 tablespoons butter, cut into small pieces

FOR THE SAUCE:

2 cups orange juice

1 cup sugar

½ vanilla bean

1 small knot fresh ginger

¼ pound (1 stick) butter

FOR THE CREPE BATTER:

1 cup milk

2 tablespoons granulated sugar

2 tablespoons butter, melted, plus additional butter for pan

3 large eggs

¾ cup flour, sifted

¼ cup confectioners' sugar

⅛ teaspoon salt

2 teaspoons lemon zest

2 drops lemon oil (optional)

FOR ASSEMBLY:

3 tablespoons butter

8 scoops vanilla ice cream

Crystallized ginger, cut into fine strips, for garnish

1. *Prepare the lemon curd:* Place a few inches of water in a saucepan and bring to a simmer over medium heat. In a stainless steel bowl, whisk together the eggs and sugar. Place the bowl in the saucepan and whisk slowly until the sugar dissolves. Add the orange juice, lemon juice, and ginger. Continue whisking until the mixture is thick and the whisk leaves tracks in the curd, 2 to 3 minutes. Add the butter and stir until blended. Remove from the heat and allow to cool. Cover and refrigerate.

2. *Prepare the sauce:* Place the orange juice in a small saucepan over medium heat and simmer until reduced by half. Skim off and discard any cloudy scum. In a medium saucepan, combine the sugar with 1 cup water. Place over medium-high heat and stir constantly until amber in color. Working at arm's length to avoid spattering, slowly add the orange juice. Add the vanilla bean and ginger, raise the heat, and boil for 2 to 3 minutes. Strain, add the butter, and stir to blend. Cool, cover, and refrigerate.

3. *Prepare the crepe batter:* In a small saucepan, combine the milk and sugar. Place over medium-high heat until the milk just begins to bubble. Remove from the heat, add the butter, and stir until melted. Set aside to cool. In a medium bowl, whisk the eggs until blended. Gradually add the flour, confectioners' sugar, and salt to make a paste. Slowly whisk in the milk until combined. Strain through a fine sieve and add the lemon zest and lemon oil.

4. Place a 6-inch nonstick omelet or sauté pan over medium-low heat. Heat about 1 teaspoon butter in the pan. Pour a scant ¼ cup batter into the pan. Swirl to cover the bottom completely. When the edge of the crepe begins to turn golden, flip with a plastic spatula. Cook about 1 minute more. Transfer to a rack to cool completely. Repeat to make a total of 16 crepes.

5. *To assemble:* Spread about 1 tablespoon lemon curd on a crepe. Fold the crepe in half and again in half, to make a triangle. Repeat until all the crepes are filled. Wrap the filled crepes tightly and refrigerate overnight.

6. In a nonstick skillet, heat 1 tablespoon butter over medium-high heat until bubbly. Roll the pan to coat it. Sauté the folded crepes, 4 at a time, until lightly browned underneath. Turn to heat through. Transfer to a plate and keep warm. Repeat to heat the remaining crepes. Place 2 crepes on each of 8 serving plates. Top each serving with 2 tablespoons warm sauce, a spoonful of ice cream, and a few strips of crystallized ginger. Serve immediately.

WINE: Eiswein

TO MAKE AHEAD

Up to two days before serving: Make lemon curd. Make sauce. Cover and refrigerate.
The day before serving: Make and assemble crepes. Cover and refrigerate.
To serve: Reheat crepes and sauce. Serve with ice cream.

TEN MENUS
FOR WINTER

· · · · · ·

MENU 1
[PAGE 206]
Endive with Salmon Dill Mousse
Asparagus Salad with Walnut Oil
Braised Lamb Shanks with Apricot Curry Sauce
Toasted Crushed Potatoes
Chocolate-Coffee Crème Brûlée

MENU 2
[PAGE 212]
Martini Olives
Caramelized Onion, Leek, and Fresh Thyme Tart
Duck Gumbo
Garlicky Rice
Georgia Pecan Cream Cheese Pound Cake

MENU 3

[PAGE 218]

Banderillas

Arugula Salad with Sweet Onion and Chèvre

Loin of Pork Stuffed with Prunes

Roasted Butternut Squash with Pumpkin Seed Oil

Zabaglione with Strawberries and Balsamic Meringue

MENU 4

[PAGE 224]

Chilled Herbed Mussels on the Half Shell

Asparagus and Brie in Puff Pastry

Curried Scallops with Tomatoes

Jasmine Rice with Lemon and Parsley

Chocolate Fantasy Tart

MENU 5

[PAGE 231]

(VEGETARIAN)

Roasted Cauliflower with Lemon, Capers, and Olives

Involtini

Escarole with Pan-Roasted Garlic

Apricot Strudel

MENU 6

[PAGE 236]

Spiced Almonds

Seared Foie Gras with Caramelized Pears and Balsamic Vinegar

Chicken with a Thousand Cloves of Garlic

Roasted Beets

Herbed Rice in Wine

Cranberry-Orange Upside-Down Pie

MENU 7

[PAGE 242]

Skordalia

Iceberg Wedges with Blue Cheese Dressing

Deviled Short Ribs with Pumpkin, Chickpeas, and Kale

Walnut Lace Cookies

MENU 8

[PAGE 247]

Crispy Mushrooms with Ginger Sauce

Lobster Ravioli in Wontons with Lemongrass Butter Sauce

Chicken with Wild Rice and Tarragon

Anna's Easy Fudge Torte with Berry Puree

MENU 9

[PAGE 253]

Asparagus Wrapped in Prosciutto

Butternut Squash Risotto

Baked Cod with Wine and Feta

Roasted Broccoli Rabe

Alexander Cake

MENU 10

[PAGE 259]

Parmesan Cheese Crisps

Salmon Tartare

Roasted Rabbit with Polenta

Wild Mushroom Sauté

Pears in Red Wine

MENU I

. . . .

Endive with Salmon Dill Mousse

For this recipe it's helpful to have a pastry bag with a decorative tip. They are quite inexpensive and can be found in housewares stores and some supermarkets.

8 ounces cream cheese

4 ounces smoked salmon, sliced

2 teaspoons freshly squeezed lemon juice

1 tablespoon minced fresh dill

Salt

2 large heads Belgian endive

1. In a food processor or blender, combine the cream cheese, salmon, lemon juice, and dill. Puree until very smooth. Season to taste with salt and puree to blend.

2. Place the decorative tip of your choice in the end of a pastry bag. Fill the bag with mousse, twist the bag closed, and cover the tip with a bit of plastic wrap to make it airtight.

3. Separate the leaves from the heads of endive, rinse well, and pat dry with paper towels. Remove the plastic wrap from the bag of mousse and pipe the mousse down the length of each leaf. Arrange on a platter, cover lightly with plastic wrap, and refrigerate. Serve well chilled.

TO MAKE AHEAD

One day before serving: Prepare salmon mousse.

One hour before serving: Pipe mousse on endive leaves, arrange on platter, and refrigerate.

Asparagus Salad with Walnut Oil

This salad is also very good with hazelnut or other strongly flavored nut oils. It isn't necessary for the oil to be made from the same kind of nut that is chopped for the salad.

1½ pounds fresh asparagus spears,
   trimmed of woody ends

2 tablespoons walnut oil

1 tablespoon red wine vinegar

1 tablespoon finely diced red bell
   pepper

2 teaspoons minced shallots

Salt and freshly ground black pepper

2 or 3 tablespoons finely chopped
   walnuts, pecans, or hazelnuts

Parmigiano-Reggiano cheese curls
   (see Note)

1. In a vegetable steamer or in a pot with 1 or 2 inches of water, steam the asparagus until the color changes to bright green and it takes on a bit of tenderness. Be careful not to overcook. Drain, rinse with cold water to stop the cooking, and drain again.

2. In a small bowl, combine the walnut oil, vinegar, red bell pepper, and shallots. Season with salt and pepper to taste. Place the asparagus in a flat dish and pour the dressing over it, tossing gently to coat the spears well. Cover and refrigerate or set aside at room temperature.

3. Remove from the refrigerator in time to lessen the chill. (The salad may be served lightly chilled, at room temperature, or slightly warm.) Place equal portions on serving plates and garnish each serving with a sprinkling of nuts and some curls of Parmigiano-Reggiano.

TO MAKE AHEAD

Up to two hours before serving: Steam and dress asparagus. Cover and refrigerate or set aside
   at room temperature.

Shortly before serving: Arrange salad on plates and garnish with chopped nuts and
   Parmigiano-Reggiano.

NOTE: Use a vegetable peeler to make curls of Parmigiano-Reggiano. Don't worry if the curls break; long shreds are just as decorative. Alternatively, a microplane grater will produce tiny flakes of cheese that can be sprinkled on the asparagus and around the edge of the plate.

Braised Lamb Shanks with Apricot Curry Sauce

You can adjust the flavor of this dish by the kind of dried apricots you choose. Turkish apricots, the kind commonly sold in supermarkets, are sweet with just a hint of tang. California apricots, available in specialty food markets, have a much more assertive, tart flavor. Either kind will work well in this recipe adapted from chef Charlie Trotter.

1½ cups small diced dried apricots

3 teaspoons hot curry powder

1 cup rice wine vinegar

2 tablespoons Dijon mustard

8 lamb shanks (12 to 16 ounces each), bones cracked

⅓ cup grapeseed, canola, or other unflavored oil

4 carrots, peeled, cut in 1½-inch chunks

4 stalks celery, cut in 1½-inch chunks

2 Spanish onions, peeled, cut in 1½-inch chunks

2 red, green, or yellow peppers, cored, seeded, and diced

16 large cloves garlic, peeled

2 sprigs fresh thyme, and more for garnish

4 bay leaves

1 teaspoon black peppercorns

1. In a blender, combine the apricots, curry powder, vinegar, mustard, and 2 cups water. Purée until smooth, about 3 minutes. Place the lamb shanks in a glass or other nonreactive dish and add the apricot sauce. Turn to coat the lamb well. Cover and refrigerate overnight, turning the meat occasionally.

2. Preheat the oven to 275 degrees. Place a large, deep, heavy sauté pan over medium-high heat and add 3 tablespoons oil. Remove the lamb from the marinade, reserv-

ing the liquid. Working in batches, brown the lamb, turning it often to prevent burning. Transfer to a platter. Add the remaining oil to the pan. Add the carrots, celery, onions, bell peppers, and garlic. Sauté over medium heat until softened but not browned, about 10 minutes. Transfer the vegetables to a large roasting pan.

3. Place the lamb shanks on the vegetables and add the thyme sprig, bay leaves, peppercorns, and all but 1 cup marinade. Add water to come up almost to the top of the pan. Lay a sheet of parchment paper over the pan and carefully transfer to the oven. Braise until the meat is so tender it almost falls off the bone, 5 to 6 hours. Remove the pan from the oven. Transfer the meat to a platter and allow to cool, then cover and refrigerate overnight. Strain the cooking liquid, discarding the solids. Cover and refrigerate overnight.

4. Preheat the oven to 300 degrees. Place the lamb in a roasting pan, brush with the remaining marinade, and return to the oven to crisp. Place the cooking liquid in a sauté pan and cook over high heat, reducing it by four-fifths. To serve, place the lamb on plates and spoon some cooking liquid around and over. Garnish each plate with a sprig of thyme.

WINES: Sauvignon Blanc (ideally, Steiermark), Crozes-Hermitage (preferably red), Brunello di Montalcino

TO MAKE AHEAD
Two days ahead: Marinate lamb and refrigerate overnight.
One day before serving: Brown lamb, then braise. Reduce cooking liquid. Refrigerate overnight.
Thirty minutes before serving: Preheat oven. Reheat sauce. Bake lamb until reheated. Serve hot.

Toasted Crushed Potatoes

Crushing potatoes before baking them gives them nicely browned edges.

Salt
8 large Yukon Gold or other baking potatoes, peeled and halved
¼ cup extra-virgin olive oil, or as needed
Hot Hungarian paprika
Fleur de sel or other large-crystal sea salt

1. Bring a large pot of lightly salted water to a boil. Add the potatoes, boil until tender, and drain well. Place in a large bowl and crush lightly with a potato masher. Allow to cool, cover, and refrigerate.

2. Preheat the oven to 400 degrees. Spread the potatoes evenly in a baking dish. Brush with olive oil and sprinkle with hot paprika and sea salt to taste. Bake until the edges of the potatoes are browned, about 20 minutes. Serve hot.

TO MAKE AHEAD

Up to twenty-four hours before serving: Boil potatoes, crush, cool, and refrigerate.
Thirty minutes before serving: Brush with oil and bake until browned.

Chocolate-Coffee Crème Brûlée

Adapted from chef Christian Delouvrier.

FOR THE CHOCOLATE CUSTARD:
3½ tablespoons sugar
1 tablespoon plus 1 teaspoon unsweetened cocoa powder
1 cup heavy cream
2 large egg yolks
¼ vanilla bean, halved lengthwise, seeds scraped out and reserved

FOR THE COFFEE CUSTARD:
2 large egg yolks
2½ tablespoons granulated sugar
1 tablespoon instant coffee
1 cup heavy cream
¼ vanilla bean, halved lengthwise, seeds scraped out and reserved
3 tablespoons extra-fine granulated sugar

1. *Prepare the chocolate custard:* Whisk together 2 tablespoons sugar and the cocoa in a small bowl. Bring the cream to a simmer in a small saucepan. Add the cocoa mixture and whisk well. Return to a simmer, then turn off the heat and let cool.

2. In a medium bowl, whisk together the egg yolks, remaining 1½ tablespoons sugar, and vanilla bean scraping with seeds. Whisk in the cooled cream mixture. Strain the custard

through a fine sieve and divide among eight 4-ounce ramekins or custard cups. Cover with plastic and freeze overnight.

3. Preheat the oven to 350 degrees.

4. *Prepare the coffee custard:* In a medium bowl, whisk together the egg yolks, sugar, and instant coffee until the coffee dissolves. Whisk in the cream and vanilla bean scraping with seeds. Strain the mixture and pour it over the frozen chocolate custard in the ramekins.

5. Arrange the ramekins in a baking pan and place the pan in the oven. Pour enough very hot water into the pan to reach two-thirds of the way up the sides of the ramekins. Cover the baking pan with foil and prick it in a few places with a knife. Bake the custards for 40 to 45 minutes, until set around the edges but still slightly jiggly in the center. Transfer to a rack and let cool. Cover and refrigerate overnight.

6. Just before serving, sprinkle a thin, even coating of extra-fine granulated sugar on each custard. Using a preheated broiler or kitchen blowtorch, caramelize the sugar. It will take about 1 to 2 minutes under a broiler, about 30 seconds with a blowtorch.

WINE: Setúbal

TO MAKE AHEAD

Two days before serving: Make chocolate custard and freeze overnight.
One day before serving: Make coffee custard, bake, and refrigerate overnight.
To serve: Sprinkle with sugar, broil, and serve.

MENU 2

· · · · · · ·

Martini Olives

Some people think that the best part of a martini is the olive.

12 ounces pitted green olives, drained
1 cup vodka or gin
2 tablespoons dry vermouth
1 teaspoon finely grated lemon zest

1. In a small container, mix together the olives, vodka or gin, vermouth, and lemon zest.

2. Cover and refrigerate for 48 hours, mixing once every 12 hours. Serve well chilled.

WINES: Frozen vodka (neat), Beaujolais Blanc, Sherry (Fino, Manzanilla)

TO MAKE AHEAD

Two days before serving: Mix olives with marinade, cover, and refrigerate.

Caramelized Onion, Leek, and Fresh Thyme Tart

Italian 00 flour can be found where baking supplies are sold and in specialty food markets. It is worth looking for because it will produce a pliable yet flaky crust. It may be ordered from King Arthur Flour (Resources, page 267).

1½ cups Italian 00 flour
Salt
¼ pound (1 stick) plus 1 tablespoon unsalted butter
¼ cup cold milk
2 tablespoons extra-virgin olive oil
2 onions, peeled and thinly sliced
2 leeks, white and light green parts only, thinly sliced into rings, washed, and dried
2 teaspoons chopped fresh thyme
Freshly ground black pepper

1. In a large bowl, combine the flour and ½ teaspoon salt. Using a pastry blender or 2 knives, cut in ¼ pound butter until the mixture resembles bread crumbs. Stir the milk in with a fork until the dough is cohesive. Shape into a ball, cover with plastic wrap, and refrigerate overnight.

2. Preheat the oven to 400 degrees. Roll out the dough slightly larger than a 10-inch tart pan. Fit the dough into the pan and trim the edges. Prick the dough all over with a fork and bake until light golden brown, about 12 minutes. Remove from the heat and allow to cool.

3. Place a large nonstick skillet over low heat and add 1 tablespoon butter and the olive oil. When the butter has melted, add the onions and leeks. Sauté until softened and golden in color, about 20 minutes.

4. Preheat the oven again to 400 degrees. Add the thyme to the onion and leek mixture, and season with salt and pepper to taste. Spread the mixture evenly in the baked tart shell. Place the tart in the oven just to heat through, 1 to 2 minutes. Serve warm.

WINES: Rioja (white or red), Chardonnay de Pays d'Oc, Merlot (Chile)

The night before serving: Prepare dough, wrap, and refrigerate.
One to two hours before serving: Bake tart shell. Caramelize onions. Assemble tart.
To serve: Preheat oven. Heat tart.

Duck Gumbo

This recipe is time-consuming, but all the work can be done a day or two ahead of time. Adapted from Steve Manning from Bayou in New York City.

1/4 teaspoon cayenne pepper	1 small carrot, finely chopped
3/4 teaspoon ground black pepper	1 bunch scallions, chopped
2 1/2 teaspoons paprika	1 tablespoon chopped Italian
1 teaspoon kosher salt	(flat-leaf) parsley
One 5-pound duck	Juice of 1/2 lemon
1 medium Spanish onion, cut in	1/4 teaspoon ground allspice
1/2-inch dice	1 teaspoon dried oregano
1 carrot, cut in 1/2-inch dice	1 teaspoon dried thyme
3 celery stalks, cut in 1/2-inch dice	3 bay leaves
2 quarts chicken broth	4 tablespoons tomato paste
1 large red bell pepper, cut in	1/2 cup flour
medium dice	1/2 cup canola oil
3 cloves garlic, minced	3 cups trimmed and sliced okra

1. Preheat the oven to 400 degrees. Combine the cayenne, 1/2 teaspoon pepper, 1/2 teaspoon paprika, and salt, and sprinkle liberally over the duck. Arrange the diced onion, diced carrot, and 1 diced stalk of celery in a roasting pan. Place the duck on a rack in the pan. Roast for 1 1/2 hours.

2. Transfer the duck to a platter and pour off and reserve about 3 tablespoons duck fat. Remove the duck meat from the bones and reserve the bones. Cover and refrigerate both the duck meat and the duck fat.

3. Place the bones in a large stockpot and add the broth and 1 quart water. Place over medium-low heat and simmer for 1 hour. Allow to cool, then strain, cover, and refrigerate overnight.

4. Heat 1 tablespoon duck fat in a large skillet over medium heat. Add the bell pep-

per, remaining 2 diced stalks of chopped celery, garlic, carrot, scallions, parsley, lemon juice, remaining 2 teaspoons paprika, allspice, remaining ¼ teaspoon pepper, oregano, thyme, and bay leaves. Sauté until soft, about 8 minutes. Stir in the tomato paste. Remove from the heat and set aside at room temperature.

5. Whisk the flour and oil together in a heavy-bottomed pot and simmer over moderate heat, whisking constantly, until the mixture turns chocolate brown, about 20 minutes. Set aside.

6. Place the stock in a large pot and add water to make a total of 3 quarts of liquid. Bring to a boil and vigorously whisk in the browned flour, 1 spoonful at a time, until the liquid thickens. Add the vegetable mixture. Simmer for 30 minutes. Remove from the heat and allow to cool. Add the duck meat and refrigerate overnight.

7. Remove the gumbo from the refrigerator and transfer to a large pot. Reheat gently over medium-low heat. Meanwhile, in a large skillet, melt 1 tablespoon duck fat over medium-low heat. Fry the okra gently about 15 minutes, turning often to avoid scorching. When the okra is crisp, drain on paper towels and add to the gumbo. Serve hot.

WINES: Grüner Veltliner, Ramitello (red), Syrah

TO MAKE AHEAD
Two days before serving: Roast duck. Remove duck meat and refrigerate. Make duck broth. Strain and refrigerate overnight.
The day before serving: Sauté vegetables and finish stock. Simmer, then allow to cool. Add chilled duck meat and refrigerate overnight.
Twenty minutes before serving: Reheat gumbo. Fry okra until crisp. Add to gumbo and serve.

Garlicky Rice

This rice takes about twenty-five minutes to prepare.

3 tablespoons butter
1 tablespoon olive oil
4 cloves garlic, peeled and minced
3 cups long-grain rice
6 cups chicken broth

1. Place a large saucepan over medium-low heat and add the butter and olive oil. When the butter has melted, add the garlic and stir until translucent; do not allow it to brown.

2. Add the rice and stir until well coated with oil, about 1 minute. Stir in the broth, cover, and simmer until the liquid is absorbed, about 15 minutes. Remove from the heat and allow to rest, covered, for 5 minutes before serving.

Georgia Pecan
Cream Cheese Pound Cake

Adapted from Gwen Arrendale, Arrendale Farm, Quitman, Georgia.

¾ pound (3 sticks) unsalted butter, soft, in pieces
2 tablespoons all-purpose flour
8 ounces cream cheese
3 cups sugar
6 large eggs
1½ teaspoons vanilla extract
½ teaspoon almond extract
3 cups cake flour
1½ cups finely chopped pecans

1. Preheat the oven to 325 degrees. Use a little butter to grease a 10-inch tube pan. Dust with flour and shake out the excess.

2. Place the remaining butter and the cream cheese in an electric mixer and beat briefly to combine. Add the sugar and beat at medium-low speed until light and fluffy, about 5 minutes. Beat in the eggs, 1 at a time. Stir in the vanilla and almond extracts.

3. Add the cake flour, about ½ cup at a time, beating at the lowest speed to blend it in until there is only about ¼ cup flour remaining. Toss the pecans with this flour and then fold them into the batter by hand.

4. Spoon the batter into the pan, smooth the top, and rap the pan once or twice on the counter top to even it. Bake about 1 hour and 45 minutes, until the top is golden brown, the cake begins to shrink from the sides of the pan, and a cake tester inserted in the middle comes out clean.

5. Allow to cool on a rack for 40 minutes, then remove from the pan to finish cooling. When the cake is completely cool, cover with plastic wrap and refrigerate for up to 2 days. Alternatively, wrap securely in freezer wrap and freeze for up to 1 month. Bring to room temperature before serving.

WINE: Muscat de Beaumes-de-Venise

TO MAKE AHEAD
May be stored, covered and refrigerated, for up to two days, or frozen for up to one month. Serve at room temperature.

MENU 3

. . . .

Banderillas

Banderilla *is a Spanish word meaning spike or spear. For this recipe you will need skewers several inches long. Short bamboo skewers may be found at many supermarkets, and decorative skewers may be found in Asian markets, specialty food stores, and mail-order catalogs. Bandilleras require no cooking and can be assembled shortly before serving.*

Cherry tomatoes

Tiny fresh mozzarella balls

Sun-dried tomato halves packed in oil

Fresh basil leaves

Cooked shrimp, chilled

Rolled anchovies

Soppressata (dry cured salami)

Melon balls or cubes

White asparagus, steamed, chilled, and cut into 2-inch pieces

Chunks of canned or cooked fresh tuna, chilled

Skewers 3 to 4 inches long

1. Alternate any of the ingredients on the skewers, matching flavors as desired. For example: shrimp, folded basil leaf, sun-dried tomato, asparagus, rolled anchovy.

2. Arrange the filled skewers on a plate. Serve immediately or cover and refrigerate until needed.

Arugula Salad with Sweet Onion and Chèvre

Try this salad with different kinds of vinegars, such as fig-flavored balsamic or orange-infused white wine vinegar.

> 1½ pounds baby arugula leaves
> 1 Vidalia or other sweet onion, peeled, halved root-to-stem,
>   and very thinly sliced
> 1 pint ripe grape tomatoes, or cherry tomatoes, halved
> 8 ounces chèvre cheese
> 2 tablespoons best-quality extra-virgin olive oil
> 1½ tablespoons Jerez (sherry) vinegar
> Salt and coarsely ground black pepper

1. In a large mixing bowl, combine the arugula, onion, and tomatoes. Toss, cover tightly, and refrigerate.

2. Using a small knife, cut small dollops of chèvre into the salad. Toss lightly to mix. Drizzle the salad with olive oil and vinegar, and season to taste with salt and pepper. Toss again and serve.

Loin of Pork Stuffed
with Prunes

Adapted from the New York City restaurant Lespinasse.

2 cups pitted prunes

1 cup Armagnac

One 5½-pound loin of pork, boned

Salt and freshly ground black pepper

4 tablespoons duck fat or vegetable oil

1 carrot, finely diced

1 medium-size onion, finely diced

3 cloves garlic, crushed

½ cup dry white wine

2 medium-size ripe tomatoes, diced

1 sprig thyme

1 bay leaf

2 cups veal or chicken stock

1. Place the prunes in a bowl, add the Armagnac, cover, and refrigerate.

2. Make a deep cut lengthwise down the middle of the pork. Spread the meat out flat like a book. Season with salt and pepper. Drain the prunes well, reserving the Armagnac for another use. Place the prunes in a double layer down the center of the pork. Close the meat over them and tie at 1½-inch intervals with butcher's twine. Dust with salt and pepper.

3. Heat the oven to 400 degrees. In a large, heavy skillet or casserole, preferably enameled cast iron, add the duck fat. Sear the meat over medium-high heat until lightly browned on all sides. Remove the meat and reduce the heat to low. Add the carrot, onion, and garlic, and cook until softened but not browned. Add the wine and reduce by half. Stir in the tomatoes, thyme, and bay leaf.

4. Return the meat to the pan and add the veal stock. Bring to a simmer and then place the pan in the oven. Cook for 30 minutes, basting every 10 minutes. Lower the heat to 325 degrees, turn the meat, and continue cooking about 1 hour more, basting every 10 to 15 minutes. Add water as needed to keep 1 inch of liquid in the pan.

5. Remove from the oven. Place the meat on a cutting board and tent with foil to keep warm. Gently simmer the liquid in the pan for 5 minutes or so, then force it through a sieve into a saucepan. Season to taste with salt and pepper.

6. Slice the pork and arrange it on a platter. Reheat the sauce, spoon a little over the meat, and pass the rest alongside.

WINES: Duoro (red), Pacherenc du Vic Bilh (dry or semi-dry), Riesling Spätlese

TO MAKE AHEAD
Two days before serving: Soak prunes in Armagnac.
Two and a half hours before serving: Stuff pork with prunes, sear, and bake for 1½ hours. Reduce sauce and sieve.

Roasted Butternut Squash with Pumpkin Seed Oil

Pumpkin seed oil has an astonishingly rich flavor and a fragrance to match. It can be found in specialty food stores or ordered by mail.

> 2 pounds butternut squash, cut in chunks (often available already seeded and peeled in supermarkets)
> 2 tablespoons pumpkin seed oil (available in specialty food stores)
> Salt and freshly ground black pepper

1. Preheat the oven to 400 degrees. Place the squash in a roasting pan or baking dish large enough to hold the pieces in a single layer (see Note). Rub the squash all over with the oil and season to taste with salt and pepper.
2. Roast until the squash is tender and the surface is browned and caramelized, 20 to 30 minutes. Transfer to a warm dish and serve.

NOTE: A heavy metal pan is preferable for roasting squash because it will conduct heat evenly and brown the squash nicely. If you do not have two ovens and can't fit a metal pan into the same oven as the pork for this menu, you can crowd the squash into a small ceramic or glass baking dish. It won't brown as well but will still be delicious.

Zabaglione with Strawberries
and Balsamic Meringue

Balsamic vinegar, which is naturally fruity and sweet, is often paired with strawberries. This recipe is adapted from David Pasternack of Esca in New York City.

10 large eggs, separated into whites and yolks, at room temperature
Pinch of salt
1 cup confectioners' sugar, sifted
2 teaspoons plus 2 tablespoons aged balsamic vinegar (at least 12 years old)
1 teaspoon vanilla extract
1 cup granulated sugar, or to taste
⅔ cup prosecco or champagne
1½ cups heavy cream
1 quart ripe strawberries, rinsed, hulled, and diced

1. Heat the oven to 250 degrees. Line a baking sheet with parchment paper.

2. Using an electric mixer, beat the egg whites with salt until very foamy. Add the confectioners' sugar gradually and continue beating until stiff and shiny. Beat in 1 teaspoon vinegar and the vanilla. Spread the meringue about ½ inch thick on the parchment paper. Place in oven and bake for 2 hours. Turn off the oven and allow the meringue to cool in oven at least 1 hour, until crisp. Break into bite-sized pieces. Place in an airtight container and store in a dry place until ready to use.

3. Have a large pot of simmering water 1 to 2 inches deep on the stove. The pot should be able to hold a large metal mixing bowl without the bowl's touching the water. Have a large bowl of ice water ready.

4. Place the egg yolks in a mixing bowl away from the heat. Add ½ cup granulated sugar and beat with a large balloon whisk about 3 minutes, until the yolks have lightened in color and start to thicken. Place the mixing bowl in the pot of simmering water. Gradually add the prosecco and continue beating until the yolks have thickened to a custard, 10 to 15 minutes. When the custard is very thick and the whisk leaves a trace in the bottom of the bowl, place the mixing bowl in the bowl of ice water to cool. Transfer to a covered container and refrigerate.

5. Beat the cream just until it holds peaks. Fold it into the custard and refrigerate.

6. Sweeten the strawberries with ½ cup granulated sugar, or to taste. Fold in the remaining vinegar. Divide the strawberries among 8 old-fashioned glasses or goblets. Top with

the crumbled meringue and then with the zabaglione. Garnish with a few pieces of crumbled meringue and serve.

WINE: Vin Santo

TO MAKE AHEAD
Up to one week before serving: Make and store meringue.
Two days before serving: Make custard, cover, and refrigerate.
Up to four hours before serving: Whip cream and fold into custard. Refrigerate.
To serve: Sweeten strawberries. Assemble layers of strawberries, zabaglione, and meringue in glasses.

MENU 4

. . . .

Chilled Herbed Mussels
on the Half Shell

These mussels can be arranged on a platter, covered, and refrigerated for up to several hours before serving. If you wish, finely shredded lettuce or rock salt can be spread across the platter first to help keep the mussels in place.

FOR THE MUSSELS:

2 tablespoons olive oil

2 shallots, peeled and chopped

1 clove garlic, peeled and chopped

2 pounds rope-grown mussels (see page 225)

1 cup dry white wine

FOR THE VINAIGRETTE:

1 tablespoon champagne vinegar or cider vinegar

½ teaspoon Dijon mustard

1½ tablespoons extra-virgin olive oil

1 tablespoon finely chopped fresh tarragon leaves

¹/₂ teaspoon finely chopped fresh mint leaves
Salt and freshly ground black pepper

Fresh herb sprigs for garnish

1. *Prepare the mussels:* Place a large, wide pot over medium heat. Add 1 tablespoon olive oil, shallots, and garlic. Sauté until the shallots are tender, 1 to 2 minutes. Add the mussels and wine. Cover and steam the mussels just until they open, checking frequently so as not to overcook them. Remove from the heat, drain, and allow to cool.

2. Remove the mussels from the shells, placing them in a small container and reserving one side of each shell (discard the other side). Cover the container of mussels and refrigerate. Rinse the reserved shells and place them in a large bowl. Drizzle with the remaining 1 tablespoon olive oil and toss until all the shells are covered with it. Transfer the shells to an airtight plastic bag and refrigerate.

3. *Prepare the vinaigrette:* In a small mixing bowl, combine the vinegar and mustard. Whisk vigorously and drizzle in the olive oil. Stir in the tarragon and mint, and season to taste with salt and pepper. Add the vinaigrette to the mussels and toss until the mussels are coated. Cover and refrigerate.

4. Place each mussel in an oiled shell half and arrange the mussels decoratively on a platter. Garnish the platter with fresh herbs. Serve chilled.

WINES: Gros Plant du Pays Nantais, Sauvignon Blanc (Chile), Verdicchio dei Castelli di Jesi; alternative: Pilsner beer

---

ROPE-GROWN MUSSELS

Mussel larvae float freely in the ocean, eventually attaching themselves to the bottom of the sea or to rocks along the shore. What we know as rope-grown mussels are cultivated mussels grown on ropes that are suspended from rafts. The ropes attract wild-mussel larvae, which attach themselves and feed off microscopic plankton in the ocean water. The mussels are harvested from the ropes after about eighteen months, when they are mature. Some mussel farmers raise mussel larvae in hatcheries, later attaching them to ropes with narrow tubular nets.

Because rope-grown mussels are suspended above the sandy bottom of the ocean, they are free of sand and grit, unlike bottom-cultured or wild mussels.

One day before serving: Steam mussels and remove from shells. Refrigerate mussels and half of mussel shells.

On serving day: Prepare herbed vinaigrette. Toss with mussels and refrigerate. Arrange shells on a platter with a mussel in each one.

Asparagus and Brie in Puff Pastry

I was served a dish similar to this at a wine-tasting dinner and thought it was an ingenious combination. I especially like the way the asparagus spears are inserted in the center of the pastry. Do not use thin asparagus because it will cook too quickly and begin to brown.

> All-purpose flour
> One 1-pound package puff pastry (containing two 8-ounce sheets of dough)
> 16 asparagus spears, medium thickness, trimmed
> 8 ounces Brie cheese, cut into 8 pieces of equal size

1. On a lightly floured surface, roll out each rectangle of dough to a thickness of about ⅛ inch. Cut each rectangle into 4 equal pieces. Dust the pieces with flour and stack, placing a sheet of waxed paper between them. Place in a sealed plastic bag and refrigerate.

2. Place the asparagus spears in a bowl of water and set aside.

3. Preheat the oven to 400 degrees. Remove the dough from the refrigerator. Place a rectangle of dough on a lightly floured surface and put a piece of Brie in the center. Place 2 spears of asparagus on the cheese, pressing them in slightly to help them stand upright. Bring up the sides of the dough around the bottom of the spears to make a bunched purse with the spears sticking out from the center. Pinch the dough around the spears so that it holds its shape. Place on a baking sheet and repeat to make a total of 8 purses.

4. Bake until the puff pastry is risen and golden, about 10 minutes. Serve immediately.

WINES: More Pilsner, or Kriek; Sparkling (extra dry), Beaujolais (lightly chilled)

TO MAKE AHEAD

Two hours before serving: Roll, cut, and stack pastry squares; refrigerate. Wash and trim asparagus spears.

Thirty minutes before serving: Preheat oven. Assemble pastry, cheese, and asparagus. Bake.

Curried Scallops
with Tomatoes

This recipe by The New York Times *columnist Mark Bittman is a favorite that I make on a regular basis. Although tomatoes aren't at their best in winter, cooking them in curried cream makes the most of their flavor. Lime juice keeps the creaminess from being overwhelming.*

6 medium ripe tomatoes
2 tablespoons peanut or vegetable oil
3 to 4 pounds large sea scallops
Salt and freshly ground black pepper
¼ cup curry powder
1 cup heavy cream, sour cream, or yogurt
Juice of 2 limes
1 cup chopped fresh cilantro or basil leaves

1. Core the tomatoes (cut a cone-shaped wedge out of the stem end), then squeeze and shake out the seeds. Chop the flesh into ½-inch pieces. Cover and refrigerate.

2. Heat the oil in a 12-inch nonstick skillet over medium heat about 3 minutes. While the oil is heating, place the scallops in a large mixing bowl and season with salt and pepper to taste. Toss gently. Sprinkle the scallops with the curry powder and toss until evenly coated. When the oil is hot, add the scallops to the pan. When the undersides of the scallops are nicely browned, about 2 minutes, turn the scallops and cook 1 minute more.

3. Add the tomatoes and cream. (If using yogurt, lower the heat and do not allow it to boil.) Simmer until the tomatoes are heated through, about 1 minute. Adjust the salt and pepper to taste and sprinkle with the lime juice. Add the cilantro and toss to mix. Serve immediately.

WINES: Sauvignon Blanc (Chile, from first course), Pinot Noir, Chablis

TO MAKE AHEAD
Up to four hours before serving: Core, seed, and chop tomatoes. Cover and refrigerate.
Ten minutes before serving: Season scallops. Sear in skillet, add tomatoes and cream, and
    cook. Add seasonings and cilantro.

Jasmine Rice with
Lemon and Parsley

3 cups jasmine rice

1 tablespoon finely grated lemon zest

2 tablespoons minced parsley leaves (see Note)

1. Place 5 cups water in a large saucepan. Bring to a boil over medium-high heat and add the rice. Reduce the heat to very low and simmer until the water is absorbed, about 15 minutes. Stir the lemon zest into the hot rice, cover, and allow to sit until completely cool. Transfer to an airtight container and refrigerate.

2. Place the rice in a large saucepan. Sprinkle with ¼ cup water, cover, and place over very low heat until reheated. Stir once during heating, adding another tablespoon of water if the mixture seems too dry. Add the parsley, remove from the heat, and keep warm until serving.

NOTE: Flat-leaf parsley, also known as Italian parsley, is generally considered the best parsley for cooking. Curly parsley, though used primarily as a decorative garnish, is not as flavorless as many make it out to be. In this recipe either parsley may be used.

Chocolate Fantasy Tart

This recipe is adapted from Nicky Morse, who is the private chef for a family of professional car racers. This is a beautiful tart with a glossy coat of icing, and the flavor actually improves if the tart is made a day or two before serving.

FOR THE DOUGH:

Nonstick spray for pan

1 cup all-purpose flour

¼ cup light brown sugar

¼ cup finely ground pecans

½ ounce unsweetened chocolate, finely grated

½ ounce semisweet chocolate, grated

9 tablespoons (1 stick plus 1 tablespoon) chilled butter, cubed

2 tablespoons whole milk

1 teaspoon vanilla extract

1 teaspoon Kahlúa

FOR THE BATTER:

3 ounces unsweetened chocolate

3 ounces semisweet chocolate

¼ pound (1 stick) butter, cubed, at room temperature

1½ cups sugar

3 large eggs, well beaten

¾ cup all-purpose flour

FOR THE ICING:

5 tablespoons unsalted butter

3 tablespoons heavy cream

2 tablespoons whole milk

3½ tablespoons sugar

3½ ounces semisweet chocolate, finely chopped

1½ ounces unsweetened chocolate, finely chopped

1. *Prepare the dough:* Coat an 1½-inch tart pan (with removable bottom) with non-stick spray. In a large bowl, combine the flour, brown sugar, pecans, unsweetened chocolate, and semisweet chocolate. Cut in the butter until the mixture resembles coarse meal. Add the milk, vanilla, and Kahlúa, and mix just until blended. Pat the dough evenly into the pan and set aside.

2. *Prepare the batter:* Preheat the oven to 350 degrees. In a double boiler, melt the unsweetened chocolate and semisweet chocolate. Add butter a little at a time, stirring to mix. Remove from the heat. Add the sugar and mix well; the mixture will be granular. Add the eggs, 1 at a time, mixing well after each addition. Add the flour and mix well. Pour into the pastry shell. Bake until a toothpick in the center comes out clean, 40 to 45 minutes. Cool to room temperature.

3. *Prepare the icing:* In a medium saucepan, combine the butter, cream, milk, and sugar. Bring to a simmer and immediately remove from the heat. Slowly add the semisweet chocolate and unsweetened chocolate, stirring slowly with a wooden spoon. Pour evenly over the pie and allow to rest until set; the icing will be slightly soft when set. Cover with foil or plastic wrap (do not allow the wrap to rest on the icing) or place in an airtight pie container. Refrigerate.

WINE: Maury

TO MAKE AHEAD

Two hours to two days before serving: Prepare dough and pat into pan. Prepare batter and pour into pastry. Bake and cool. Prepare icing, pour onto pie, and cool. Cover and refrigerate.

MENU 5

. . . .

Roasted Cauliflower with Lemon, Capers, and Olives

In this recipe, adapted from Babbo and Otto chef Mario Batali, browned, tender cauliflower has a richness not normally associated with this vegetable.

1 large head cauliflower, cut into large florets
Kosher salt and freshly ground black pepper
2 cups best-quality olive oil, or as needed
Grated zest of 2 lemons
3 cloves garlic, peeled and green germ removed
2 tablespoons fresh thyme leaves
2 tablespoons salt-cured capers, rinsed well and drained
¼ cup pitted Kalamata olives
Lemon olive oil or freshly squeezed lemon juice for sprinkling

1. Preheat the oven to 375 degrees. Place the cauliflower in a large bowl and season to taste with salt and pepper. Toss by hand to distribute the seasonings. Add about ½ cup olive oil and toss again until the florets are well coated; add more oil if needed. Spread the

cauliflower on a baking sheet and roast until browned and tender, 30 to 35 minutes. Rotate the baking sheet halfway through. Remove from the heat and allow to cool.

2. While the cauliflower is roasting, combine the lemon zest, garlic, thyme, and 1 cup olive oil in a small saucepan. Place the pan over medium-low heat until bubbles form on the edge; do not boil. Cook until the garlic is soft, about 20 minutes, then remove from the heat and allow to cool. Pour the cooled mixture in a blender and blend on the lowest speed to puree.

3. In a separate small saucepan, combine the capers, olives, and ½ cup olive oil. Warm over medium-low heat for 5 minutes. Transfer the cauliflower to a large serving bowl. Pour about half of the lemon-garlic oil over it and toss gently to coat. (Reserve the remainder for another use.) Add the caper-olive oil mixture and toss once more. Adjust the salt and pepper to taste. Cover and refrigerate.

4. Transfer the cauliflower mixture to a decorative platter and allow to come to room temperature. Just before serving, sprinkle with lemon olive oil or lemon juice to taste.

WINES: Sparkling or Champagne (demi-sec), Chenin Blanc (South Africa), Savoie (white)

TO MAKE AHEAD

Up to one day before serving: Roast cauliflower. Make seasoned oil. Combine cauliflower and oil with capers and olives. Refrigerate.

To serve: Bring to room temperature. Sprinkle with lemon olive oil or lemon juice.

Involtini

This is one of my favorite recipes from Nigella Lawson. It can be made ahead of time and only needs to be put in the oven shortly before guests arrive. Pine nuts and raisins give just the right piquancy to the filling, and nonvegetarians will never notice the absence of meat.

3 large eggplants (about 1 pound each), trimmed and cut lengthwise
into ¼-inch thick slices (about 16 slices total)
¾ cup olive oil, or as needed
8 ounces feta cheese, crumbled
½ cup pine nuts
⅓ cup raisins, soaked in hot water for 10 minutes and then drained
¼ cup extra-virgin olive oil, plus additional for drizzling

2 tablespoons bread crumbs

1 clove garlic, peeled and minced

Finely grated zest of 1 lemon

1½ teaspoons dried mint

2 tablespoons chopped Italian (flat-leaf) parsley

1 large egg, beaten

Salt and freshly ground black pepper

2½ cups canned crushed tomatoes, drained

3 large balls fresh mozzarella cheese, cut into ¼-inch slices

1. Place a heavy skillet over medium-high heat. Working in batches, brush the eggplant slices on both sides with olive oil and cook, turning, until soft. Set aside and allow to cool.

2. In a large bowl, combine the feta, pine nuts, raisins, extra-virgin olive oil, bread crumbs, garlic, lemon zest, mint, and parsley. Mix in the egg and season to taste with salt and pepper.

3. Spread the eggplant slices on a work surface and divide the stuffing evenly among them, placing 1 or 2 tablespoons at one end of each slice. Roll up the slices tightly to secure the filling and place in a 9 × 13-inch baking dish or other shallow baking pan in which the rolls fit snugly in a single layer. Pour on the crushed tomatoes. Arrange the mozzarella slices in 3 rows lengthwise down the pan. Drizzle olive oil evenly over the pan and season to taste with salt and pepper. Cover and refrigerate.

4. Preheat the oven to 375 degrees. Bake, uncovered, until the cheese has melted and the eggplant is bubbling and fragrant, 25 to 30 minutes. Remove from the heat and allow to stand for 5 to 10 minutes. Serve hot.

WINES: Gamay (United States), Bardolino, Bourgueil

TO MAKE AHEAD

One to six hours before serving: Fry eggplant and make filling. Assemble involtini and top with tomato and cheese. Refrigerate.

One hour before serving: Preheat oven. Bake involtini.

Escarole with Pan-Roasted Garlic

The secret to this recipe is in cooking the garlic very slowly over low heat so it becomes very soft and sweet. Do not be impatient; if the garlic browns, it will be bitter. You can make this easy recipe even easier by slicing, rinsing, and drying the escarole a few hours ahead of time. Store in a sealed bag in the refrigerator until needed.

2 medium heads escarole
8 to 10 cloves garlic, peeled
⅓ cup extra-virgin olive oil
Juice of ½ lemon, or to taste
½ lemon, cut into 6 wedges

1. Slice the escarole crosswise into ribbons about 1½ inches wide. Rinse the escarole well, drain, and pat dry with paper towels. Set aside. Halve lengthwise any large cloves of garlic; the cloves should be of uniform size. Set aside.

2. Place a large (12 inches or larger) sauté pan over medium-low heat and add the olive oil. When the oil is warmed, reduce the heat to as low as possible. Add the garlic and toss to coat well with oil. Cook, partially covered and stirring occasionally, until the garlic is translucent and very tender, about 25 minutes. Do not allow the garlic to brown, which will cause it to be bitter. It may be desirable to use a "flame-tamer" disk (available in kitchenware stores) over the source of heat.

3. When the garlic is tender, raise the heat to medium-high and immediately add the escarole. Toss the escarole until it is well coated with oil and just begins to wilt, about 1 minute. Add lemon juice to taste and toss again. Add the lemon wedges and toss until the escarole is barely tender and still green, about 2 minutes. Serve immediately.

Apricot Strudel

FOR THE ALMOND CREAM:

¼ cup plus 1 tablespoon sugar

¼ cup finely ground blanched almonds

4 tablespoons unsalted butter, softened

2 tablespoons beaten egg

1 tablespoon flour

FOR ASSEMBLY:

8 sheets filo dough

¼ pound (1 stick) butter, melted

Confectioners' sugar

8 fresh apricots, pitted and quartered

1. *Prepare the almond cream:* In a medium mixing bowl, combine the sugar, almonds, unsalted butter, egg, and flour. Whisk until smooth.

2. *To assemble:* Preheat the oven to 400 degrees. Place a sheet of filo dough on a work surface and brush with melted butter. Sprinkle evenly with confectioners' sugar. Top with another sheet of filo dough, melted butter, and confectioners' sugar. Spoon the almond cream in a narrow strip along one of the narrower edges of the dough. Top the cream with a row of apricot quarters. Starting with this edge topped with apricots, roll the dough to encase the apricots and cream. Repeat to make 3 more rolls.

3. Place the rolls on a baking sheet and brush with melted butter. Sprinkle with confectioners' sugar. Bake until golden brown, 15 to 20 minutes. Cut the rolls into the desired portions and serve warm.

WINES: Cadillac or Botrytised Chardonnay

TO MAKE AHEAD

Up to two hours before serving: Make strudel. Cool, cover tightly, and store at room temperature.

MENU 6

. . . .

Spiced Almonds

1 teaspoon ground fennel

½ teaspoon ground cumin

¼ teaspoon ground coriander

¼ teaspoon cayenne pepper

¼ teaspoon salt

2 tablespoons butter

2 cups whole almonds

2 tablespoons sugar

1. In a small bowl, combine the fennel, cumin, coriander, cayenne, and salt. Place a small skillet over medium-low heat and add the spice mixture. Stir with a wooden spoon until fragrant, about 1 minute.

2. Add the butter, almonds, and sugar, and stir until the sugar melts and the almonds are coated with the seasonings, 1 to 2 minutes. Remove from the heat and transfer the almonds to a plate to cool. Place in an airtight container, breaking apart any almonds that have stuck together. Store at room temperature.

BEVERAGES: Beer, cider, ginger ale

TO MAKE AHEAD

Up to one week ahead: Prepare almonds, cool, and store.

Seared Foie Gras with Caramelized Pears and Balsamic Vinegar

To do justice to this marvelous recipe, use the best-quality balsamic vinegar you can afford.

2 tablespoons grapeseed or other flavorless oil
4 large, firm Bosc pears, peeled, halved, and cored
½ cup honey
Three 3-inch sprigs fresh rosemary, each sprig cut into 3 pieces
⅓ cup port wine
1 large fresh foie gras, very well chilled
Coarse salt and freshly ground white pepper
2 tablespoons aged balsamic vinegar (*balsamico tradizionale*)
8 sprigs fresh thyme

1. Preheat the oven to 450 degrees. Place a large ovenproof sauté pan over medium-high heat and add the oil. When the oil is hot but not smoking, add the pears. Immediately transfer the pan to the oven. Roast the pears, turning often, until they begin to caramelize, about 10 minutes. Stir in the honey and rosemary, and continue to roast until the pears are golden and caramelized on all sides, 6 to 8 minutes more.

2. Transfer the pan to medium heat on the stove top and add the port. Stir briefly to scrape the bottom of the pan and coat the pears with the syrupy mixture. Drain the pears in a colander, discarding the rosemary and cooking liquids.

3. By hand, carefully separate the 2 lobes of the foie gras. If there is any fat at the separation point, trim and discard it. Using a sharp, thin-bladed knife, dipping it into hot water and drying as necessary, cut each lobe of foie gras crosswise into ½-inch-thick slices. Cover the slices snugly with plastic wrap and refrigerate.

4. Preheat the oven to 350 degrees. Remove the foie gras from the refrigerator. Lightly oil a baking sheet, place the pears on it, cut side down, and set aside.

5. Place the pears in the oven briefly while cooking the foie gras. Heat a large non-stick sauté pan over medium-high heat. Season each slice of foie gras with salt and white pepper and, working quickly, slip the slices into the pan. If necessary, work in batches; do not overcrowd the pan. Sauté the slices for 1 minute, then turn them and sauté 1 minute more.

6. To serve, arrange 1 pear half in the center of each of 8 warm plates. Top each pear

half with slices of foie gras and drizzle with about 1 teaspoon balsamic vinegar. Garnish each plate with a sprig of thyme and serve immediately.

WINES: Moscato d'Asti, Riesling Spätlese, Gewürztraminer (Alsace), Sauternes or Barsac

TO MAKE AHEAD

One day before serving: Caramelize pears. Slice foie gras. Cover and refrigerate.

Thirty minutes before serving: Preheat oven. Remove pears and foie gras from refrigerator. Place pears on baking sheet.

Fifteen minutes before serving: Heat pears. Sear foie gras. Arrange on plates and garnish.

Chicken with a Thousand Cloves of Garlic

This is a classic French recipe traditionally called Chicken with Forty Cloves of Garlic, *the name being a charming exaggeration of the number of garlic cloves actually used. I have taught this recipe to children and so have exaggerated the name even further. Children love the idea that they can cook a real dinner for their families. One boy proudly reported that the roasting food smelled so good, the neighbors came over to see what was cooking. Whenever I move to a new house, even if just for a vacation, I make this recipe the first night I am there. The herbed chicken and garlic fill the house with a tantalizing aroma that makes it feel like home.*

> Two 3½- to 4-pound free-range chickens, rinsed and dried
> Salt and freshly ground black pepper
> 2 tablespoons dried thyme leaves
> 2 tablespoons dried rosemary
> 5 tablespoons extra-virgin olive oil
> 2 to 3 heads garlic, cloves separated but not peeled
> Fresh thyme and rosemary sprigs for garnish

1. Preheat the oven to 350 degrees. Place the chickens in a large roasting pan. Season the inside and outside of each chicken with salt and pepper to taste. Sprinkle 1 tablespoon thyme and 1 tablespoon rosemary over each chicken. Pour 2 tablespoons olive oil over each

chicken and rub them well with the mixture, making sure to get some seasonings into the cavity of each bird. Place about 6 cloves unpeeled garlic in each cavity as well.

2. Roast the chickens until the juices run clear when the leg is pierced at the joint, about 1½ hours. After the chickens have roasted for 1 hour, toss the remaining garlic cloves in 1 tablespoon olive oil and add them to the pan.

3. Remove the chickens from the oven and cut them into serving pieces. Arrange on a platter and scatter the roasted garlic cloves on top. Garnish with fresh thyme and rosemary, and serve.

WINES: Continue with Riesling Spätlese or Gewürztraminer, Rioja (red), Chianti Classico, Burgundy (white, red)

TO MAKE AHEAD

Two hours before serving: Preheat oven. Rub chicken with herbs. Roast.
To serve: Slice and arrange on a platter. Garnish.

Roasted Beets

The flavor of fresh roasted beets is much better than canned beets, and the texture is firmer and more appetizing. This recipe works equally well with red or yellow beets. Red beet juice will stain your hands, so wear rubber gloves to peel them or peel them under running water. Baby beets are nice if you can find them, but large beets are also delicious. When you trim the leaves from the beets, remember that they also can be eaten. Use tender baby beet greens in salads; sauté larger leaves in a little olive oil and garlic.

> 8 large fresh beets or 16 small beets, trimmed
> 2 tablespoons extra-virgin olive oil
> 2 tablespoons balsamic vinegar
> Salt and freshly ground black pepper

1. Preheat the oven to 375 degrees. Wrap the beets in foil and place on a baking sheet. Bake until tender when pierced with a knife. This will depend on the size of the beets: Baby beets may take only 30 minutes, while large beets may take as long as 1½ hours. Leave the beets in the foil until ready to peel.

2. To peel the beets, remove them from the foil while they are still very warm. Peel the beets under running water by gently rubbing the skin with your fingers (wear gloves to avoid staining).

3. Cut the beets into wedges or slices. Place in a bowl and drizzle first with olive oil and then with vinegar. Season well with salt and pepper, and toss to mix well. Serve hot, warm, or chilled.

Herbed Rice in Wine

This is one of my favorite recipes for rice. It uses an unusually small amount of liquid in proportion to the rice, and the rice retains a slight chewiness.

$\frac{1}{4}$ pound (1 stick) butter
2 cups finely chopped onions
1 cup finely chopped carrot
1 pound long-grain white rice
$1\frac{1}{4}$ teaspoons dried marjoram
1 cup beef stock or canned beef broth
$1\frac{1}{2}$ cups dry white wine
Salt and freshly ground black pepper

1. Place a large sauté pan or casserole over medium-low heat and melt the butter. Add the onions and carrot, and sauté until golden brown, 15 to 20 minutes. Add the rice and stir until well coated with butter.

2. Add the marjoram, beef stock, and wine. Season with salt and pepper to taste. Stir well, cover, and reduce the heat to very low. Simmer for 15 minutes, remove from the heat, and serve.

TO MAKE AHEAD
Eight hours before serving: Prepare rice, cook, and cool. Cover and refrigerate.
Thirty minutes before serving: Preheat oven to 350 degrees. Stir rice mixture and add enough water ($\frac{1}{4}$ to $\frac{1}{3}$ cup) to moisten mixture. Place covered pan in oven until mixture is thoroughly reheated.

Cranberry-Orange Upside-Down Pie

This recipe was inspired by Laurie Colwin's Nantucket Cranberry Pie. In this version I have added orange slices and inverted the pie.

Nonstick vegetable oil cooking spray
About 7 paper-thin slices of orange with rind, seeds removed
2 cups whole cranberries, rinsed and thoroughly dried
½ cup chopped walnuts
2 teaspoons very finely grated orange zest

1½ cups granulated sugar
2 large eggs
4 tablespoons melted butter
1 cup flour
1 teaspoon almond extract
Confectioners' sugar (optional)

1. Preheat the oven to 350 degrees. Spray the bottom and sides of a 10-inch glass pie plate with nonstick vegetable oil cooking spray. Arrange the orange slices in a single layer on the bottom of the plate; set aside.

2. In a large bowl, combine the cranberries, walnuts, orange zest, and ½ cup granulated sugar. Carefully pour into the pie plate and pat down gently so as not to disturb the orange slices.

3. In a medium bowl, combine the eggs, butter, flour, almond extract, and remaining 1 cup granulated sugar. Mix well. Pour over the cranberry mixture and smooth gently until level and touching the edges of the plate. Bake until light golden brown on top, about 40 minutes.

4. Remove the pie from the oven. While the pie is still hot, run a thin-bladed knife around the edge between the crust and the plate. Place a serving platter on top of the pie and, using oven mitts, turn the pie over so it is reversed onto the platter. Lift off the pie plate. If any cranberries or orange slices stick to the plate, remove them and pat them back into place on the pie.

5. Allow the pie to cool to room temperature. When the pie is completely cool, it may be covered with plastic wrap. If desired, just before serving sprinkle a small amount of confectioners' sugar in the center of the pie and around the edges of the platter.

WINES: Orange Muscat or one of the wines from the second course

TO MAKE AHEAD
One to eight hours before serving: Prepare pie. Bake.

MENU 7

. . . .

Skordalia

Skordalia is a Greek garlicky potato puree used as a dip for bread or as a side dish for fish and other light dishes. This recipe is adapted from Molyvos restaurant in New York City.

2 ounces sliced blanched almonds (about ¾ cup)
2 large cloves garlic
1 large potato (such as a russet; about 10 ounces), unpeeled and
  cooked in lightly salted water until tender
1 cup olive oil (not extra-virgin)
3 to 4 tablespoons fresh lemon juice
½ to ¾ cup very cold sparkling water or seltzer
Salt
1½ teaspoons freshly ground white pepper

1. In a food processor, pulse the almonds until finely chopped. Add the garlic and pulse until the mixture is very fine.

2. Peel and quarter the potato quickly while still very hot. Transfer to a food mill or potato ricer positioned over a food processor bowl and mill the potato. Add to the almond mixture and pulse briefly just to mix together.

3. Add the olive oil in a slow stream while pulsing the food processor. Add 2 tablespoons lemon juice, then pulse in the sparkling water. Skordalia should be very white and have the consistency of light mashed potatoes. Add more water if too thick. Season with salt and pepper and adjust the seasoning, adding more lemon juice if desired. Do not overprocess. Chill overnight. Serve as a dip with pita triangles.

WINES: Amalia Brut, Sauvignon Blanc (Greece or South Africa), St.-Péray (still or sparkling)

TO MAKE AHEAD
The day before serving: Prepare skordalia, cover, and refrigerate.

Iceberg Wedges with Blue Cheese Dressing

The often-scorned iceberg lettuce has a crunch that other lettuces do not have. It also holds its shape nicely, allowing it to be cut into wedges. Here, chilled lettuce is paired with bacon and crumbled Roquefort cheese. Adapted from John Schenk, executive chef at Clementine in New York City.

4 ounces smoked slab bacon, cut into ¼-inch cubes
8 slices white bread, crusts removed and cut in half
1 cup buttermilk
4 ounces Roquefort cheese, crumbled
2 tablespoons lemon juice
1 tablespoon red wine vinegar
1½ tablespoons minced shallots
1 tablespoon chopped parsley
Pinch of cayenne pepper
Kosher salt and freshly ground black pepper
1½ heads chilled iceberg lettuce, trimmed
3 scallions, green part only, cut diagonally in thin slices

1. Preheat the oven to 350 degrees. In a medium skillet over medium heat, cook the bacon until crisp. Remove with a slotted spoon and drain on paper towels; reserve the bacon

fat. Brush the bread slices on both sides with bacon fat. Place the bread on a baking sheet and bake until golden brown, turning once, about 5 minutes per side. Remove from the oven and allow to cool completely, then place in an airtight plastic bag.

2. In a small bowl, combine the buttermilk, Roquefort, lemon juice, vinegar, shallots, parsley, and cayenne. Whisk to blend. Season to taste with salt and pepper. Cover and refrigerate.

3. Cut the lettuce through the core into 16 thin wedges. On each of 8 plates, place 2 slices of bread. Arrange a lettuce wedge on each slice. Stir the dressing and pour over the wedges. Sprinkle with bacon and scallions.

TO MAKE AHEAD

Up to eight hours before serving: Cook bacon. Brown toast. Make dressing.
Immediately before serving: Cut lettuce wedges and arrange on toast. Drizzle with dressing and sprinkle with bacon and scallions. Serve immediately so the toast doesn't become soggy.

Deviled Short Ribs with Pumpkin, Chickpeas, and Kale

This hearty dish combines the best of winter flavors. Adapted from Anne Rosenzweig, chef at the Lobster Club.

8 short ribs (about 1 pound each)
2 tablespoons kosher salt
2 tablespoons cracked black peppercorns
¼ cup vegetable or light olive oil
3 cups chopped onions
6 cloves garlic, finely chopped
2 tablespoons brown sugar
12 ounces porter or stout
4 cups beef, veal, chicken, or vegetable stock, or water
3 cups diced fresh pumpkin or winter squash (butternut or acorn)
2 cups canned chickpeas, drained
3 tablespoons Dijon mustard
1 teaspoon dry mustard

2 tablespoons white wine
2 cups fresh bread crumbs
¼ cup chopped fresh parsley
2 cups chopped fresh kale or Swiss chard
Freshly grated horseradish root (optional)

1. Preheat the oven to 325 degrees. Rinse the short ribs and dry thoroughly with paper towels. Season with salt and pepper. Heat the oil in a large ovenproof casserole over high heat and add the ribs. Sear until well browned and crusty on all sides.

2. Remove the ribs from the casserole and lower the heat to medium. Add the onions and sauté until just beginning to brown, about 10 minutes. Add the garlic, brown sugar, porter, and stock. Return the ribs to the casserole, cover, and bake in the oven until the meat is very tender, about 3 hours. Remove from the oven and allow to cool to room temperature. Refrigerate for up to 3 days.

3. Transfer the ribs to a platter and set aside. Preheat the oven to 475 degrees or preheat a broiler with a rack 3 inches from the heat. Add the pumpkin to the casserole and place over medium-high heat. Cook until the liquid has reduced and thickened, and the pumpkin is just tender, 5 to 7 minutes. Reduce the heat to low and add the chickpeas.

4. Meanwhile, in a small mixing bowl, combine the Dijon mustard, dry mustard, and white wine. Brush the mixture on all sides of the short ribs. In a bowl, combine the bread crumbs and parsley. Pat on the short ribs. Place the ribs on a baking sheet and place in the oven or under the broiler. Cook until hot and crispy, being careful to avoid burning, about 5 minutes. While the ribs are browning, stir the kale into the pumpkin and chickpea mixture. Simmer until heated. If desired, serve with freshly grated horseradish as a condiment.

WINES: Minervois, Teroldego (red, but try the rosé if you like), Syrah (California, Central Coast, Santa Barbara County); alternative: Porter or Stout

TO MAKE AHEAD

Up to three days before serving: Sear ribs. Sauté onions. Make sauce. Refrigerate.
Thirty minutes before serving: Preheat oven and broiler. Add pumpkin to casserole and heat. Bread ribs and broil. Add kale to casserole and heat.

Walnut Lace Cookies

When I was a child growing up on the as-yet-ungentrified Upper West Side of Manhattan, one of my greatest delights was buying lace cookies from the neighborhood bakery. Those cookies had apricot jam layered between two cookies, and a rim of chocolate. I've been meaning to try the same with these cookies, but they always get eaten too fast.

¼ pound (1 stick) butter
½ cup light corn syrup
⅔ cup (packed) light brown sugar
1 cup flour
1 cup chopped walnuts
4 ounces semisweet chocolate
⅓ cup nonpareils or sprinkles (optional)

1. Preheat the oven to 350 degrees. Line a baking sheet with a nonstick liner or parchment paper and set aside.

2. In a medium saucepan over low heat, melt the butter. Add the corn syrup and brown sugar. Bring the mixture to a boil, then remove from the heat and add the flour and walnuts. Stir until well mixed.

3. Place rounded teaspoons of the mixture on the baking sheet about 3 inches apart; the batter will spread quite a bit during baking. Bake until the batter has spread and is full of air bubbles and light golden brown, about 8 minutes. Be careful not to overbake. Remove from the oven and allow to cool completely before removing from the baking sheet.

4. In a microwave oven or a double boiler, melt the chocolate and transfer it to a small, shallow bowl. Place the nonpareils in another small, shallow bowl. Roll the very edge of one side of each cookie in the warm chocolate, then immediately in the nonpareils. Lay the cookies on a baking sheet to cool. Store the cookies in an airtight container.

WINE: Tokay Pinot Gris Vendange Tardive

TO MAKE AHEAD
One day before serving: Make cookies. Store in airtight container.

MENU 8

. . . .

Crispy Mushrooms
with Ginger Sauce

These mushrooms are crisp and golden brown on the outside, moist and tender inside. Offer toothpicks or small forks so the mushrooms can be skewered for easy dipping. The dipping sauce can be made ahead and refrigerated for up to two days, but bring it to room temperature before serving.

FOR THE SAUCE:

⅓ cup low-sodium soy sauce

1 scallion, trimmed and thinly sliced
  diagonally

1 teaspoon sugar

1 teaspoon finely grated ginger

2 teaspoons rice wine vinegar

2 teaspoons dry sherry

FOR THE MUSHROOMS:

½ cup all-purpose flour

3 eggs, beaten until smooth

1½ cups panko (Japanese bread
  crumbs, available in many
  supermarkets)

Vegetable oil for frying

32 small white button mushrooms,
  wiped clean

1. *Prepare the sauce:* In a small bowl, combine the soy sauce, scallion, sugar, ginger, vinegar, and sherry. Cover and refrigerate for up to 2 days. Allow to come to room temperature before serving.

2. *Prepare the mushrooms:* Place the flour, eggs, and panko in 3 small bowls. Set a large plate near them to hold the breaded mushrooms. Fill a large skillet with enough oil to come about ¾ inch up the sides of the pan and place the pan over medium-high heat.

3. Dip the mushrooms first in the flour, turning to coat well, then in the egg, and then in the panko. Place the breaded mushrooms on the plate. When the oil is simmering, carefully place all the mushrooms in the pan and allow them to sit until they are golden brown on the bottom halves. Turn the mushrooms to brown on the other side. Drain the mushrooms on paper towels, then transfer to a serving platter. Serve warm with the dipping sauce in a separate bowl.

WINES: Moscato d'Asti, Vouvray/Chenin Blanc, demi-sec, Pinot Noir

Lobster Ravioli in Wontons with Lemongrass Butter Sauce

Luxurious lobster made easy to eat. Adapted from chef Gerd Knaust.

FOR THE RAVIOLI:

6 ounces scallops

1 teaspoon olive oil

12 ounces chopped lobster meat or crabmeat

2 large cloves garlic, minced

2 tablespoons minced onion

1 scallion, finely chopped

1½ tablespoons finely chopped cilantro

1½ tablespoons dry white wine

2 tablespoons brandy

⅛ teaspoon salt

32 wonton squares

1 egg mixed with 1 teaspoon water

Flour for dusting

FOR THE SAUCE:

1 teaspoon olive oil

2 tablespoons finely chopped leeks, white part only

1 large shallot, finely chopped

1 clove garlic, minced

4 mushrooms, finely chopped

1 large stalk lemongrass, trimmed and soft bulb
  finely sliced

1 kaffir lime leaf

¼ cup dry white wine

6 tablespoons fish stock

1 cup heavy cream

½ pound (2 sticks) unsalted butter

Salt

1 teaspoon olive oil

Cayenne pepper

1. *Prepare the ravioli:* Mince the scallops and set aside. In a large skillet, heat the olive oil and sauté the lobster meat or crabmeat with the garlic, onion, scallion, and cilantro until just hot. Stir in the white wine, brandy, and salt. Remove from the heat. Add the minced scallops and mix well to combine the filling ingredients.

2. Divide the filling into 16 equal portions and place 1 portion in the center of 16 wonton squares. Brush the edges of the wontons with egg wash and place the remaining wontons on top of those with the filling. Press the sides down firmly to seal. Dust the wontons very lightly with flour, cover, and refrigerate.

3. *Prepare the sauce:* Heat the olive oil in a nonstick skillet over low heat. Sauté the leeks, shallot, garlic, mushrooms, lemongrass, and lime leaf. Cook for a few minutes, stopping before the ingredients begin to take on color. Add the wine, bring to a boil, and then reduce by two-thirds. Add the fish stock and reduce by two-thirds. Add the cream and simmer for 10 minutes. Strain the sauce and place in a small saucepan over medium-low heat. When the sauce is simmering, whisk in the butter, 1 tablespoon at a time. Remove from the heat and keep warm.

4. Place a large pot of water over high heat. Add salt and 1 teaspoon olive oil. When the water is boiling, add the ravioli and boil for 2 minutes. Drain and transfer to a bowl.

5. Pour the sauce over the ravioli and stir gently until coated. Season with a slight sprinkling of cayenne and serve.

WINES: Vouvray/Chenin Blanc (demi-sec from first course), Riesling (Alsace), Chardonnay

TO MAKE AHEAD

The day before serving: Make ravioli; refrigerate. Make butter sauce; refrigerate.

Twenty minutes before serving: Bring water to a boil. Cook ravioli. Reheat butter sauce and combine with ravioli.

Chicken with Wild Rice and Tarragon

1½ cups raw wild rice

2 tablespoons olive oil

4 ounces pancetta, coarsely chopped

2 pounds boneless, skinless chicken breasts

Salt and freshly ground black pepper

3 shallots, peeled and sliced

½ cup finely chopped carrot

½ cup finely chopped celery root (celeriac)

4 cloves garlic, peeled and minced

8 ounces shiitake mushrooms, trimmed and sliced

3 cups chicken stock

2 tablespoons flour

½ cup dry white wine

1 cup heavy cream

2 tablespoons chopped tarragon leaves

1 tablespoon chopped Italian (flat-leaf) parsley

Whole tarragon sprigs for garnish

1. In a large saucepan, bring 4 cups water to a boil. Add the wild rice, cover, and reduce the heat to low. Simmer for 25 minutes, then remove from the heat and set aside. While the rice is simmering, place the olive oil in a large skillet over medium heat. Add the pancetta, sauté until lightly browned, and then transfer to a plate. Season the chicken breasts with salt and pepper to taste and add to the skillet. Sauté until golden brown on both sides, about 5 minutes per side. Transfer the chicken to a plate and allow to cool. Slice the chicken into ½-inch-wide strips and set aside.

2. Return the pancetta to the skillet and add the shallots, carrot, celery root, and garlic. Sauté until the vegetables are softened, about 5 minutes. Add the shiitake mushrooms and sauté for 1 minute. Stir in the chicken stock. Mix the flour with 2 tablespoons wine until smooth. Add the flour mixture and remaining wine to the skillet. Stir until thickened, about 5 minutes, then remove from the heat.

3. Preheat the oven to 350 degrees. In a large decorative casserole, combine the rice mixture and chicken strips. Add the cream, tarragon, and parsley. Season with salt and pepper to taste. Toss gently until everything is well mixed. Bake until the mixture is bubbling and fragrant, about 20 minutes. Garnish with tarragon sprigs.

WINES: Vouvray/Chenin Blanc, Riesling, or Chardonnay from the previous course; for a red, Pinot Noir from first course, or sip Pastis (chilled, neat, or with five parts water)

TO MAKE AHEAD

The day before serving: Cook rice. Brown chicken. Prepare sauce. Cover and refrigerate.
One hour before serving: Preheat oven. Combine rice and chicken. Add seasonings and cream. Reheat.

Anna's Easy Fudge Torte with Berry Puree

Anna Avellar was born in Budapest, raised in Israel and Chile, and spent most of her adult life in Provincetown, Massachusetts. For fifteen years she and her late husband operated the Dolphin Fleet Whale Watch, the first whale watch company on the East Coast. She and her husband, writer Peter Manso, now divide their time between Truro, Massachusetts, and Berkeley, California. They are both excellent cooks and love to entertain. Anna's flourless chocolate cake is a classic. She likes to make it with blackberries. I use raspberries. Either way, it's marvelous.

> 12 ounces semisweet chocolate chips
> 4 ounces unsweetened chocolate, broken into pieces
> 1 pound (4 sticks) unsalted butter
> 1 cup light brown sugar
> 1 cup strong coffee
> 8 large eggs, at room temperature
> 1 pint fresh raspberries, blackberries, or strawberries
> Confectioners' sugar

1. Preheat the oven to 325 degrees. Grease a 9-inch springform pan and line the sides with a strip of parchment paper.

2. In a large heat-proof bowl, combine the semisweet chocolate and unsweetened chocolate.

3. In a saucepan, combine the butter, brown sugar, and coffee, and bring to a boil. When the liquid is hot, pour it into the chocolate and mix to melt it. Set aside and allow to cool.

4. By hand or using an electric mixer, beat the eggs until smooth. Add the cooled chocolate mixture and mix at low speed (to avoid aerating the mixture) until very smooth. Pour into the springform pan and place in the oven. Bake for 1 hour, remove from the heat, and allow to cool. Refrigerate.

5. Using a food processor or blender, puree the berries until liquefied. Add the confectioners' sugar until sweetened to taste (the mixture should remain somewhat tart). Line a fine-meshed strainer with cheesecloth and place over a bowl. Pour the puree into the strainer and stir gently with a wooden spoon until the pulp has passed through and the seeds are left behind. Cover and refrigerate the strained pulp.

6. Remove the wall of the springform pan and discard the parchment paper. The cake may be left on the springform base or be carefully removed by passing a large knife under the cake to loosen it and then sliding it onto a platter with the aid of a large spatula. Cut the cake with the knife heated in hot water and garnish each slice with a spoonful of fruit puree.

WINE: Moscato d'Asti (from the first course)

TO MAKE AHEAD

The day before serving: Prepare cake, bake, cool, and refrigerate. Make berry puree; refrigerate.

To serve: Remove cake from pan and transfer to platter. Cut with hot knife. Serve with fruit puree.

MENU 9

. . . .

Asparagus Wrapped in Prosciutto

This simple hors d'oeuvre needs no additional seasoning or dressing and can be picked up and eaten without utensils. If the asparagus spears are thick, you may wish to peel the bottom third of each one with a vegetable peeler before steaming.

> 24 asparagus spears, medium thickness, trimmed of tough ends
> 24 paper-thin slices prosciutto

1. Place asparagus in a steamer or pot with about 1 inch of water. Place over high heat to bring to a boil and steam asparagus just until bright green and barely tender; be careful not to overcook. While the asparagus steams, set aside a large bowl of ice water. When the asparagus is ready, drain and immediately plunge into the ice water to stop further cooking and retain bright green color.

2. Drain the asparagus and pat dry with paper towels. Wrap the middle portion of each spear with prosciutto and arrange in a neat pile on a small oval serving dish. Cover with plastic wrap and refrigerate until serving.

WINES: Rosé di Alghero, Sauvignon Blanc (Alto Adige or Friuli), Valpolicella

Up to four hours before serving: Steam asparagus and chill. Wrap with prosciutto, cover, and refrigerate.

Butternut Squash Risotto

This recipe is adapted from chef Jamie Oliver, who makes it with a variety of winter squashes, including hubbard and kabocha. I like the sweetness and color of butternut squash. This recipe makes a generous quantity of risotto for a first course. If you have leftovers, you may wish to shape the cooled risotto into small cakes that can be dusted with flour and fried in vegetable or olive oil.

FOR THE SQUASH:

2 tablespoons extra-virgin olive oil

1¼ cups finely diced fresh butternut squash

½ cup finely chopped onion

1½ teaspoons ground nutmeg

1¼ teaspoons freshly ground white pepper

Salt

¾ cup medium-dry California Riesling

½ cup freshly grated Parmesan cheese

FOR THE FINISHING THE RISOTTO:

7 cups chicken stock or low-sodium canned chicken broth

5 tablespoons unsalted butter

1½ cups Arborio rice

½ cup finely chopped onion

3 tablespoons chopped fresh parsley

1. *Prepare the squash:* In a medium saucepan over medium heat, warm the olive oil and add the squash, onion, nutmeg, white pepper, and salt to taste. Sauté, stirring frequently, until the squash is almost tender, about 7 minutes. Add the wine and cook, stirring occasionally, for 15 minutes. Remove from the heat and allow to cool. Using a food processor or blender, puree until smooth. Transfer to a covered container and refrigerate.

2. *Finish the risotto:* Remove the squash from the refrigerator and set aside at room temperature. Place the stock in a medium saucepan and bring to a boil. Reduce the heat to very low, just to keep the stock hot. In a medium heavy-bottomed saucepan over medium

heat, melt 2½ tablespoons butter. Add the rice and onion, and stir well with a wooden spoon until the onion is translucent, about 5 minutes. Immediately add about 1½ cups hot stock or just enough to cover the rice. Simmer gently for 10 minutes, stirring occasionally, adding a cup of stock about every 3 minutes.

4. Add the squash puree and stir well. Simmer another 9 minutes, continuing to add stock every few minutes until all the stock has been used. Add the remaining 2½ tablespoons butter and the parsley. Cook, stirring constantly, until the butter has been completely absorbed, about 3 minutes. Adjust the salt and pepper to taste.

5. Spoon equal portions of risotto on 8 warm plates. Sprinkle each plate with Parmesan and serve immediately.

WINES: Continue with the Valpolicella; Sangiovese (United States or di Romagna), Collioure

TO MAKE AHEAD

One hour to one day before serving: Sauté squash and puree. Cover and refrigerate.
Thirty minutes before serving: Heat stock. Make risotto and serve.

Baked Cod with Wine and Feta

This recipe is from Brian Engel, a former chef at Dock's seafood restaurant in Manhattan.

8 pieces of cod fillet (5 to 6 ounces each)
Salt and ground white pepper
6 plum tomatoes, trimmed and very thinly sliced
⅓ cup finely diced red onion
½ cup finely chopped Italian (flat-leaf) parsley
2 cloves garlic, peeled and finely chopped

1 tablespoon chopped oregano leaves
6 ounces feta cheese, crumbled
2 tablespoons clam broth, or as needed
2 tablespoons fresh lemon juice
3 tablespoons extra-virgin olive oil, plus additional as needed
3 tablespoons dry white wine
About 1 cup fresh bread crumbs

1. Arrange the cod fillets in a single layer in a large baking dish. Season with salt and white pepper to taste. Cover each fillet with a layer of tomato slices.

2. In a small bowl, combine the onion, parsley, garlic, oregano, and feta. Sprinkle evenly over the cod fillets. Cover the dish with plastic wrap and refrigerate. In a small container, combine the clam broth, lemon juice, olive oil, and white wine. Cover and refrigerate.

3. Preheat the oven to 400 degrees. In a small bowl, toss the bread crumbs with just enough olive oil to moisten them, about 1 tablespoon. Unwrap the baking pan and pour the liquid mixture over all the fish and around the pan. Sprinkle the fish evenly with bread crumbs. Bake until the fish is opaque in the center and browned on top, 10 to 15 minutes. Serve hot.

WINES: Rioja (white), Graves or Pessac Léognan (white), Fiano di Avellino

TO MAKE AHEAD

The day before serving: Arrange fish and seasonings in baking dish; cover and refrigerate.
Combine liquids; cover and refrigerate.
Twenty-five minutes before serving: Preheat oven. Pour liquid over fish. Bake.

Roasted Broccoli Rabe

Broccoli rabe, also known by its Italian name rappini, *has long thin leaves that should be left attached to the stalks. For this recipe choose the leafiest bunches you can find. Roasting crisps the leaves, providing a nice textural contrast to the tender florets.*

> 3 to 4 pounds broccoli rabe with leaves, dry ends of stalks trimmed
> Extra virgin olive oil
> Freshly ground black pepper
> Fleur de sel or other salt, optional

1. Preheat the oven to 400 degrees. Wash the broccoli rabe well and shake off excess water. Spread in a large roasting pan or across a baking sheet. Drizzle with olive oil and sprinkle with pepper to taste.

2. Roast until the florets are lightly browned and the leaves are crisp, turning once halfway through, 20 to 30 minutes. (The stalks should be tender and the leaves crisp but not burned. If the leaves are browning too quickly, reduce heat as needed.)

3. Remove from the heat and transfer broccoli rabe to a serving platter. If desired, sprinkle sparingly with Fleur de sel or other salt.

Alexander Cake

This rich cake is made of two thin layers of shortbread nicely offset by raspberry filling and a slightly tart icing.

Pastry chef Eva Baughman brought this cake to a meeting of the garden club to which we both belong. As everyone was exclaiming over it, Eva whispered to me that it was an old family recipe that had been given to her by her mother and that she hoped she would not be asked for the recipe. Of course, I had been about to ask for it myself. After several weeks of puzzling over how to duplicate the recipe, I finally confessed to Eva how much I wanted it. I offered to give her one of my own special recipes in return and promised not to pass her recipe to anyone else. Eva laughed and within an hour delivered the recipe to my door. She kindly suggested that I might like to publish the recipe in my book, and that is how the secret Baughman family recipe came to the Exeter Garden Club and to you.

FOR THE CAKE:

Vegetable oil or nonstick spray

2 cups all-purpose flour

1½ teaspoons baking powder

½ teaspoon ground cinnamon

¾ cup sugar

¼ pound (1 stick) unsalted butter

¼ pound (1 stick) margarine

1 large egg

About ½ cup seedless raspberry jam

FOR THE ICING:

1½ cups confectioners' sugar, sifted

2 to 3 tablespoons fresh lemon juice

1. Oil or spray a 9 × 13-inch baking pan and line with parchment paper, allowing the ends of the paper to extend over the ends of the pan by several inches. Set aside.

2. In a mixing bowl, combine the flour, baking powder, cinnamon, and sugar. Using a pastry blender or 2 knives, cut in the butter and margarine until the mixture resembles coarse crumbs. Using a fork, mix in the egg until well blended. Shape into a ball and cover it with plastic wrap. Refrigerate for 30 minutes.

3. Preheat the oven to 350 degrees. Using the plastic wrap as an aid in handling the dough, press the dough evenly into the bottom of the prepared pan. Bake until evenly golden across the center (the edges may be a bit darker), about 20 minutes. Remove the pan from the oven and allow to cool on a rack for 10 minutes. Run a knife along the long edges of the pan to loosen the cake. Using the paper extending from the ends of the pan, carefully lift the cake onto a rack to cool.

4. Place a cutting board over the cake on the rack and invert it so that the rack is on top. Remove the rack and paper. Using a sharp knife, cut the cake in half to make two squares. Spread one half evenly with jam. Carefully invert the other half on top, sandwiching the jam between the 2 layers. Trim off the browned edges so they are neat and even.

5. In a medium bowl, whisk together the confectioners' sugar and lemon juice to make a thin, smooth icing. Spread it evenly across the top of the cake, right to the edges. Allow to sit until completely dry, about 1 hour. Cover with plastic wrap and set aside at room temperature.

6. Using a sharp knife, cut into bars, squares, or diamonds and arrange on a serving platter.

WINES: Rivesaltes or Framboise

TO MAKE AHEAD
One day before serving: Bake cake. Spread with icing, cover, and store at room temperature.
To serve: Cut into bars, squares, or diamonds.

MENU 10

. . . .

Parmesan Cheese Crisps

It's possible to make these crisps a day or two before serving, but there is a risk that they will soften somewhat. To keep them crisp, make sure they are stored in a dry, airtight container.

$1\frac{1}{2}$ cups grated Parmesan cheese

1. Preheat the oven to 375 degrees. Line baking sheets with nonstick liners or parchment paper.

2. Place tablespoons of Parmesan on the baking sheet and spread them several inches apart from one another. Bake until the Parmesan melts and turns light golden brown, about 5 minutes. Be careful not to overcook.

3. Remove the baking sheet from the oven and allow the crisps to cool until firm. Use a spatula to transfer them to paper towels to finish cooling. Store in an airtight container at room temperature.

WINES: Sparkling (sec), Chardonnay, Rioja (red)

TO MAKE AHEAD
Up to four hours before serving: Make crisps. Cool and store in airtight container.

Salmon Tartare

Use caution when seasoning the tartare. There should be a bare hint of wasabi and soy, allow-ing the flavor of the fresh fish to dominate.

> 4 ounces fresh sushi-grade salmon, finely diced
> ½ teaspoon wasabi paste, or to taste
> Soy sauce
> 1 or 2 heads Belgian endive, separated into individual leaves

1. In a small mixing bowl, combine the salmon and wasabi. Add a few drops of soy sauce and toss to mix.

2. Place about ½ tablespoon on each endive leaf and arrange the leaves in a circular flower-petal pattern on a serving plate. Cover and refrigerate until serving, up to 1 hour.

WINES: Sake, Sparkling wine or Champagne (demi-sec, or sec from first course), Sancerre; alternative: India Pale Ale

TO MAKE AHEAD

Up to one hour before serving: Prepare tartare. Cover and refrigerate.

Roasted Rabbit with Polenta

Rabbit is not as hard to come by as you might think. Many supermarkets carry rabbit in their frozen meats section. This recipe is from Christian Delouvrier, chef at the Essex House in New York City.

> FOR THE RABBIT:
> 6 tablespoons extra-virgin olive oil
> 4 tablespoons butter
> 4 rabbits, hind legs and forelegs separated from loins, hind legs cut
>   in 2 at joints, trimmings reserved
> Kosher salt
> 8 white button mushrooms, quartered

2 large onions, chopped

2 carrots, sliced

24 cloves garlic, smashed and peeled

3 tablespoons tomato paste

1½ cups white wine

4 medium tomatoes, cubed

2 bunches tarragon

2 bunches thyme

6 shallots, peeled and sliced

FOR THE POLENTA:

10 cups milk

2 cups quick-cooking polenta

2 teaspoons salt, or to taste

1 cup grated Parmesan cheese

6 tablespoons butter

1. In a large, deep skillet over high heat, heat 2 tablespoons olive oil and 2 tablespoons butter. Add the rabbit forelegs, trimmings (except liver), and salt to taste. Cook over high heat, stirring and turning, until golden brown on all sides. Add the mushrooms, onions, carrots, 8 cloves garlic, and tomato paste. Cook, stirring, until the vegetables are tender, about 10 minutes. Add 1 cup wine and simmer until it evaporates. Add tomatoes, 1 bunch tarragon, 1 bunch thyme, and water to just cover. Simmer until reduced by half, about 1 hour. Strain, pressing on the solids. Discard the solids.

2. Place the loins on a work surface with the cavities facing up. Lay the remaining tarragon, thyme, and garlic on the centers of each loin. Roll up the loins so that the filling is enclosed and tie with kitchen twine.

3. Preheat the oven to 450 degrees. Season the rabbit pieces with salt to taste. Place a large ovenproof skillet over high heat and add the remaining 4 tablespoons olive oil and 2 tablespoons butter. Add the loins and hind legs, and sear until golden brown. Transfer the skillet to the oven and roast for 5 minutes. Turn the rabbit pieces, lower the temperature to 425 degrees, and roast until the meat is slightly pink at the bone, 15 to 20 minutes. Transfer the rabbit to a carving board, reserving the skillet and its drippings. Cut the twine from the loins and discard the garlic and herbs. Place the legs and loin meat in a plastic bag, seal, and refrigerate.

4. To make a sauce, place the skillet with the drippings over medium heat. Add the shallots and sauté until tender, about 5 minutes. Add the remaining ½ cup wine and cook

until it evaporates. Add sauce and simmer for 10 minutes. Strain sauce, pressing hard on the shallots. Place the strained sauce in a covered container, seal, and refrigerate.

5. Preheat the oven to 300 degrees. Place the rabbit in a small baking dish, cover tightly with foil, and reheat until warm, about 15 minutes. Meanwhile, reheat the sauce in a small saucepan over medium-low heat and keep warm.

6. *Prepare the polenta:* In a large saucepan, bring the milk to a simmer. Slowly add the polenta and salt, whisking well, until the polenta absorbs the milk but is still soft, 5 to 7 minutes. Stir in the Parmesan and butter. Keep warm.

7. Arrange the loin and leg meat over the polenta. Pour the sauce around the meat and serve.

WINES: Pinotage, Saint-Joseph, Barbaresco

TO MAKE AHEAD

The day before serving: Make sauce. Roll loins with herbs. Brown rabbit. Finish sauce. Refrigerate.

Thirty minutes before serving: Preheat oven. Reheat rabbit and sauce. Make polenta. Arrange rabbit on polenta. Serve with sauce.

Wild Mushroom Sauté

Any mushrooms can be used for this recipe, but try to choose a variety, including some with earthy flavor. Slice or cut them into pieces of a similar size. To clean the mushrooms, wipe them with a damp paper towel.

> 1/4 cup extra-virgin olive oil
> 2 cloves garlic, peeled and finely sliced
> 8 ounces oyster or hen o' the woods mushrooms
> 8 ounces shiitake mushrooms, trimmed and sliced
> 4 ounces crimini (or baby Portobello) mushrooms, thinly sliced
> Salt and freshly ground black pepper
> 3 tablespoons chives sliced into 1/2-inch lengths

1. Place a large skillet over medium-low heat. Add the olive oil and allow to heat. Add the garlic and sauté for 1 minute.

2. Add all the mushrooms and toss until they begin to soften, 1 to 2 minutes. Increase the heat to high and continue to toss the mushrooms until they throw off their liquid and begin to brown on the edges. Season with salt and pepper to taste. Transfer to a serving bowl, add the chives, and toss again.

Pears in Red Wine

There are many recipes for pears poached in red wine. I like this one flavored with a touch of vanilla.

1 750 ml bottle dry red wine
⅓ cup superfine sugar
2 whole star anise
1 strip lemon peel, about 2 inches long and 1 inch wide
1 strip orange peel, about 2 inches long and 1 inch wide
1 vanilla bean, split lengthwise (optional)
8 Bosc, Comice, or other firm pears, peeled with stems intact

1. In a large saucepan over medium-low heat, combine the wine, sugar, star anise, lemon peel, orange peel, and vanilla bean. Bring to a simmer and stir until the sugar has dissolved. Remove from the heat.

2. In a wide flameproof casserole, arrange the pears so they are in a single layer (some may be placed upside down). Pour the wine mixture, including the solids, over the pears. Place the casserole over medium heat and bring to a simmer. Reduce the heat to low and simmer until the pears are tender, 30 to 40 minutes. Allow to cool, then refrigerate.

3. The pears may be served chilled or at room temperature with a little of the poaching liquid drizzled over. To serve warm, reheat the pears in the poaching liquid until hot. Transfer the pears to serving dishes and boil the poaching liquid until it is reduced and thickened. Drizzle the pears with hot syrup and serve.

WINES: Ruby Port or Poire William

TO MAKE AHEAD
The day before serving: Poach pears. Cool and refrigerate.
To serve: May be chilled, at room temperature, or reheated.

Afterword

. . . .

WHAT IS THERE to say about the aftermath of a dinner party? My husband jokingly refers to the "post-party depression" that sets in when the guests are gone and the table must be cleared and the kitchen cleaned.

I am not one of those people who is compelled to go to bed with a spotless kitchen. While all the plates must be rinsed and leftover food put away immediately, I have no trouble leaving a sink full of soaking pans and a counter filled with glasses to be washed. In the morning I will put on some of my favorite music and set to work.

There is always the next dinner party to plan. If friends are planning a visit to us and say, "Don't go to the trouble," I am disappointed—not because they can keep me from entertaining them in style (they can't), but because it shows they don't see how much pleasure it gives me to do it.

Eight is the perfect number for a dinner party. It's not much more trouble to cook for eight than it is for four. Eight allows for an interesting mix of old friends and new. The evening will be lively, conversation will never lag, and you will have brought people together to share their stories and their lives over a table of good food and drink.

Resources

. . . .

Adriana's Caravan (spices and specialty foods)
78 Grand Central Terminal Market
New York, NY 10017
(800) 316-0820
www.AdrianasCaravan.com

AlsoSalt (high-quality salt substitute)
P.O. Box 953
Maple Valley, WA 98038
(800) 381-7258
www.AlsoSalt.com

Berkshire Meats, Inc. (ham and all cuts of pork
   from the Berkshire breed of hogs)
P.O. Box 266
Geneva, MN 56085
(507) 256-7231
www.berkshiremeats.com

Capriflavors, Inc. (imported Italian foods)
1012 Morrisville Parkway
Morrisville, NC 27560
(800) 861-5440
www.capriflavors.com

Champlain Valley Honey (raw honey, beeswax
   candles, and gift items)
P.O. Box 127
Middlebury, VT 05753
(800) 841-7334
www.champlainvalleyhoney.com

Dean & DeLuca (specialty food products)
560 Broadway
New York, NY 11101
(800) 999-0306 (store)
(800) 221-7714 (catalog)
www.deananddeluca.com

Ducktrap River of Maine (smoked fish and
   other smoked seafood)
57 Little River Drive
Belfast, ME 04915
(800) 828-3825
www.ducktrap.com

Formaggio Kitchen (cheese, spices, specialty
    foods)
244 Huron Avenue
Cambridge, MA 02138
(617) 354-4750
www.formaggiokitchen.com

Hansen Caviar Company (caviar, foie gras,
    truffles, smoked fish)
881 Route 28
Kingston, NY 12401
(800) 735-0441
www.hansencaviar.com

Hess Pottery (fine red clay pie plates)
P.O. Box 214
Reeds Spring, MO 65737
(417) 272-3283
www.hesspottery.com

John Cope's Food Products, Inc. (dried corn)
P.O. Box 419
Rheems, PA 17570-0419
(800) 745-8211
www.copefoods.com

Kalustyan's (spices and other products)
123 Lexington Avenue
New York, NY 10016
(800) 352-3451
www.kalustyans.com

The King Arthur Flour Company, Inc. (flour,
    bakeware, cooking classes)
P.O. Box 1010
Norwich, VT 05055
(802) 649-3881
www.KingArthurFlour.com

Martha Hoey (ceramic apple bakers and other
    handcrafted bakeware)
Elm Tree Centre
R.R. #1
Moffat, Ontario, Canada L0P1J0
(519) 823-5091
www.ElmTreeCentre.com

MexGrocer.com (nonperishable Mexican foods
    and cookware)
7445 Girard Avenue, Suite 6
La Jolla, CA 92037
(858) 459-0577
www.MexGrocer.com

North American Vegetarian Society
    (information about vegetarianism)
P.O. Box 72
Dolgeville, NY 13329
(518) 568-7970
www.navs-online.org

Oriental Trading Company, Inc. (toothpicks,
    skewers, novelty party supplies)
P.O. Box 2308
Omaha, NE 68103
(800) 875-8480
www.oriental.com

Pearl River, Inc. (toothpicks, skewers, Asian
    foods, and kitchenware)
477 Broadway
New York, NY 10013
(800) 878-2446
www.pearlriver.com

Penzeys, Ltd. (spices)
P.O. Box 1448
Waukesha, WI 53187
(800) 741-7787
www.penzeys.com

The Vegetarian Resource Group (information
    about vegetarianism and veganism)
P.O. Box 1463
Baltimore, MD 21203
(410) 366-8343
www.vrg.org

Zingerman's (breads, spices, and specialty foods)
620 Phoenix Drive
Ann Arbor, MI 48108
(888) 636-8162
www.zingermans.com

Recipes from
The New York Times

. . . .

The following recipes from the pages of the *Times* have been adapted from their original published form and are used with permission. See the index for specific page references.

Acknowledgments

· · · · · · ·

IN SIXTEEN years of testing and editing recipes I have learned from countless people in the worlds of food and publishing. I was fortunate to be associated with top-notch writers and editors from the start. Maria Guarnaschelli was the first to hire me and became both teacher and friend. I am grateful to Julie Sahni, who introduced me to the late Carol Shaw at *The New York Times*. Having heard there might be an opening for a recipe tester for the "Living" section of the paper, I phoned Carol every week or two until, after my fourth or fifth call, she good-naturedly agreed to give me a try. We worked together for many years and I will always miss her.

The New York Times has been a congenial place for me to work. I have enjoyed the spirit of friendliness among the staff and writers of the "Dining In/Dining Out" section (formerly the "Living" section). Michalene Busico was the first to offer me writing assignments. Among many other writers and editors who offered support and encouragement were Regina Schrambling, Amanda Hesser, Nick Fox, Sam Sifton, and Kathleen McElroy. I am particularly grateful to Patricia Gurosky, my editor and daily contact at the *Times*, for her availability, her sense of humor, and, most of all, her brilliant editing of my work.

When I told Mike Levitas at *The New York Times* that I wanted to write a cookbook, he suggested a book on entertaining and offered the idea and name for *Dinner for Eight*. For that, for his encouragement, and for many courtesies and kindnesses I am truly grateful.

Many thanks to Elizabeth Beier at St. Martin's Press for being the perfect editor for me. She has been encouraging, smart, and kind, and it was a pleasure to hear her insights and suggestions about my work. I quickly felt I had a new friend as well as an excellent editor, and I feel so lucky that fate brought us together.

Although I have tested other cooks' recipes for sixteen years, I knew it would be important to have my recipes looked at with new eyes. Jim Collins, the instructor of the culinary arts classes at the Seacoast School of Technology, a vocational high school in Exeter, New Hampshire, allowed his classes to test some of my recipes. The students were charming and intelligent, and their comments were of great value.

I can't imagine what I would do without my assistant, Amber Walker. She is organized and knowledgeable, and is invariably cheerful as well. Thanks also to Alanna Callendrello, who assisted in testing some of these recipes and was both a help and a pleasure to be around.

Thanks are due to all the restaurant chefs who took the time to talk to me about food, cooking, and the business of serving the public. I am particularly grateful to Thea and John Shaw of Frankie and Johnny's in Cape Neddick, Maine. John is a brilliant and creative chef and I learn something new every time I eat his cooking.

I often make requests of my local food markets for information and special orders. For his gracious help I am especially grateful to Fred Daley of Fresh Fish Daley, who is always good-natured about hunting down small amounts of obscure fish for me. Thanks as well to Kathy Gallant of Blue Moon Market in Exeter, New Hampshire, and Sor Lo of Lo's in Portsmouth, New Hampshire. I would also like to acknowledge the staff, particularly in the produce and meat departments, of the two New Hampshire supermarkets where I make an almost daily appearance: Shaw's and Market Basket in Stratham. And thanks to Sean Morrissey in the produce department of Shaw's in North Hampton, New Hampshire.

While I learned about the food business from professionals, I became more keenly aware of the fine cooking I enjoyed in the homes of my family and friends. My parents, William P. and Diana R. Tillar, are both excellent cooks who introduced their children to all kinds of foods from an early age, and I have followed their example with my own children. My sister is one of the best cooks I know, and some of my favorite recipes have been inspired by, borrowed from, or stolen from her. I'm grateful to my brother for insisting that we siblings get together with our families once a year for a vacation, the highlight of which is our shared meals.

Friends who have taught me about hospitality include Sarah and Herb Heller (whose memorable meals include caviar hors d'oeuvres and bellinis made with frozen white peach puree), Florence Ruffner (who sets a breathtaking table and taught me what a *charger* is), and Margaret Gram (whose grandmother's Italian wedding soup takes a full three days to make). Vasilka Nicolova shared with me some of her favorite recipes, which are now among my own favorites. I am grateful to Danny and Hilary Goldstine for not thinking it a waste to share fresh black truffles with our children when they were young, serving ample portions in lightly scrambled eggs and teaching them lessons about food, taste, and generosity that they have never forgotten. Many thanks to Elena and Nicholas Delbanco for a long and dear friendship that has included picnics and wedding feasts. Year-round, Wendy, Bob, and Nell Pirsig share my family's most important celebrations, which inevitably begin or end at a dinner table. And thanks to Anna Avellar and Peter Manso for much warm hospitality in Provincetown and Truro.

Eva Baughman, fellow recipe-tester and professional baker, is a true friend who is always ready to give advice or share a recipe. Diane Zatz and I have exchanged recipes and tales regarding entertaining, and our conversations have inspired many ideas for articles.

Thanks to Betsy and Michael Bacon, Alexis Balkonis, Grace Savage, and Penelope Smith Berk for deep and abiding friendship and support, and to Lavanya Joshi for both friendship and her lessons about Indian food.

I am grateful to the members of the Exeter (New Hampshire) Area Garden Club, who made me feel that I instantly had seventy-five new friends when I joined ten years ago and who remain a small community of caring that goes beyond gardening. And many thanks to Jay Perkins, a talented gardener, landscaper, and stonemason, for creating my beautiful garden. Thanks also to Justin K. Hall and Paul Javaruski for helping to keep it growing.

To my dear friend Margie Kaplan, I am grateful for a twenty-year friendship that only deepens with time. For providing me with a home in New York City whenever I choose to show up at her door, for her advice and encouragement, and for the great bag lunches she packs for me for the bus ride back to New Hampshire, a thousand thanks would not be nearly enough.

My family have always been, and still are, my favorite people to feed: my daughter, Sara, who is married to Luke and now has a baby of her own; my son Jacob, who has an extraordinary ability to be able to identify ingredients in a dish by taste and smell; and my younger son, Benjamin, who as a small child once asked me if there was such a thing as love at first sight and then quickly corrected himself, saying there couldn't be *"because how would you know what they eat?"*

And my thanks and love to my husband, Jim. He has encouraged me to cook and to write, has edited my work, and let me persuade him to write the wine pairings for this book. He is the best of companions at dinner and always.

Index

· · · · · · ·